Building Literacy
Through
Classroom Discussion

Research-Based Strategies for Developing Critical Readers and Thoughtful Writers in Middle School

Mary Adler & Eija Rougle

New York • Toronto • London • Auckland • Sydney
Mexico City • New Delhi • Hong Kong • Buenos Aires

Teaching
Resources

Dedication

For Ethan and Lucy, the best conversationalists, with love. — M.A.

For my mother, who taught me how to listen and value dissidence, and my father, who taught me how to negotiate ideas and build human bridges. — E.R.

The work on which this book is based was supported by the Center on English Learning & Achievement through the U.S. Department of Education Research and Development Center Program (Grant No. R305A960005), as administered by the Office of Educational Research and Improvement (now the Institute of Education Sciences). However, the contents do not necessarily represent the positions or policies of the department.

Photographs in this book do not come from Partnership for Literacy classrooms.

Cover design by Maria Lilja
Interior design by LDL Designs
Cover photos by © Maria Lilja (top and bottom) and © Ellen B. Senisi (center)
Interior photos by © Ellen B. Senisi, with the exception of photos on pages 87, 90, 120, 130, 155, 159, and 162 which are by © Maria Lilja
A special thanks to Kelly Millet-Wilson, who invited us into her extraordinary classroom in the Niskayuna school district.
The poem, "Scaffolding" by Seamus Heaney, is from *Death of a Naturalist* .
Faber & Faber, (1966/1985). © copyright by Seamus Heaney.

ISBN 0-439-61650-6
Copyright © 2005 by Mary Adler and Eija Rougle
All rights reserved. Published by Scholastic Inc.
Printed in the U.S.A.
2 3 4 5 6 7 8 9 10 40 12 11 09

Contents

Acknowledgments

Scaffolding

Seamus Heaney

Masons, when they start upon a building,
Are careful to test out the scaffolding;

Make sure that planks won't slip at busy points,
Secure all ladders, tighten bolted joints.

And yet all this comes down when the job's done
Showing off walls of sure and solid stone.

So if, my dear, there sometimes seem to be
Old bridges breaking between you and me

Never fear. We may let the scaffolds fall
Confident that we have built our wall.

We came upon this poem somewhere in the middle of writing this book and loved it, both for its beautiful simplicity and for the way it shows the careful human planning and relationships that go into creating something durable. In preparing for this project, we worked alongside numerous "masons" to develop ideas, tighten connections, and test out plans. Our collective work formed the scaffolding for this book.

Thank you to the middle school teachers we worked with, who have been so generous with their time, ideas, enthusiasm, and spirit. It has been a privilege to be able to partner with you. We also want to thank your wonderful students and supportive administrators; together with them you have created literate communities that shine with thoughtfulness and glitter with warmth. We hope that you will hear your voices in this book.

We owe a great debt of gratitude to the facilitators who worked shoulder-to-shoulder with us throughout the project: Eileen Kaiser, Samantha Caughlan, Ester Salasoo and Barbara Ring. Your weekly collaboration and innovative ideas shaped our collective direction and knowledge.

There would not have been a Partnership for Literacy or a Center for English Learning and Achievement (CELA) without the work of its directors, Arthur Applebee and Judith Langer in New York, and Martin Nystrand in Wisconsin. We thank them not only for their research, which was

foundational to the project and to this book, but also for their ongoing support throughout the Partnership project. Researchers Carol Rodgers, Mark Jury, Jim Collins, Cheryl Dozier, Adam Gamoran, Peter Johnston, George Kamberelis, Gloria Ladson-Billings, and Mary Louise Gomez were also instrumental in helping us discover effective ways to share research findings with teachers.

The Partnership for Literacy also relied upon a dedicated and knowledgeable staff, including (in Albany), Janet Angelis, Jacqueline Marino, Betty Close, Laura Morrill, Jenna Stortz, Meg Cashen-Martin and Holly Wik. Classroom data were collected and organized by a tremendous group of graduate students, including Marta Albert, Stefanie Bellack, Jinsook Choi, Paula Costello, Stacy Denton, Marea Gordett, Sam Harb, Tara Lee, Paula Orlando, Elsiana Ortiz, Ilene Rutten, Karen Trainor, Steve Westbrook, Jenn Wolfe, Christine Woodcock, and Liz Yanoff.

Mary would like to thank the faculty and administration at California State University Channel Islands for a Faculty Development Grant and a Smith Family Faculty Innovation and Excellence Grant, both of which provided support for my continued work on this book. Thank you also to my colleagues who provided valuable feedback on chapters from this book: Bob Mayberry, Julia Balen, Jill Leafstedt, Paul Rivera, Jeanne Grier, Kevin Volkan and Merilyn Buchanan; and to two student assistants, Wendy Primicerio and Carol Pond, for your timely help. Finally, thanks to my friends and family for your unswerving support, especially to Bryan—reader, writer, husband, and friend.

Eija would like to thank her teacher friends and colleagues in Albany, New York. Warm thanks, *kiitos*, to my sister, Pirjo, in Finland, for her solid support. Thank you also to my children, Jaakko and Ida-Marie, for their love and for all the honest conversations today and in the future. A special thank you is due to my husband, Charlie; his gourmet cooking, humor and verbal wit have energized me all along.

A final thank you goes out to our Scholastic family, including Margery Rosnick and Wendy Murray, for your thoughtful responses, careful editing, and unflagging encouragement. With your help and those of the many others involved in the process, we can be "confident that we have built our wall"—or in this case, a bridge.

photo: Bryan Adler

Foreword

Middle school students are on the edge—sometimes teetering, sometimes strutting on that fine line between childhood and adulthood. Recent research has shown that the brain grows just before puberty, giving adolescents new capacity to reason and make judgements. Cognitively, adolescents' brains are ready to use newly acquired capacity for abstract thought and analytical thinking. Socially and psychologically, middle schoolers crave connection. They jockey to be part of a peer group. Peer approval and peer interaction are highly important. And yet they are also at an age when they are eager to make their marks as individuals, to be recognized for who they are.

As educators of middle school students, how do we best harness what we know of this phase of adolescence to help our students become literate thinkers and writers? With *Building Literacy Through Classroom Discussion*, Mary Adler and Eija Rougle make a strong case for discussion-based learning.

This book is the result of a very exciting and successful research project, the Partnership for Literacy, whose goal was to offer both a coherent theoretical framework and interrelated instructional approaches that could increase teacher knowledge about students' literacy needs and support successful literacy learning in a systematic and engaging manner.

The Partnership for Literacy was directed by the two of us, at the University at Albany, and by Martin Nystrand at the University of Wisconsin, and grew from the many studies we and our colleagues at the Center on English Learning and Achievement had already done to identify specific features of curriculum, professional context, instruction, classroom activities, and interactions that lead to higher student literacy. Mary Adler and Eija Rougle were among the key instructional facilitators in the project who played a vital role in turning the research knowledge into the kinds of engaging activities that excite teachers, motivate students, and improve learning. Adler and Rougle were masterly in developing activities that worked for the diverse range of students in the range of schools we studied.

In sum, Mary and Eija bridged theory and practice, helping us to organize what we know about adolescent literacy into a coherent learning experience that can guide teaching decisions and that students can experience across each year and across the grades. Their book comes at a crucial time, for the high-stakes testing movement has left many highly professional educators with questions about which instructional programs to follow, what teaching approaches to adopt, and toward what ends. With the Partnership for Literacy's extensive research as their bedrock, Adler and Rougle have

created a resource that will give middle school teachers much peace of mind. They show you how to orchestrate thought-provoking classroom discussions that will make the halting, go-nowhere conversations you may have had a thing of the past. Working from the simple but profound belief that adolescent readers and writers need to talk to one another and the teacher as they learn, they show you how to build your curriculum around this need. Give students interesting texts, pose rich, provocative questions, ramp up their thinking skills with comments and questions that require analysis and reasoning, and watch high literacy come into bloom. With each chapter, they guide you deeper into the process of linking your lessons and units into a coherent curriculum, one that is fueled by dynamic discussions about authentic questions and the issues of our time.

Adler and Rougle are teachers to the core. That is where their hearts are. Because they have worked so closely with teachers during this project, they are in the powerful position of knowing the numerous questions that arise among teachers as they move to a dialogue-based approach. They set up their book beautifully—it's like a semester-long professional development course within book covers. The goal: to help teachers help students gain the ability to engage in both thinking like a highly literate person and using the skills and knowledge such thinking entails.

We particularly marvel at the ways in which they have anticipated the kinds of questions their readers may have; they ask these questions and offer useful scaffolding throughout the book. We urge you to step into their book and follow the professional journey they have set for you. From past experience, we're certain you will enjoy it and your students will benefit.

Judith A. Langer
Arthur N. Applebee
Directors, Center on English Learning and Achievement

Introduction

Meeting the Push-Me Pull-You Needs of the Adolescent Learner

By all accounts, middle school is a tumultuous time. Peer groups are pivotal and powerful (Hamburg, 1992; Kinney, 1993; Finders, 1997). Identity is being negotiated and shaped by the influences of race, class, and gender (Fine & Macpherson, 1993). Moreover, adolescents sit on an odd perch; they are no longer children, and yet they are not yet adults. They are eager to fly, and yet terrified at the thought of being out in the world on their own. As Finders writes: "In one breath, a student lunges forward with, 'Hey, don't treat me like a baby. I can do this myself,' and in the next, recoils with, 'How do you expect me to do this? I'm just a kid'" (p. 14).

We like Finder's description because it captures the spirit of budding independence—and the neediness—that young adults bring into the classroom. Middle school students require our support as they navigate the social, cognitive, and emotional terrain stretching out in front of them, and yet we have to fashion our ways of teaching and learning to meet their desire for independence and peer interaction too.

Middle school students need dialogue. They need to be able to talk about their learning with other students and with their teacher. This book is based upon this truth. We'll even go so far as to say that dialogic forms of instruction are ideally suited to this age group. Why? Because these students are now capable of independent thinking; because they are impassioned—they have strong opinions about their social, intellectual, and political worlds; because they pay keen attention to what their peers do and say. They are finding their voices on many levels, and classroom dialogue provides a forum for them to do so.

Giving Teachers a Role: How Dialogic Discussion Allows Teachers to Guide Talk Effectively

With dialogic discussion, students are given opportunities to take independent stances and yet receive the teacher guidance they need. Middle schoolers are still developing cognitively, still learning to navigate complex social relationships in and out of the classroom.

While the teacher has a central responsibility in a dialogic discussion, he or she is not necessarily at its center. Rather, the teacher orchestrates discussion by taking up the questions, ideas, and connections that are generated by students. The teacher expects these understandings—or envisionments—to change over time. The teacher helps students to take an active role in their own learning by preparing them to listen to and connect to one another's ideas. In this way, students from a variety of backgrounds are helped—and are helping one another—at the same time. The teacher also stretches student thinking by connecting it to larger issues or topics that students need to know to develop literacy skills in English language arts. A dialogic discussion, therefore, extends throughout the curriculum into writing assignments and across texts. We'll show you this dimension in later chapters.

This kind of discussion differs from the teacher-led classrooms that predominate in practice as well as from the student-led (teacher-absent) discussions advocated by some education professionals. This is not to say that the use of cooperative learning groups (literature circles or book groups, for example) is ineffective for student discussion—quite the contrary. However, as is true in any learning group, participants initially need lots of coaching for the dialogue to unfurl smoothly, and for it to be intellectually rigorous. For example, many of the teachers with whom we work are frustrated with their student-led, small-group discussions because they find that the exchange often gets stuck in a question-and-answer mode, and the students never really engage in a free-flowing conversation that goes much beneath the surface of a text. Research suggests that this kind of pattern occurs because students in small groups tend to replicate the kind of talk that takes place in their whole-class sessions (Marshall, Smagorinsky, & Smith, 1995). To truly change how talk functions in the classroom, then, we must consider the whole-class dynamic. Once students are engaged in a dialogic

pattern of discussion, it is likely that they will find it easier to participate in smaller book groups or literature circles because they will have a model to emulate.

Closing the Gap: Using Dialogic Discussion to Bring In All Voices

In addition to concerning themselves with issues of adolescent psychological growth, educators have also been concerned for some time that student achievement tends to dip during the middle school years. Students move from self-contained elementary classrooms to subject-specific instruction in different classrooms, which brings on different expectations for the adolescent learner. Research conducted by the National Assessment of Educational Progress (NAEP) has demonstrated that while fourth graders as a group have improved their reading achievement scores during the last five years, eighth graders have showed no such growth (Plisko, 2003). Moreover, gaps in the performance of students from different ethnic groups have remained disappointingly constant among eighth graders, as was noted by a member of the National Assessment Governing Board (Stevens, 2003),

> The average scores of whites and blacks, as well as those of Hispanics, have shown no change. The racial gaps in eighth-grade reading are just about as wide as they were five years ago, and, in fact, they haven't budged since the current version of the NAEP reading assessment was first given in 1992. (pp. 2–3)

Raising the Bar: Developing Students' Reasoning Skills

Middle school students continue to struggle with higher level reading—in short, they aren't able to infer, to analyze a text, and to apply what they read to other situations. Eighth graders are having difficulty achieving a score of Proficient on the NAEP exams. This is not a new problem; in the NAEP's statistics for 1999, 75 percent of adolescents were able to read and write on the basic level but only 5 percent performed at an advanced level (Alvermann, 2000). As Stevens (2003) explains, the NAEP expects middle school readers to be able to do more than comprehend the text:

> The Proficient achievement level requires something more. Again, as in math, it is the ability to analyze and reason and extend, to draw inferences and make trenchant summaries, not just to provide details. At the Proficient level in 8th grade reading, students should be able to discern themes and analyze motives, and to draw connections between what they read on the test and other things they have read and learned. In other words, Proficient reading requires the ability to analyze and interpret, to apply what is read not just retell it.

And it is at this level that many students fall short, that progress has been slow, and where the racial/ethnic gaps are most disturbing. (p. 4).

Through dialogic discussion, students develop analytical thinking and reasoning skills as well as the ability to make connections in their learning—skills that the NAEP has indicated are critical to student success. Indeed, one of the reasons that we advocate this kind of classroom is we know that students retain and achieve more through dialogic methods of instruction than through lecture or question-and-answer sessions (Applebee, Langer, Nystrand, 2003; Nystrand, 1997). Consequently, dialogic discussion is a more efficient way for students to gain and retain the skills they need to succeed on local, state, and national exams. More important, it simultaneously helps students develop a proficiency in thinking that they will need throughout their lives if they are to become educated and productive members of a larger society.

> Dear Eighth Grade Teacher,
>
> During seventh grade, I have grown as a writer and a person. When we looked at our portfolios, I truly realized it. My writing, speaking, and reading has developed a lot. I have accomplished many things this school year.
>
> My work will prove that my writing has grown. I was amazed at the difference. I think a lot more critically. I am able to describe what I want to say in less words. Not only less words, but more sophisticated words, my vocabulary has changed for the better. When we did the vocabulary packets not only did I write down the definitions on paper, I wrote them in my head. The readers marks and writing formula worksheets also helped me. As Ms. _____ said in the beginning of the year we had been playing the game of writing without knowing the rules. This year we learned the rules. We now know the format and it made it a lot easier for me. I could write before, but now if you were to read my writing, you can hear my voice. You can hear my voice because I learned to organize my writing. Not only have I learned to organize, I have learned to edit! This was the first year we had peer editing it was really cool! I saw the difference it made. So now I encourage myself to edit even more. I have learned how to express myself. Not only in an essay, in poetry also. I have found my creative side too. Some people write journals, I write poems.
>
> This year I was in the Cela class and I had the opportunity to participate in many interesting discussions. Theses discussions taught me a lot not only of English but of life. I also learned a lot about others that I didn't know. One of the last assignments was to evaluate yourself and write a paragraph about another student and how they developed over the year. Nine people wrote about me! This really amazed me, that others noticed my change in discussions and as a writer. I am now one of the main speakers. I have learned to say what I think, and people respect it. I'm not afraid of what others will think. I have also learned to listen more, because you can not learn while talking. Listening to others thoughts really interested me, because that's the beauty of English, it can be interpreted in so many different ways, not like math or science, where there's only one way. I gained more knowledge of the book or poem or topic that we were discussing. Not only has Ms. _____ taught me a lot but my whole class has as well.
>
> Ms. _____ also taught us to use sticky notes to write wonder questions on. The sticky notes also made it easier for me to write journals. My journals slowly became longer and longer because my thoughts became more developed. When we read The Giver it would've been pretty hard to go back and read it all over just to look for wonder questions. This method helped me to think while reading, not just read. It has also interested me to read different types of books. Now when I go to a bookstore I'll check out the historical fiction or science fiction. Now I feel I can understand books more. My reading has also increased, now I don't just sitting around watching television; I will go and read instead. I have also learned to not judge a book by the cover. For example during the book I may decide that I don't like it, but I will keep on reading. Even if it's not the best book, there's always a message or lesson. I have become a critical thinker.
>
> Cela is just one of the examples of the wonderful opportunities I've had this year. The knowledge I have gained from these experiences will stay with me forever. I have learned a lot and I'm looking forward to learning more next year with you !
>
> Sincerely,

A student's evaluation of herself as a learner shows the gains she made in a discussion-based classroom.

The Research That Informs This Book

The material for this book comes from the Partnership for Literacy, a research-based instructional and professional development program developed by the Center on English Learning and Achievement (CELA; http://cela.albany.edu). CELA's project directors, Arthur Applebee, Judith Langer, and Martin Nystrand, designed the program as a collaboration between CELA and groups of middle school teachers. CELA would provide research on effective practice; teachers would develop ways to implement it in real classrooms, and instructional facilitators would develop research-based instructional strategies and techniques that would assist teachers in their work. The federally funded project began in 2001 and continued for two and a half years. (CELA maintains a related version of the Partnership today for school districts in New York State.)

More than 70 urban, suburban, and rural middle school teachers in New York and Wisconsin participated alongside a large CELA staff that included researchers, facilitators, and field researchers. The teachers were organized into two groups, one beginning the facilitation process a year before the other. Field researchers collected data from both cohorts throughout the two years. For teachers, the facilitation process began with an intensive summer institute week that was reinforced during a fall institute day and another in the spring—a total of seven full days of collaborative work. Additionally, teacher groups met with a facilitator every two weeks throughout the school year. These sessions, held after school on-site, lasted approximately two hours and provided time for regular reflection and ongoing development of the ideas begun during the summer institute. Facilitators also visited teachers' classrooms and met one-on-one with teachers to help with curriculum planning and provide feedback on classroom interactions (for more about the facilitation of the project, see Adler, Rougle, Kaiser, & Caughlan, 2003/2004).

As instructional facilitators for the Partnership, we had the unique vantage point of being able to work with individual teachers, teacher groups, fellow facilitators, field researchers, and university researchers at CELA to progress toward a shared goal: improving student achievement in English language arts. We bring collective experience from our work with more than 40 of the Partnership teachers from ten middle schools, as well as our shared knowledge from cross-site conversations and institutes in New York and Wisconsin. Additionally, we apply a research perspective developed from in-depth work on previous CELA studies.

Six Key Characteristics of Successful Teaching and Learning

The studies that served as a foundation for the Partnership for Literacy are drawn from more than a decade of work by CELA researchers and others, including Judith Langer, Martin Nystrand, Arthur

Applebee, Peter Johnston, Gloria Ladson-Billings, Mary Louise Gomez, Peter Smagorinsky, and Pamela Grossman. Collectively, this research offers teachers six findings about ways to successfully approach curriculum and instruction (Applebee, 2002):

1. **Engage students in higher-order talk and writing about the disciplines of English**

2. **Ensure the cohesiveness of curriculum and instruction**

3. **Use diverse perspectives to deepen discussion and enhance learning**

4. **Align curriculum with assessment**

5. **Scaffold skills and strategies needed for new and difficult tasks**

6. **Provide special help to struggling readers and writers** (p. 2)

These six characteristics informed our work on a regular basis and helped us target specific, research-based goals for the Partnership project. Over time, however, we came to see these characteristics as most useful when they are embedded within three key concepts, or classroom-based practices. These concepts are so central to the work we did with teachers, we chose to organize this book around them. They are:

- **Dialogic instruction** (Nystrand, 1997)—instruction that builds on student ideas and questions in dialogue with the teacher and other students,

- **Envisionment building** (Langer, 1995)—a description of the way readers make meaning from texts and experiences, both alone and with others,

- **Curriculum as conversation** (Applebee, 1996)—a metaphor for curriculum as a larger conversation that gains shape and coherence from dialogic interactions within and across texts.

Discussion-Based Approaches: The Benefits, the Realities

Although analysis continues on data collected during the Partnership, a recent report from a previous CELA study confirmed the importance of the three central concepts to improving student achievement (Applebee et al., 2003). Participants in this study included more than 1,400 students from 64 middle and high school classes in 19 schools across 5 states, representing rural, suburban, and urban schools. The researchers collected data on classroom discourse patterns, student and teacher background information, and student performance on literacy tasks. Within this data set, they looked for characteristics of dialogic interactions, envisionment building, and curricular coherence. They found the following:

- The amount of discussion and the level of academic work required of students were significantly related to student performance on the assessments (when initial differences among students were accounted for).
- Results were consistent across grade level, type of school, and academic level of the students. (p. 719)

Reflecting on the results, the researchers concluded that:

the approaches that contributed most to student performance on the complex literacy tasks that we administered were those that used discussion to develop comprehensive understanding, encouraging exploration and multiple perspectives rather than focusing on correct interpretations and predetermined conclusions. (p. 722)

Despite the encouraging relationship between discussion-based approaches and student achievement, open discussion—a free exchange of information among three or more participants lasting at least 30 seconds (Nystrand, 1997)—was infrequent in these classrooms—averaging just 1.7 minutes per hour. Authentic questions (those without a prespecified answer) were uncommon as well, averaging only 19 percent of teacher questions. (p. 707)

Although these statistics may be discouraging, they are not surprising. Actually, they are higher than Nystrand's (1997) findings from a previous large-scale study on discussion, which reported the following:

- Authentic questions accounted for only 10% of questions in eighth grade classrooms and 27% of questions in ninth grade.
- Teachers asked 92% of the questions in eighth grade classes and 91% in ninth grade.
- Across both eighth and ninth grade classes studied, discussion accounted for less than one minute of instructional time per day.
- While discussion was rare, it had a large effect on achievement when it did occur. (p. 58)

Similarly, Ramirez, Yuen & Ramey (1991) found restricted opportunities for limited English speakers to produce language: "Teachers do most of the talking in classrooms, making about twice as many utterances as do students" (p. 8). They also found that the kind of talk produced by second-language learners was largely restricted to answering teacher questions by filling in the blank with a word or two, or often with no words at all, but just a gesture. From all of these statistics, we can see that it is largely the teacher who dominates classroom talk and who asks questions;

furthermore, the questions tend to be test questions that do not promote further thinking or understanding. In these classrooms, authentic student voices are not heard.

Rich Discussion: Why a Needle in a Haystack?

With studies showing that discussion is an important contributor to student achievement, why is it that discussion is so rare in classrooms across the country? One reason, as we came to understand during the Partnership, is that facilitating discussion is a challenging, absorbing task. Without supportive strategies and guiding principles, it can be overwhelming. It runs counter to what teachers have probably experienced in their schooling as well as to what their students expect from their experience. Marshall, Smagorinsky, & Smith (1995) put it this way:

> Classroom talk is shaped by traditions that are centuries old and held dear by teachers, administrators, parents, and other members of the community . . . it is not surprising, therefore, that teachers who seek change are likely to be thwarted not only by institutional structures but also by their own deeply instilled sense of the "right" way for schooling to proceed. (p. 131)

Changing Practice: Renewed Energy and Engagement

Given these traditions of teacher-led classrooms, it is not surprising that teachers often feel awkward when they begin to change patterns of classroom discourse. Teachers in the Partnership had many questions as they began their work, and they expressed how vital it was to have regular support through the help of their teacher colleagues and university facilitators. Our research in this area has shown that a number of supports were helpful to teachers as they worked to make these changes in the Partnership classrooms (for more on this, see Adler et al., 2004). Throughout this book you will hear the voices of more than 70 of your colleagues—middle school teachers who have struggled with these concepts and who have shared their successes with each other, and now with you.

Here is one urban teacher group's reflection of how the process changed its practices and beliefs:

> Our group has been involved in new strategies and interaction since CELA began two years ago. Here are some observations about teaching prior to CELA's involvement:
>
> How it used to be:
>
> • more teacher-directed Socratic method lessons

- more teacher involvement, less student involvement
- more teacher-directed questioning, less student participation
- more memorization, less thinking

How it is now:

- Students more involved and willing to be part of lesson and learning. Engagement is stronger!
- Conversations in classroom now different—more sophisticated, multiperspective answers from students. Ambiguities are recognized.
- Students more comfortable to share and listen to each other. Students create meaning and develop their own understanding.
- Students now willing to question openly ... more intense, sophisticated thinking and questioning.
- Students now attending to the higher expectations in reading/writing.
- More student understanding across the board!! Concept development by students.

In addition to noticing improvements in their students' thinking, teachers across sites often commented on the renewed energy they felt in their teaching as a result of their involvement in an ongoing dialogue with their peers, with the facilitators, and with the researchers on the project. If you are able to read and discuss this book with others, we hope you'll also feel the renewed sense of satisfaction with your profession that comes about through collegial focus and shared commitment.

Is a dialogic classroom for you? Take a look at some of the characteristics of such classes in the following chart. You can infer from this chart that a dialogic classroom supports many kinds of literacy activities, including a number of those identified by the National Reading Panel (2000) as critical for student achievement: comprehension monitoring, cooperative learning, the use of graphic and semantic organizers, question generation, and summarization (p. 15).

This Book: A Professional Development Course

Based on our professional development work, we've organized this book to reflect the process teachers go through as they shift to dialogue-based instruction. Our goal is to give you the right support, right when you need it! In Part 1, "Beginning Discussion," we focus on the things you can do to create an environment in which true discussions, or dialogues, can happen. In Part 2, "Sustaining Discussion," we share ways to enrich the quality of the conversation so it is meaningful and productive. In Part 3, "Extending Discussion," we look at the curriculum itself and suggest ways to create bridges between isolated conversations and content areas, so that students perceive all their learning as a coherent, expansive conversation.

In a middle school, dialogic classroom:	In a traditional middle school environment:
The classroom culture is one where student work is posted, books are available, and thoughtfulness is expected and rewarded.	The focus is on reminders of rules and requirements or generic English skills.
Discussion time is used to develop students' changing understandings about a text or topic.	Class time is primarily used to review information already presented.
Students learn how to speak, listen, respond to and challenge one another in effective ways.	Students take turns answering questions to develop the teacher's ideas on a topic.
Students are taught to look for multiple perspectives to enrich their understanding of a text or topic.	Students learn the dominant interpretation of a text or topic.
Students are challenged to support ideas on a regular basis in discussion and in writing.	Students are asked to support their ideas primarily in essays and in end-of-unit exams.
Teachers scaffold each student's learning of new and more difficult tasks.	Students receive the same level of support on similar tasks throughout the year.
Texts and discussions build on previous ideas; these ideas link back to significant larger topics.	Texts are assigned without apparent links to previous works; ideas often are not revisited.
Students reflect on what has been learned through discussion and how understandings have changed over time.	Ideas and understandings are fixed at the end of the class session, rarely to be revisited.

Within each of these three parts you will find three chapters. The first chapter is always conceptual and research based, so you get the "why" behind the "how". The second chapter is practical and classroom based, providing teaching techniques and activities that bring the concepts to life. The third chapter gives you troubleshooting advice, with the question-and-answer format based on the questions teachers often raise. We hope to honor the integrity of middle school teachers by offering a text that provides classroom-based strategies built upon conceptual and research-based ideas, with the ultimate goal of helping students build literacy.

Part One

Beginning Discussion

A New Fable of Bidpai

In one of the fables of Bidpai that has somehow escaped the diligence of the translator, we are told how once a young sandpiper was sent by its parents to the great college of birds in the Forest of Childar to learn the art of nidification. Arriving at the edge of the forest, the fledgling was presently halted by a brisk young woodpecker, but little older than himself, who let it be known that he was the college examiner. "And we will soon discover," said he, "whether you are so grounded in the essentials of nidification as to be ready for admission to the venerable forest."

"My tutors," began the sandpiper—

"Are doubtless very pretty fellows as sandpipers go," interrupted the woodpecker. "But I do not know them, and pardon me, I do not care to know them. So we will proceed to the test. And first you may answer me this: Out of all the trees in the forest, which one would you select as most suitable for a nest, taking into account, of course, accessibility to destructive animals, vertical and lateral movement of the boughs, remoteness from food supply, and particularly the grade and variety of ornithological environment?" To this question the candidate replied humbly that in the country he came from trees were unknown. "What? No trees?" screamed the woodpecker. "Where, then, do you wretched birdlings nest?"

"Why," returned the sandpiper, "we build our nests hard by the breakers in the yellow sands. They are not so lofty as your tree nests, nor as beautiful, but we sandpipers have always built them so, and we like them as they are."

"Dear me," said the woodpecker fretfully. "Here's a nice beginning. No trees! Why, half my questions are about trees. How do you suppose I am to examine such a blockhead? Well, well, we must get on some-how. Perhaps you can tell me how many straws there are in the nest of the great auk."

"Indeed, I cannot," replied the sandpiper. "I never had a chance to count them."

"Nor anybody else, you little fool," cried the woodpecker, "for the great auk lays its egg on the bare rock and makes no nest at all. And now if that is all you know about the great art of bird-nesting, you will see that we cannot admit you to the forest."

"But," pleaded the sandpiper, "you have not asked me about the nests that I am acquainted with—the nests that are built on the sands and in the fens and marshes. These nests I know and love. I have visited hundreds, and watched them in building, and I can tell you about them."

"That may be," replied the woodpecker, yawning, "but I am not interested in those inferior sorts of nests myself. Besides, as I hear a worm moving under the bark, I shall soon be too busy to make out a proper set of questions. So run along home and tell your people that if they mean to send their young ones to this college, they will do well to build their nests in boughs thereafter, or better, bore holes in trees as we woodpeckers do." So saying he broke off the examination.

As for the young sandpiper, after a few unavailing tears, he withdrew and sought the advice of a wise owl in a tree just outside the forest, who in a few hours instructed him so adroitly in the favorite questions and answers of the woodpecker, that on the very next day he was admitted to the forest with the highest honors.

—Editorial, published in the *English Journal*, February 1912

Chapter One

Good Discussion

A conceptual/theoretical overview of the benefits of dialogic discussion—and why middle schoolers are ripe for it

"**A** New Fable of Bidpai" needs no explanation, because we recognize in it an exaggerated version of the educational climate today. Unfortunately, in too many American classrooms, teachers have settled into a role not unlike the woodpecker's. The woodpecker holds all of the important knowledge and perceives that he represents the gateway to higher learning, college. The sandpiper, though possessing much knowledge about a particular kind of nest building, finds that he has somehow learned the wrong thing his whole life. When he sets aside his own experience and memorizes the right answers to the woodpecker's favorite questions, he is admitted to the forest and his family can be proud of his accomplishments. But in this traditional enactment of schooling, what has he accomplished? What has he learned? Does this fable really have a happy ending?

While we intend a comparison between the sandpiper and middle school students, we have found that middle school teachers who are seeking to build literacy through discussion are not at all like the woodpecker. Rather, they *are* interested in finding out what students know. They *want* to hear what students have to say. However, often this desire gets back-burnered by the need to cover information, to teach the discipline, and to meet the standards. As Connie, a seventh-grade teacher, put it, "When I lead a discussion in my classroom, I am always two people." She went on, "I'm a person, but I'm also a teacher. The person part of me is interested in what the kids have to say, interested in them as people and in helping them explore and think about their ideas. But the teacher part of me knows that they need to know character traits and a plot outline and figurative language for the state exams and for high school. So whenever I facilitate a discussion, I have these two voices in my head."

How do we make it so that the "two voices" are harmonious? How do we make it so that a teacher doesn't feel quite so much tension between her role as a curious person who wants to know her students and her identity as a teacher responsible for conveying knowledge? In this book, we hope to show you how comfortably to bring in both your personal and professional self through classroom discussions that are vigorous and sustained over days, weeks, even months.

In most classrooms, the teacher's voice predominates (Langer, 2002; Nystrand, 1997). Rarely does a voice emerge that genuinely responds to students as true participants in a free-flowing discussion of ideas. Rather, the teacher, rightly concerned that students learn about essential literary elements such as character, plot, and language, *presents* the correct form of knowledge or "truth" *to* students, often through question-and-answer sessions. Researchers have coined this kind of question and answer I-R-E: The teacher *initiates* a question, students *respond*, and the teacher *evaluates* (Mehan, 1979). The I-R-E pattern of interaction is so prevalent in classrooms that Cazden (2001) calls it the "default option—doing what the system is set to do 'naturally' unless someone makes a deliberate change" (p. 31).

Yet we also know that when the teacher and students make a deliberate change, dialogue happens and learning intensifies. Research has shown that even as little as one minute of discussion per day can produce positive effects on student achievement! (Nystrand, 1997). It is not always clear *how* a verbal discussion among many translates into individual growth, though Cazden (2001) suggests some likely reasons:

- The discussion format helps make thinking overt and public so that the thinking process is visible to all (adapted from Bruer, 1994). Teachers in particular may help students to clarify their thinking, which in turn gives students concrete ideas for refining their arguments and thoughts in subsequent discussions.

- Because speaking is harder than listening, it may force the speaker to process the information in a more meaningful way (adapted from Bruer).

- Over time, when teachers listen carefully to students' words and incorporate them into a subsequent question or rephrase them for the class (known as *uptake*), they help learners connect their thinking to the bigger picture. That is, the bigger picture of the curricular conversation—and of the world. Students feel more confident, more intellectually surefooted, when they perceive that their ideas have a real place in the world.

- Speakers may use the discussion as an opportunity to try on, or appropriate (using Bakhtin's [1981] term), an idea. They then gradually develop the idea and make it part of their ongoing thinking, or they may reject it. Either way, discussion may entice students to think freely, to take risks with half-baked thoughts, and to readily take on other points of view.

As you can infer from this list, good discussions have particular features that lead to higher thinking, including time for speakers to develop their thoughts, a skilled facilitator who can use students' responses to promote further thinking, active involvement among student participants, and an environment in which it is acceptable to try out ideas that may not yet be fully formed or "right." In other words, discussions that produce higher literacy skills among students are not simply serendipitous happenings. Rather, they are the result of planning and orchestration on the part of the teacher, and active, thoughtful participation on the part of the students.

Creating this kind of productive discussion requires both of the teacher's selves. On the one hand, the classroom environment benefits greatly from teachers who feel comfortable being themselves in the classroom, bringing in their sense of humor, their curiosity, and their listening ability. On the other hand, it demands that teachers use their professional knowledge to model, guide, and develop student knowledge in appropriate ways.

When you think about your own discussion-leader style, consider how much of your personal

self you bring into your professional stance. One excellent and enjoyable way to get a feel for how a good discussion relies upon an interplay between the two "selves" is to get together with colleagues to discuss a story or an article. This is a strategy that we have used again and again in the Partnership.

Let's Listen In

In the following segment, let's listen in on a group of urban seventh and eighth-grade teachers. In this transcript, Sarah, June and Marissa are sitting in Sarah's classroom after school, discussing the short story "Thank You Ma'am" by Langston Hughes. In the story, a young man learns a lesson from Mrs. Jones when she catches him trying to steal her purse. Grabbing him around the shoulder, she takes him into her home, and ends up showing him a kindness he never expected. Sarah initiates the first topic.

SARAH: One thing that I was wondering about was if the whole situation with Mrs. Jones sounds realistic. Would a woman really do that? I read it a couple of times and every time I read it, that's one question that I always kind of . . . think about.

> Sarah wonders about the realism of the story. It's a real question to which she does not know the answer—hence, it's authentic.

JUNE: I jotted down some similar things that are sort of related to it . . . um . . . do you want to hear them?

> This question starts a thread as June and Marissa offer their thoughts on the topic.

EVERYONE: Sure.

JUNE: Okay. I just thought, I can't imagine a woman grabbing a strange boy and dragging him into her home! So that made me think that this must be written some time in the past, where you know, where people wouldn't respond and call the police if they saw a woman dragging a kid in a half nelson into her home [laughs]. That wouldn't happen now, I hope . . . And then later on . . . it's similar. It said, "She did not embarrass him"—it was nice of her not to do that, but would I do the same thing if I were her? Probably not. The boy just tried to steal from me—would I be that nice to him? I don't think so. So that goes back to whether or not it's realistic—the whole situation, or her treatment of him.

> The group gives June time to think through a lengthy response.

SARAH: Well, I mentioned that line about that she doesn't want to embarrass him. And for me that scene pointed out that she really understands him and where he's coming from. Because she said that she had been in his shoes before and it seems that she really

> Sarah picks up on a quote that June uses—"She did not embarrass him"—and extends it further from her own perspective.

does understand like his . . . I want to say . . .

JUNE: Like his situation?

SARAH: Yeah, like his family situation and the fact that he really wants something and he can't have it—so it sounds like she's been there before, needing something or wishing she had something. She doesn't ask him questions about his family—she just talks to him like if I invited Marissa over to my house and we were just kind of chatting. I wouldn't pry into her life.

MARISSA: That's what makes it seem realistic to me, though.

SARAH: You're saying because she does that, it seems realistic?

MARISSA: Yeah. Because it's like she really does see herself in him. It's almost like she doesn't want him to go in the same direction that she went in.

In that one part . . . it's on page 101. [*The group turns to look at the passage. Marissa reads aloud*]: "But I didn't snatch people's pocketbooks." So she's kind of saying, "I've done these things, I don't want you to do them too."

By thinking of the story from Mrs. Jones's perspective, Sarah offers evidence that while the situation *might not be realistic judging from today's perspective (June's point), Mrs. Jones's* treatment *of the boy in the story is realistic because she has walked in his shoes.*

Marissa feels comfortable disagreeing with her colleagues.

Sarah clarifies Marissa's point.

Marissa extends this shift of perspective by considering possible future consequences for the character.

So what have these teachers learned about discussion by participating in one themselves? They are reminded that a natural place to begin conversation is by asking questions in order to make sense of the story. They learn that by voicing what they wonder about and what confuses them, they start the engines of the conversation. Their questions provoke thought in themselves and others, and the questions arise out of the intersection between the teachers' own life experiences and their knowledge of literature. Sarah, Marissa, and June naturally stay away from the more recitation-type questions that are typical of classroom literature discussions. They don't, for example, ask a teacher question like, "What are the three character traits of Mrs. Jones?" Such a question would be obviously artificial and out of place in the discussion these people are having.

From this process the teachers also learn the importance of listening to one another attentively with the purpose of finding a point to comment on, or even argue against. Ideas are not dropped as completed but are picked up again in different ways. Participants naturally use uptake to build on one another's words, connecting and sustaining the conversation. By contrast, in many typical classroom discussions, students' words serve as finite answers, not likely to be revisited.

Finally, this excerpt shows how the teachers learn to consider the threads of the discussion from a number of perspectives—from their own, as individuals living in a certain time and place, from the perspectives of the author and the characters, and from the point of view of their colleagues, who have had different experiences.

Unlike more-scripted discussions that follow teacher or textbook-prepared study guide questions, conversations that incorporate multiple perspectives offer diverse voices and experiences—including those voices disenfranchised by gender, race, culture, class, and age. A male teacher or one who had grown up in an earlier time, for instance, might have introduced insights that may not have been considered by the others. We refer to this interaction of voices as *multi-voicedness* (Wertsch, 1991, p. 67). As we leave this dialogue behind us now, we can imagine that Marissa's words still actively live in Sarah's and June's minds as they think further about the story, helping them to develop a deeper understanding—of the piece of literature as well as of human behavior—than they would have had they not discussed the story.

This real-life experience is an important tool to understanding how theory leads into principle-led practice (Applebee, 1986; Smagorinsky, 2002). If it's not possible to organize a discussion with your colleagues, we encourage you to pay particular attention during a discussion among friends, or with your family. It's fascinating to notice the interactions, the human need to have our ideas affirmed, the types of comments that open folks up, the things that hinder talk, and so on. Bring what you notice back to your classroom.

In addition to this informal research, it is equally important to examine the concepts and principles that form this theory and that help shape the decisions teachers make on a daily basis. In the next section we take a more conceptual look at the principles that underlie discussion-based teaching.

Principles of Discussion-Based Teaching

Imagine a prism in your hand. A ray of light hits the glass, refracting a rainbow of colors. Similarly, a dialogic exchange refracts ideas. They deflect, bend, and break into an array of hues. The concept of dialogic exchange was developed by the Russian literary theorist Mikhail M. Bakhtin (1929/1973, 1981).

Principles of Dialogic Theory

Dialogue is intentional. Those who engage in dialogues do so for a particular purpose, in order to focus in on content: a text, an issue, an experience or a concept.

Even the most basic words spoken in dialogues—what Bakhtin calls *utterances*—are always part of a larger context, relating to previous comments (voiced or thought) and addressed to others for a response.

Dialogue is largely used to refer to an exchange of thoughts and feelings between and among people. However, it can also describe other kinds of conversations, such as those in one's own mind between an "older" self and a present self, between the reader and the text, or between the writer and the text.

Not all talk is dialogue. Dialogue is more than oral presentations, or sharing answers in a group. Rather, think of dialogue as a dynamic flow of ideas occurring among a majority of the participants.

All discussion is not equal. Particular types of dialogue, such as a debate or a Socratic seminar, are useful for learning because they offer an opportunity to examine issues that are intellectually stimulating. In these cases students speak from more-defined roles—their goal may be to make or win a point—whereas in dialogic discussions speakers focus on developing a holistic understanding of the issues at hand. Langer (1995) calls this process envisionment building. (We return to this concept in Part 2.)

Bakhtin (1981) used the term *dialogic* to characterize the *interactive* and *responsive* interplay of diverse characters' voices in Dostoyevsky's novels. While Dostoyevsky worked within a fictional environment, creating an interaction of multiple voices, here we apply the term to the interplay of students' and teachers' voices. In such exchanges, we can think of "words as having a side-ward glance" (Bakhtin, in Wertsch, 1991, p. 144). They take direction from the listener with a promise of something in return. The dialogic intent is the openness to imagine what words will be heard in response to what has been spoken.

Now contrast the image of the prism with that of a rubber stamp, touching an ink pad and leaving an imprint—an exact copy. Rather than producing the multiple refractions of light in a dia-

Building Literacy Through Classroom Discussion

logic exchange, *monologic* talk marches forward with a particular expectation, that of transmitting content as a permanent imprint on the mind of the listener. The table below shows some essential differences between these two kinds of talk in a classroom context.

An Overview of Dialogic vs. Monologic Instruction		
	Dialogic	**Monologic**
Chief characteristics:	Multidirectional talk; questions used to explore issues or ideas	Unidirectional talk; questions used to check information
Primary benefit(s):	☀ Depth—A few topics opened to students for analysis via multiple perspectives ☀ Higher achievement in literacy tasks (Nystrand, 1997)	☀ Breadth—A lot of material imparted to students in a short time
Primary drawback:	Time; students need instruction in technique	Passive; short-term learning; easily tuned out
Purposes for use:	☀ To support thinking with evidence ☀ To build a reasoned understanding of a topic ☀ To consider alternative viewpoints concurrently ☀ To develop speaking and listening abilities	☀ To remember basic information ☀ To follow directions ☀ To understand appropriate behaviors ☀ To make procedures and processes explicit ☀ To listen to a story
Teacher role(s):	Supporter of student thinking and facilitator of learning	Knowledge-holder and transmitter of information
Appropriate student role:	Listens, responds, and asks questions of peers and the teacher; considers multiple points of view	Listens to the teacher; strives for the correct answer

How Dialogue Relates to Learning

When you make discussion central to your instruction, it's as though the windows and doors of the classroom are thrown open, so students' understanding can reach outward—and so the ideas of the world can blow in.

Through talk we come to know for ourselves and we start articulating what we know for others. When you create a dialogic classroom, you provide students with the opportunity to tell, share, and explain what they know about the topic under discussion. You also motivate students to come up with new and unexpected ideas and insights, especially in reaction to those they hear around them. As Bakhtin writes, "Truth is not born and does not reside in the head of an individual person; it is born of the dialogical intercourse between people in the collective search for the truth" (1973, p.90). Ultimately, this interaction in the search for the truth can produce a synergy of active questioning and answering among all participants. Students sit forward, minds on, listening for ideas to add substance and perspective to their own thoughts or questions. As they listen, they compare the evidence they are hearing with what is in their own minds, in order to formulate a response. They learn how to challenge others and how to respond to challenges of their own ideas.

Consequently, teachers who create a dialogic environment promote a learning situation in which students develop rich, defensible interpretations of literature and solid, reasoned understandings of ideas and concepts under study. This kind of active meaning making through dialogue produces results in terms of student achievement. As Nystrand (1997) explains, "What ultimately counts is *the extent to which instruction requires students to think, not just report someone else's thinking*" (p. 72, italics in the original). As a student in a discussion-based classroom put it in her end of the year reflection, "There's a huge difference between being taught and learning. . . . [Here] we are interacting and learning from different situations." Or, in another student's perspective, "Here, almost every one of your classmates is a teacher because they each teach you different points of view, something you didn't know before."

First Steps: Step Away From the Podium!

The teacher as conveyor of knowledge, as wise, entertaining lecturer, is deeply ingrained in our education system and psyches. And yet we don't mean to say never, ever deliver a monologue. Monologic instruction can be helpful during times when you want listeners to quickly absorb information or when you need to explicitly teach a concept or process. However, when used as the predominant form of instruction, this approach seriously reduces students' ability to engage in active learning. As Ramirez et al. (1991) explain, "This pattern of teacher/student interaction not only limits a student's

opportunity to create and manipulate language freely, but also limits the student's ability to engage in more complex learning (i.e., higher-order thinking skills)" (p. 8). Part of our purpose in this chapter is to show how dialogic methods can offer an answer to the limitations of the monologic approach.

Yet even in typically monologic activities, students can deepen their learning by becoming involved in some kind of dialogue with the ideas they are hearing. For example, a student might offer questions and advice to the persuasive speaker at the end of his or her speech. Or you might invite students to respond in writing about an issue, which sets in motion a conversation that shapes learning in important ways (Langer & Applebee, 1987). So don't feel you have to go from zero to sixty in implementing the ideas in this book. Build dialogue in at your own pace. We've found that once dialogic discussion begins, generally in literature lessons, other, previously monologic activities may also be meaningfully opened up to dialogue—a review of a story, a grammar lesson, or even a review before the unit exam. We say "meaningfully" because when dialogue is superficial, infrequent, or easily exhausted, it can send students a message that their ideas are not truly valued. In these cases, instead of authentic, meaning-making discourse, students produce, as Nystrand (1997) puts it, "pseudo-discourse" (p. 72), as if they are acting out their part in a well-rehearsed play.

Talk Creates a Different Classroom Culture

As you devote more time to discussions, students will notice it; it's like a dramatic change in the air pressure. Literally, more students are talking—and more are listening. Quiet students may now be voicing ideas that peers deem highly valuable. And with your guidance, students learn to support their ideas and learn to link what they say to classmates' contributions. As one student put it, "You learn to respect what [other students] say because they justify it." In these classrooms, the teacher sees students not as receivers of transmitted information but as thinkers and producers of ideas. Diverse voices are valued, so these classrooms tend to be more academically equitable (Allington & Johnston, 2001; Alvermann, 2000). The collaborative nature of dialogue—whether it happens in pairs, small groups or whole-class settings—provides support for all students to develop, regardless of their skill levels in writing and reading. Dialogue-centered classrooms are also more humanistic. Noddings (1995), for example, advocates for a more caring curriculum in classrooms where teachers "spend time developing relations of trust, talking with students about problems that are central to their lives" (p. 679).

> Cultivates Respect

> Allows for Diverse Voices

Because students are allowed and even encouraged to explore multiple possibilities of meaning (Langer, 1995), they learn to be flexible in their thinking, coming to accept ideas as open for reexamination. There is not the automatic push to reach a consensus and completely close a conversation about an issue. In a democratic society, such close examination of ideas and viewpoints is a cornerstone for progress.

> **Builds Flexible Thinking**

All of these social and cognitive benefits to students accrue over time, as you and your students share and model appropriate and expected ways to act. Humor, acceptance of others, compassion, revising one's ideas, and constructive disagreement are encouraged; sarcasm, adversarial relationships, hidden agendas, and unfounded opinions are discouraged. Over time, participants gain a shared understanding of the process and come to feel invested in it.

> **Encourages Alternative Viewpoints**

In the next two chapters, we provide a variety of classroom-tested strategies and tools to help you and your students make the transition to a more dialogic classroom culture. First, though, let's look at two classroom examples of dialogic activities and discussions, in order to make the possibilities—and the contrast with more monologic classrooms—clearer.

> **Lets All Students Learn**

A Literature Discussion

As you read the following short excerpt from a seventh-grade discussion, think of the various student voices as characters in the Bakhtinian sense—coming forward on equal footing, yet expressing different ideas. Notice the teacher's role, how she orchestrates the diverse comments, much like the narrator of a novel might. With her comments, it's as though she's picking up individual strands of thought and linking them together to make a chain. The conversation is free-flowing, and yet she's imparting to it a necessary unified design, ensuring that students' comments get linked to the text world and to one another's. This helps everyone "see" the lines of thinking and add to the evolving ideas and themes.

The seventh graders and their teacher, Annie, have been reading a science fiction novel, *The White Mountains*, by John Christopher. The book describes a futuristic society in which machines have taken control over the earth. The humans have escaped these invaders, the Tripods, by retreating to the mountains.

In this section of the transcript, Jake expresses his quandary about the characters and the conflict in the story. Much like someone fishing, he is casting out a line of thought, with a hope that he will catch something—that his peers will join in the speculation and help him make sense of the story.

Notice his wonderfully open-ended phrase "I'm just wondering," which he repeats. This phrase suggests a climate in which children—and the teacher—feel free to raise an issue they are unsure of.

JAKE: I'm just wondering. Are people in *The White Mountains* technologically advanced? 'Cause they escape? So . . . . I mean do they have machines and cars there? I'm just wondering.

> Jake's question functions as an invitation to dialogue; it also makes the dialogue he is having in his own mind overt.

TEACHER: Anybody? Tell us why you think that. Well, let's take Jake's question and let's kind of jump ahead of where I thought we're going to go. Earlier, one of you said something too about where did the Tripods come from. Let's go to that area. There were two particular theories or beliefs as to where the origin of the Tripods could be.

> Annie is orchestrating the discussion by taking up a student's idea and doing something with it. Like an author creating foreshadowing to advance the plot, she builds on Jake's question, connecting it to a central ambiguity in the story.

RICK: There was a revolt of the machines against men, or they came from another world.

> Rick responds, articulating the two theories.

TEACHER: There was a revolt of machines or they came from another world. I want you to think a minute, everybody, just on your papers, jot down which of those ideas you would go with. Are they machines that took over the world? Just one choice. Or did they come from another planet. Just one word, you know. Whichever you think. (*Students writing.*) Now, no changing your minds . . . yet. Okay, if you feel that they come—came from another planet, stand up. (*Students stand up.*) Oh? Now. Why would you people feel that way? Melissa, why don't you start off and everyone can see.

> When the students reenter the conversation they have generated more ideas about the two theories under discussion.

> Annie aids the students' thinking regarding the theories and compels them to take a stand by asking them to write down their opinion regarding the origin of the Tripods.

MELISSA: Because, um, they were machines and, they—you can't really have like a brain, like to tell them what to do. Like, if they were from another planet you couldn't know what's inside of them, so how could you know if they didn't have a brain in there. So it could be from another planet and I don't think it could be a machine.

> Here Melissa seems to rely on what she knows about the difference between machines and human behavior. She reasons that if machines were cerebral, *you could tell them what to do.* She concludes that they must originate from another planet.

TEACHER: Uh-huh. How about you Rick?

> Annie acknowledges Melissa's thought by pausing and then invites Rick's opinion into the conversation.

RICK: Also in their school, they did—they didn't teach them about the stars and the planets. So. So, um, if they were

made by men uh, back a hundred years from when the story takes place, how could they come up with that kind of um, machine power and stuff? Because if, if it was like, really old back then and like, they could only make old, like a very early version of a car and not make something like this. So.

KATE: I know that they said in the book that they never knew what was inside of the Tripods. And they never find out. So. Almost, and if the machines were just machines, then they wouldn't have anyone controlling them. So that would probably—they'd probably not be machines.

TEACHER: John, you're sh—I mean Jameel, you're shaking your head no. What does that no mean?

JAMEEL: It's just—no one thinks that there's [inaudible].

JAKE: The more I think about it, the more [I think it's] possible that it could be a revolt in the machines.

TEACHER: Why are you thinking more about it?

JAKE: Because the Tripods don't really seem to have any powerful weaponry except for stomping on things.

(Students laugh.)

JAKE: And, I mean—

(Students laugh.)

JAKE: And it appears to be the time period when humans had fighter planes and tanks. So why c—and there were tons of them and they had grenades and everything. And so why couldn't humans defeat the Tripods 'cause there were tons of them? Uh 'cause they don't seem to be too awful powerful.

STUDENTS: Oh. Huh.

Rick picks up Melissa's strand of thought and adds a new thread— time—to the discussion.

Kate's words are responsive both to Rick and to Melissa. Like Rick, she looks for evidence in the book, and she returns to Melissa's idea that a machine needs a brain in order to be subject to anybody's control. In a way Kate is consolidating both lines of thought.

By asking Jameel to explain his obvious objection, Annie invites yet another view.

Jake is quick to retake the floor, and almost as if continuing his own internal monologue, he voices another possibility.

The teacher's role is critical. Annie expects whole-hearted participation from everyone. She clearly encourages children to wonder, to have hunches, to voice even the quirkiest, most tentative ideas. She is an able listener and kid watcher, picking up on her students' facial expressions, body language, and raised hands, so that she doesn't leave anyone out. She facilitates the conversation by re-voicing students' ideas. She keeps the discussion dynamic by juxtaposing two possible theories and thus opening up two perspectives for her students to consider.

The students also play essential roles in the dialogue. In fact, their thinking generates it. They are the actors in it, not a sidelined chorus reciting correct answers. The students who did not speak in this particular section of transcript were following what Bakhtin (1981) calls "the rivulets and droplets of the social heteroglossia" (p.263), or the many and diverse voices of the conversation. Everyone followed the chain of conversation in their heads, even adding their own links. In other words, the multi-voicedness we speak of includes the thoughts that continue to spin in students' minds long after students leave the classroom, regardless of who spoke and who did not. Everyone's thinking is enriched.

A Dialogic Grammar Lesson

Most middle school teachers we worked with have enjoyed the challenge of creating a more dialogic approach to literature, in part because they readily can see that dialogue is a good vehicle for exploring the complexity and ambiguity of a good text. However, when we invite them to consider building discussions into teaching nonfiction texts, study skills, writing instruction, the research paper, oral presentations, and grammar instruction—well, they look at us as though we're trying to sell them the Brooklyn Bridge.

How could something that has so many definite right and wrong rules such as grammar be negotiated in dialogue? they rightly wonder. Think about it. Consider how the teaching of mathematics, another discipline that's got little wiggle room between right and wrong answers, has evolved. The best math instructors include an exchange about process, and not a sole focus on right and wrong answers. Teachers now realize how valuable it is for a child to understand one's process in problem solving and to be able to explain that process intelligently to someone else (see, for instance, Lampert, 1990).

So let's look now at what dialogic interaction around grammar might look like in a middle school classroom. The following excerpt was inspired by a conversation heard in an urban middle school English classroom in upstate New York:

TEACHER: I want us to spend some time thinking about fragments because I noticed a lot of them when I read your essays over the weekend . . . they distract your reader from your ideas and make them pay attention to the errors in your writing instead. Let's start with this sheet about fragments. Who can remind me what a fragment is?

SAM: It's only part of a sentence.

TEACHER: Okay . . . anyone agree? Disagree? Who can build on that?

ALLIE: If it's a sentence, then it's a complete thought.

JOSÉ (reading from the worksheet): It has a subject and a predicate.

TEACHER: Great! So you're saying that a fragment is not a complete thought, that it's missing a subject or a predicate, right?

SAM: Yeah.

TEACHER: Okay. Let's try one. I'll give you a group of words and you tell me if it's a sentence or a fragment. Then we'll discuss what your reasons are. (*Writes on overhead,* "The talking student sitting backwards in his seat.") Take a moment to think about it. Then I want you to write down what steps you used to make your decision.

ALLIE: What do you mean "steps"?

TEACHER: I mean what did you do, in your mind, to help you decide?

[*When polled, students are divided; some think it's a sentence, some a fragment.*]

TEACHER: Okay. Looks like we might disagree here. That's good—gives us a chance to figure it out together. Someone start us off by telling us your process and your decision. Then others of you add to that. While you talk, I'm going to take some notes here on the overhead. Sam, want to start?

SAM: Okay. First I look for the end of the subject part, which is *student*, and then I draw a line to show that *sitting* is the predicate part. Then I know it's a sentence.

JOANNA: I did the same thing but I thought the subject ended after *seat*, and then there wasn't a predicate to put after it. So I think it's a fragment.

YOLANDA: I circled the predicates—*talking* and *sitting*—so that means that it's a complete sentence.

TEACHER: Anybody else?

MIKE: I just said it out loud to myself a couple of times. It don't sound right.

TEACHER: Mike, can you say more about that? How did it sound to you?

MIKE: It sound like . . . like you building a bridge, right? And it's hanging there over the water, like only halfway built. That's like this one. So I said fragment.

Though this conversation took more time than would correcting a grammar worksheet for right and wrong answers, the multiplicity of voices heightens student understanding of language conventions and language use. What might the teacher do next to build on the strategy-sharing that has begun here? She's tackled a huge topic—many a middle school teacher throws his or her hands in the air upon reading yet another essay full of fragments. Yet she knows that if students can gain an understanding of what makes a sentence and what signals a fragment, and, better yet, if they can arrive at a mechanism to test out their understanding, this knowledge will serve them well beyond the middle

school classroom. She's decided to invest the time to create a long-term solution. So, what next?

Some Possibilities . . . By the end of this transcript, the teacher has taken notes on four student-developed strategies for identifying fragments. In her mind, she's aware of several different directions in which she could steer the conversation. She could simply talk to the students and point out which responses were correct and explain why. This more monologic approach, as we discussed earlier, would be an economical way to use the time to get the correct information out there. Yet this approach would also limit students as learners, forcing them to think all in the same way (her way) and undo the work she has already done in opening up their understandings to different processes. At best, her students would simply memorize her directions and not really be able to apply them as the adaptable and flexible thinkers she wants them to be.

Let's imagine that the teacher decides to continue her work, having students dialogue with her and each other over this issue. Where should she focus their attention first? She notices that Sam and Joanna used the same strategy but came up with different answers, one correct, one incorrect. That observation might be a good place to start. Since Joanna used it correctly, she could ask Joanna to teach her strategy to the class and have them take notes on it to practice on other sentences. She could also praise Sam for developing a working strategy and have him and others reflect on how the right strategy could produce a wrong answer. The teacher also knows that Yolanda's strategy was not effective at identifying fragments and in fact resulted in incorrect information. She could ask Yolanda to analyze her strategy—that is, to think about why it did not work here. Finally, she's intrigued by Mike's intuitive metaphor of the sentence as a bridge, wondering if she can work with that. Perhaps a visual representation of the sentence as a bridge would help some students (for more on teaching for multiple intelligences, see Gardner, 1993).

This class's initial discussions open the floor for a variety of activities and conversations about the concept of the sentence fragment and later, by extension, the concept of the run-on sentence.

Effective Approaches: Separated, Simulated, Integrated

Langer's work (2002) with schools and teachers who are beating the odds reminds us that effective teachers use three approaches to skills instruction (such as identifying and correcting fragments): separated, simulated, and integrated. In our example above, the teacher has first provided students with a worksheet that identifies fragments in a way that is *separated* from her regular curriculum. She has taken the additional step of helping students develop their metacognitive knowledge about the thinking processes they use along the way. (For more on ways to use metacognition effectively in the classroom, see Schoenbach, Greenleaf, Cziko & Hurwitz, 1999.) After discussing and clarifying their

strategies, she plans to have students apply this knowledge to fragments presented in a *simulated* environment—that is, in short excerpts that provide practice in the skill. Finally, she plans to put the lesson to a real test by having students focus on improving fragments in their own writing and editing, *integrating* the skill into their own meaningful activities. She also wants them to be able to bring this skill into their literature discussions to help them talk about the writer's craft, such as recognizing how authors like Sandra Cisneros deliberately use fragments to create intended effects.

This multilayered approach gives students many different opportunities to learn the skills they need to succeed in their subject area. A variety of approaches are helpful, even in areas that we may consider to be largely skill based. Lampert (1990), for example, shows how this worked in her fifth-grade mathematics class:

> Sometimes, I straightforwardly told students what kinds of activities were and were not appropriate. At other times, I modeled the roles that I wanted them to be able to take in relation to themselves and one another. And at other times, I did mathematics with them, just as a dance instructor dances with a learner so that the learner will know what it feels like to be interacting with someone who knows how to do what he or she is trying to learn how to do (p. 40).

The classroom examples in this chapter are meant not as perfect examples of instruction but rather as illustrations of what a dialogic approach can do for students. In these examples we see students' voices entering into the conversation as writers and thinkers, part of a classroom culture in which they help to co-construct meaning for themselves and one another. We also see teachers using their advanced knowledge of the subject to guide students toward developing understanding.

Looking Ahead

From our work with teachers, we know that a shift to dialogic instruction often creates a ripple effect that can be both invigorating and disorienting. Your sense of balance may feel thrown off, as you come to see many things differently—including your role as teacher, your assigned curriculum, your students' contributions, even the way your classroom looks and feels. In the next chapter, we offer support for these changes by sharing some strategies and tools that teachers have used and developed to engage students in increasingly dialogic interactions. Then, in Chapter 3, we provide some solutions to common challenges that are to be expected when getting started with a dialogic transformation.

Chapter Two
Learning to Voice Ideas

Getting-started tips for arranging the room, setting the ground rules, and seeding the conversation

I n this chapter, we provide a set of strategies and tools so that you may begin to make discussion a central focus in your classroom. By strategy, we mean a plan, a course of action that will lead to a goal. For instance, in order to construct a colorful blanket by hand, you first need a visual image of what the finished blanket will look like—a pattern or a photograph from a knitting book. The blanket's design determines the materials that you will need (the wool's weight and color, the loom, and so on). In this example, the *strategy* is the series of steps that lead toward the goal, while the *tools* are the means by which you will accomplish it: the loom, and the raw materials, which you will weave together. You use the tools skillfully, guided by the strategy that you have laid out, to accomplish your goal. Tools and strategy work hand in hand.

The interplay of strategy and tools provides the structure for this chapter, because it's so important to understand that actions and changes in the classroom are strengthened by an overarching goal to give them direction and purpose.

STRATEGY: Create an environment conducive to discussion
TOOL: Restructure the physical environment of the classroom

Imagine that you open a door to a discussion-centered classroom; like a workshop, it vibrates with activity. The class is talking about a story. Comments are brought to the floor, questions are asked, and disagreements are voiced—all in an orderly fashion. The room resonates with students' words and ideas. While you eavesdrop on the teacher to learn more about how he or she orchestrates this conversation, your eyes span the room. Student-produced material—writing and drawings—adorn bulletin boards and walls. You discover books: anthologies, dictionaries, and thesauruses in bookcases, paperback novels in a book rack, poetry and picture-books in plastic crates, stacks of short stories on a desk, and books displayed on the chalkboard base. You may also notice that students' desks are grouped together in clusters—no rows in sight. This classroom feels and looks different; engagement is "minds on," upbeat, and authentic.

A teacher walking by might be inspired to wonder, "Is my own classroom conducive to talking, thinking, and learning together? Are there materials to stimulate learning? Does the appearance of the room make one think that students' words are valued? Would I feel comfortable having a conversation with my peers in this room?"

Pam, a seventh-grade teacher who works in an urban school, began her fall semester by hanging a colorful banner that read, "A Thoughtful Community." The block letters, arranged as an arch, signaled early on the aspirations Pam held for students and herself. This "thoughtful community" soon turned

into a showcase for students' thinking: Notes, essays, poems and visual representations were constantly pinned up on classroom walls and bulletin boards. Everybody had a chance to read their peers' ideas. Like an artist's studio, Pam's room provided tools and the environment for the creative process:

When students have opportunities to work side-by-side, a thoughtful community develops.

texts, computers and willing learners. A thoughtful community didn't develop overnight, but from the very beginning the teacher was committed to creating a physical environment that would stimulate sharing and invite conversations. She had a plan and developed strategies to accomplish her goal.

Although the discussion-centered classroom grows over time, from the beginning the teacher decides its architecture and culture. The first step is to figure out how to arrange the desks. You may want to avoid any rigid floor plans in which students' desks stay in rows. Sometimes we defend this arrangement for classroom management reasons: for example, in a testing situation—when students are required to work strictly by themselves with paper and pencil tasks—or at times when you decide that monologue is appropriate, such as when a guest lecturer visits.

To break away from desks in rows, we encourage you to "take the big jump," as Kurt, another urban teacher, called his first experiment with reconfiguring his seventh graders' seating. With a little bit of commotion, Kurt and his class pushed their desks into a big circle and commenced a discussion. Students who had not participated before began asking questions and making comments. Over the ensuing weeks, Kurt noticed that when students were sitting in a circle, it was easier for them to see the effect of their own words on their peers. Students naturally leaned into the center, which helped them to hear better, and also made the person speaking feel that his ideas were being carefully considered. Kurt was amazed at the intellectual energy a circle generated.

Variations of the circle also promote student exchange. No matter the shape or size of your classroom, or whether you form a square, oval, or a rectangle during discussions, the key is that stu-

dents can see one another's faces. As an eighth grader told us, "If you are staring at a person's neck you don't want to say anything, but if you sit in a circle, it's easier and much more interesting."

Try pairing two rows and turning the desks to face each other for a book discussion. Or set up a horseshoe-shape with paired desks. If you have a large class in a small room, try forming a fishbowl:

1. Create a small inner circle (those discussing the text) and an outer circle (those who take notes on what is said).

2. Students in both circles come having read the text, with notes and questions.

3. During the discussion, have two empty guest chairs in the inner circle; students from the outer circle are invited and expected to take these seats for up to two minutes to voice their comments and questions, at will.

4. After the discussion, all students write their understandings down on the right side of their t-chart or in a journal.

5. You may repeat the second day with the outer-circle participants in the inner circle, further enriching everyone's understanding.

In any of these seating constellations, you, the teacher, can participate as part of either circle.

If students will be writing during the discussion, arrange the chairs in a circle with desks in front of them. Otherwise, push the desks away, against the wall. In most of the discussion-centered classrooms we observed, the teachers practiced with students how to move desks and chairs quietly and quickly. One teacher in a very small room even marked tiny dots on the floor to ease the transition to a circle.

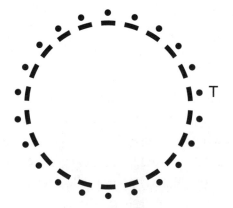

Circle: chairs outside

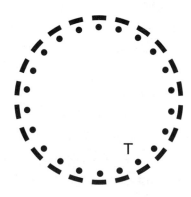

Circle: chairs inside

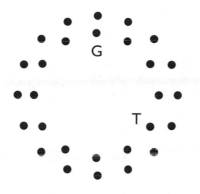

Fishbowl: a guest chair in inner circle

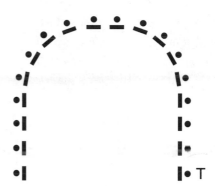

Horseshoe

Rectangular: chairs behind desk

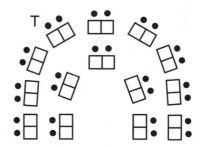

Horseshoe with paired desks

In many ways, the process of building a minds-on classroom environment resembles the world premiere of John Williams's work *Soundings*, composed for the opening of the Walt Disney Concert Hall in Los Angeles. In Williams's notes (2004) on the work, he explains how he began to see the collaborative possibilities of all the players in the piece, including the hall itself:

> As I admired the Hall and studied its interior, I wondered what it might be like if the building's brilliant exterior surfaces could be sounded and the Hall actually "sang" to us. These thoughts suggested the third section, "The Hall Responds," in which the Hall itself becomes a partner in the music making. The orchestra sounds a vibrant low D, and the Hall reverberates and responds. Three other great sails are sounded as the orchestra, led by the solo flute, sends messages which are returned to us from various locations in the Hall. (p. 1)

So as you take your first steps toward a dialogic classroom, keep Williams's vision of his concert in mind. The walls of your room and your arrangements will amplify the many vibrant notes of your voice and students' voices. You might think of yourself as an orchestra conductor and your students as co-composers and musicians.

STRATEGY: Define expectations and create buy-in
TOOL: Set ground rules

In many middle school classes, students have little opportunity to converse, so in a sense, it's beneficial to start from square one. For example, the teachers we've worked with have found it is helpful to have a brainstorming session on the very idea of conversation. Your not-so-hidden agenda is that you want your students to know how to participate actively in a discussion that will support thinking and talking about texts. The students and teacher together negotiate a plan. One way to do this is to engage your students in an activity called "Reflection on a Word" (Himley & Carini, 2000):

1. Ask your students to write a word—in this case the word "conversation" or "discussion"—in the middle of the paper.

2. For a couple of minutes, students write down associations they make with that word (not definitions). They write whatever comes to mind—metaphors, images, phrases, personal connections—using lines radiating outward, or just clustering ideas free-form on the page. The purpose is similar to that of tilling the soil after the frost; you want to loosen up ideas so there is prime ground from which to cultivate further ideas.

3. Call upon students to share their reflections on the word. Write their ideas on the board or on an overhead transparency for everyone to see.

4. Now help students engage in some critical thinking: Can they group the ideas into categories? What are the broader things to think about regarding real conversations or discussions? (Some broader outcomes for this topic may include: everyone feels valued; each participant can see and hear each other; new ideas about a topic or a book get shared; conversation gives you a better appreciation; everyone's point of view is different, and so on.

5. Ask students: Based on these categories, what sorts of ground rules would help you have satisfying discussions in class?

Involving students in generating rules is crucial, as it gives them a stake in sustaining conversations along agreed-upon lines. Reflection on a Word also promotes higher-level thinking, useful with any topic. Post the ground rules, as they offer students helpful cues.

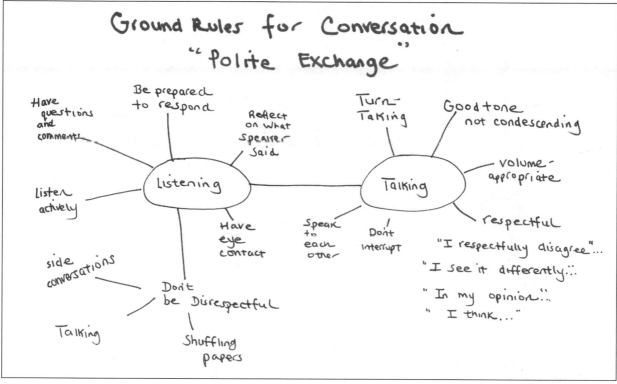

Ground Rules for Conversation "Polite Exchange"

- Have questions and comments
- Be prepared to respond
- Reflect on what speaker said
- Listening
- listen actively
- Have eye contact
- side conversations
- Talking
- Don't be Disrespectful
- Shuffling papers
- Turn-Taking
- Good tone not condescending
- Talking
- volume - appropriate
- respectful
- Speak to each other
- Don't interrupt
- "I respectfully disagree"...
- "I see it differently."...
- "In my opinion."...
- "I think..."

One class's ground rules, developed around two essential activities in discussion: listening and talking.

During our workshops, teachers sometimes ask us, "Wouldn't it be more effective to just hand out the ground rules to the students, and not waste valuable class time in creating them?" Teachers who are experienced with discussion-based classrooms respond that it is necessary for students to go through the process, for the sake of community building. It is the process of developing rules together that creates investment in the possibility of true discussions.

Reflection on a Word is not the only way to generate guidelines. For example, Kevin Miller, a seventh-grade teacher, asked his students to reflect in writing on this prompt: Have you ever been part of a good conversation? What happened? What makes a good conversation? The next day Kevin's students read aloud from their journals their ideas about what makes a good conversation. He listed them on the chalkboard, and then he and the class sorted them into categories. Based on the ideas that surfaced, the class generated their rules of discussion, casting them as a "board game" called dis-cussation. Kevin called them "The Ten Commandments of Discussion," typed them up, and had his students sign their names to it (see next page).

English
Mr. Miller
Classroom Discussion

The following rules have been compiled from the list and suggestions made by each and every one of you, the students. In some cases I have combined ideas or reworded rules to make them easier to understand.

Remember the directions and participate with an open mind and an enthusiastic heart.

Discussation: A Combination of Discussion and Conversations

Directions for this new and exciting board game that takes place right in your very own English class:

First, gather together as a class, and place chairs in a circle. Desks should be behind the chairs. Generally, the only thing you should need in your hands are any notes you have taken, or the book, story, or poem we are discussing.

Second, follow the initial directions given by Mr. Miller. After the sharing begins, don't look to me to jump in. I will call upon people to share, but don't talk to me, talk to the person you are responding to. Police yourselves and maintain the civility and order expected in any class discussion. Some of your rules follow:

1. Thou shall listen carefully to what is being said.
2. Thou shall respectfully disagree.
3. Thou shall know thy facts to support your opinions.
4. Thou shall raise your hand to share; hands down when others share.
5. Thou shall not use sarcasm, criticism, or interrupt or laugh at a fellow sharer.
6. Thou shall come to class prepared to share.
7. Thou shall share opinions, make connections, and be personal and honest.
8. Thou shall make good eye contact and avoid "sidebar" conversations.
9. Thou shall ask good questions and gently correct others when inaccuracies are voiced.
10. Thou shall not be scared to share and will be open-minded.

Lastly, be prepared by doing your homework the night before. You will not be able to add much to the discussion if you have not completed the appropriate reading assignment. Many of you mentioned some obvious rules like not shouting and the need to treat others as you would like to be treated. All I can add is: Take chances. Explore. Share. Question. Be honest and make connections to your life. Don't be afraid. Finally, don't share for too long a time.

I have read the above list of suggestions and rules and agree to them. I will play the game as well as I can, and be a polite and enthusiastic participant.

Date _____

Name _____

Signature. _____

Kevin Miller mixes students' ideas with a dose of good humor to establish working ground rules.

As you'll glean from the conversation below, it's useful to review the guidelines with students from time to time. Why? Because listening well and adeptly building on others' comments are really advanced skills that take a long time to assimilate as a habit. Here, Myra, the teacher, displays the list of rules before they begin a literature discussion:

> TEACHER: So I put this sheet up just so everybody can remember the rules that we came up with at the beginning of the year. Let's just quickly go over those expectations.
>
> Number One: Read the text before discussion. For this discussion we know that that's been accomplished.

Okay, Number Two: This is the most important one; especially today *everybody's going to participate and add something to the discussion.* Okay? And I'm going to have one of my notebooks open and I'm going to be taking notes on what people are saying, questions you're asking, and what you're actually doing during the discussion. Okay? So I'm going to be busy taking notes myself.

Number Three: You are going to have to *listen actively to others.* What do you guys think that means? You talk about reading actively, how do you listen actively? Don?

DON: Not to talk and always listening, be silent.

TEACHER: Okay. We shouldn't be talking during somebody-or-other's talking. What else? Mike?

MIKE: Make sure you're listening to what everybody has to say.

TEACHER: Okay. Make sure you're listening. Chris?

Guidelines for Discussion

✓ Everyone comes having read the text.

✓ Everyone needs to talk.

✓ Listen actively to others.

✓ Wait for quiet before you speak.

✓ Raise your hand after someone has finished.

✓ No one has a bad idea.

✓ Build on other's ideas.

✓ Maintain eye contact.

After their teacher articulated the first rule on the list, students generated other common-sense guidelines.

CHRIS: Respond to what they say.

TEACHER : Yeah, respond to what they say. And that really leads us into number four: *Build on others' ideas.* Okay? And when I think back to discussions we had in the past, I think that is the one thing we really need to work on, starting today, is really building and listening actively to others . . . You know how when you're in a conversation and your mind's busy making up your own ideas, and you have your own opinions, your own thoughts, and you're really not listening to what's being said? That's something we need to work on.

Number Five: *You are going to wait for the person to finish before you start talking.* And that's really important. Because I think we all know how annoying it is when you're saying something and someone cuts you off in the middle of it and doesn't let you finish. . . .

And lastly, maintain eye contact with *the group.* Why do you think I underlined *the group?* Who do you think you usually keep eye contact with? Kyle?

As Myra reviews the rules on the list, she reinforces the expectations for a minds-on classroom. The rules are a concrete reminder, like a contract, binding every member of the classroom with an expectation of dialogic talk.

Diving Into Dialogue: Ways to Swan Dive Rather Than Belly Flop

Think about it. When you have something to add to a conversation it's awfully hard to wait, isn't it? We may lean forward, look urgent—and then maybe just jump in, blurt out our comment, often using the word *but* to cut right in. And we stopped actively listening sever-

At the beginning of the discussion process, signs such as these help students learn how to bid for the floor.

Building Literacy Through Classroom Discussion

al moments earlier, so who knows how well what we say actually builds on things said before? Gracefully, respectfully entering a conversation is an art, and one that is learned by students when we give them rules of etiquette and effective language.

Take a look at the following prompts. They will keep a conversation pleasantly flowing like a river, rather than zig zagging haphazardly.

WAYS TO ENTER A CONVERSATION

- I think I agree with what you say because . . .
- I think I disagree with what you say because . . .
- I'm not sure I understand. Could you show me something in the text that makes you say that?
- I have another idea . . .

Prompts such as these are more easily adopted by students if they are given the opportunity to discuss them and add to them, and perhaps put them into their own language. Here, a teacher develops effective entry comments with her class:

TEACHER: I thought it would be good if you had some suggestions to get you into the conversation. These are just some ways—if you're actively listening, how to make comments and get into the discussion, if you're not sure how to start. Okay?

After you listen to somebody, you could say, "I think I agree with what you said, because . . ." and then get your opinion out there that way, if it is because you agree with what's being said. Next, "I think I disagree with what you said, because . . ." But make sure that if you have an opinion, you explain it, and use the text as much as possible to support what you are saying. The next one, "I'm not sure I understand—could you show me something in the text that makes you say that?" So use that prompt if somebody just gave an opinion but didn't back it up with what they read, or the text. And then lastly, "I have another idea..." but in some way showing that even if you want to change the topic a little, acknowledge somehow, that you heard what the last comment was. Make some connection to it even if you think you want to change what's being discussed. Okay? Does anybody have any questions?

These first two strategies—setting up the environment and establishing the ground rules—should take you only a class period. For the next class period, you'll want to immerse your students in an actual discussion, which we'll look at next.

> ## STRATEGY: Create successful early experiences with discussion
> ## TOOL: Provide rich, accessible texts

Just as theater directors—with dreams of Broadway in their heads—want their play's opening night to receive rave reviews, it's important that you make your students' first discussions successful and satisfying for them. They may be initially more comfortable in the monologic "theater" of learning. Success now may mean something different than it will later, when you're all well-versed in dialogue. Now, what you're trying to achieve is good participation—as many children as possible listening well and speaking constructively.

A critical tool at this point is a high-quality text. A short story that is a couple of pages long or an intriguing poem works well. A good rule of thumb is to choose a text about which you feel excited. Of course, you will want a text that will appeal to and be appropriate for your students as well. Look for ambiguity, something to puzzle over, in your first shared piece. Some short pieces that we have seen work well in a first discussion include "The Dinner Party" by Mona Gardner, "Thank You Ma'am" by Langston Hughes, "Eleven" or "My Name" by Sandra Cisneros, "Snow" by Julia Alvarez, and "Oranges" by Gary Soto. These diverse texts work well either because they are written from a young adult's perspective or they have an intriguing ambiguity. The diversity of authors and subjects appeal to students from a variety of backgrounds and experiences—they may relate to the characters, the setting, or the situation. And you will be engaged as well, as a thinker and learner, because you find the story exciting. Let's imagine that you've picked "Oranges," a poem about a sweet memory of first love.

> ## STRATEGY: To get students talking, listening, and feeling successful
> ## TOOL: Use Wonder Questions, Passing the Hat, and other writing and speaking activities

Wonder Questions. Picture this: All your students sit in a circle. The desks are cleared; binders and other material have been placed underneath the chairs. Each student has a copy of the poem "Oranges," by Gary Soto, and a pen in his or her hand. You read the poem aloud, bringing it to life with the intonations of your voice. After reading, you pause so students may appreciate the impressions the poem left on them. You tell them you are going to read the poem aloud again, only this time they are to follow along and mark the text— underline, make question marks, jot down words or associations, and circle words they don't know.

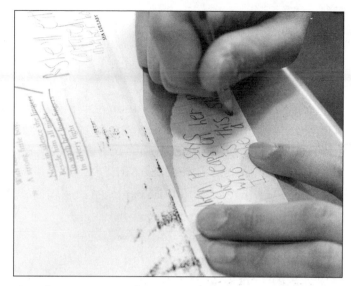

A student writes a wonder question.

Your students are actively engaged with the text as you read it aloud. When you finish, again, you give them time to savor the poem. Then you ask: "What are you wondering about? Is there a question in your mind?" You call this a "wonder question."

Passing the Hat. You ask students to write their wonder questions on slips of paper. You collect them and put them in a hat or a small basket. A student pulls a question from the hat and reads it. Or you choose to be the first reader. Once the first question is asked, you invite someone to

With anticipation, a student draws a slip of paper from the hat and prepares to read it aloud.

respond. Once the responses are diminishing, someone pulls another question and reads it out, and the conversation begins again. This way, all students have an equal opportunity to hear their questions asked and discussed.

This approach—passing the hat and having students' wonder questions drive the conversation—is dramatically different from asking study guide questions, for you are actually shifting your focus to *students'* ideas about the story. We'll discuss how to facilitate the conversation, sustain it, and make it more productive in terms of literary thinking in Chapter 5. But for now the goal is to develop some early successful experiences, to get students talking and listening, and to help you begin to distinguish, in your own mind, between students' ideas and your own ideas about a text. As you begin to tease ideas apart, you may feel that tension that Connie spoke of earlier, that tug between you as a person and as an educator. As we give the floor to students' ideas, the teacher part of us may fret that students might not be taking from the text the "correct" understandings. For now, though, keep it simple. Invite students to react to texts using prompts as jump starts, listen closely, encourage authentic responses, and build connections between comments to give students that wonderful charge they feel when their ideas are affirmed.

> What was the story supposed to tell the reader?
>
> Why did the kids care about the lady painting on the wall?
>
> Was Jimmy Lyons a real person in the author's life?
>
> What did the Wall really represent?
>
> Why was the wall so important to the children? Why was the lady ignoring the children when they were trying to talk to her?
>
> Will the painter woman ever return back to the town to paint something else?

A collection of wonder questions shows students' deep curiosity after reading "The War of the Wall."

Journal Jots. Writing goes hand in hand with reading. It helps students to clarify their thinking and make sense of the text. One good way to invite students to write about their reading is to have them do "journal jots." These quick jots can be assigned any time you wish—as homework, in the midst of a discussion, right after one, and so forth. And they can be connected with other writing venues. For example, in one eighth-grade class, the teacher connected the journal jot to her students' reading log entries. (To facilitate these entries, each time her students read a text, she asked her students to write about one of the following: their thoughts and feelings, surprises, new ideas and information, personal connections, text connections, world connections, favorite parts, important passages, questions and/or confusing words.)

From these brief, frequent comments in their logs, students created longer journal jots. In turn, the

journal jots were used as a takeoff for class discussion. Sometimes the teacher asked her students to develop their jots into an essay.

T-charts. This graphic organizer is a classic, because it's such an effective tool for helping students track their developing understanding of a text. Students divide a journal page into two halves. On the left side, they jot down their understandings of the story as they read.

Dear Journal Jot,

I have just finished chapter three of the book <u>The Call Of the Wild</u>. This chapter was called "The Dominant Primordial Beast." I thought that it was very interesting how the first words in this chapter were the title of the chapter itself. This chapter started on page 27, and ended on page 43. I still don't find this book interesting, but I'm trying to read on, hoping that something will come up that I will enjoy.

One big thing that took place in this chapter was the changing of Buck. The title explains Buck, changing into almost a beast. The words 'dominant' and 'primordial' are explaining his new character. Buck used to be a well-tamed dog that minded his own business. He changed all of a sudden, almost secretly into a beast that then soon became a killer. This poor dog learned from the rest of the team of sled dogs, and thought that if he didn't act like them, he wouldn't survive. Buck changed a lot in this chapter.

Another big thing that took place in this chapter was when a huge pack of wild dogs came and attacked the camp, looking for food. The book described the events that night as horrible and unexpected. These pathetic, savage dogs came and destroyed almost everything. These dogs were pathetic because their skin was almost transparent. You could see and count every rib. The clubs that were hitting them repeatedly injured many of these dogs, but yet they did not seem to notice, or care. They weren't even trying to fight back. All they wanted was food. That night was very eventful, and many of the sled dogs were injured badly. Buck was scratched on his throat, and one dog even lost his eye.

In my opinion, I think that the fight between Buck and Spitz was the most important part of the whole chapter. This fight determined life or death. The two dogs were basically fighting for their lives. I was very surprised when Buck came back at the end and threw Spitz down on the ground. That gave him more power, just like the law of fang states. Now that that fight is over, I am hoping that the violence will stop. Many things have happened in Chapter 3, and I hope many more exciting events happen throughout the rest of this book.

Your Friend,

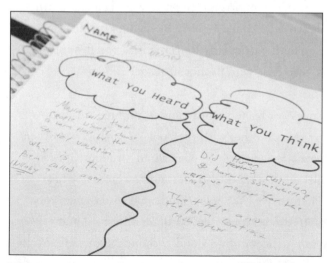

T-charts are excellent tools to take down ideas and see them grow.

Although she claims that *Call of the Wild* (London) is not interesting, this student uses her journal to develop a vivid envisionment.

These include impressions, connections, inferences, predictions, and questions they have at that point in reading. On the right side, they write their understandings *after* discussion. Here they will reflect on how some of their ideas evolved during or after the conversation. Thus the T-chart helps students to listen to one another and appreciate that their understandings change as a result of discussion.

Wait Time: Count to Ten!

There are going to be times when class discussions feel like a bad date—halting talk, low energy, uncomfortable silences. That quiet may be excruciating to you as a teacher, but listen and you'll hear the wheels of students' thoughts turning. Pausing invites thinking—for all of us. So wait ten seconds or longer after you've read aloud a text before you invite students to speak up. And initially impose at least five seconds of wait time after a student has made a comment; see if a student has anything to say before you make a "bridging" response.

You now have a number of tools to help you create early successful experiences with discussion. However, how do you help your struggling learners—those who have trouble with reading, predicting, questioning, or writing? This next strategy will provide some solutions.

STRATEGY: Involve all learners in the class discussion
TOOL: Use an array of instructional techniques for developing reading skills

During the first weeks of your class discussions, it's helpful to begin by reading the text aloud a couple of times, as this creates a shared experience that supports all students, especially your struggling readers. However, because struggling readers need to build fluency by reading on their own, and because you won't be able to read every text aloud, particularly longer works, you'll want to incorporate techniques that help these students keep pace with proficient readers.

Paired Reading. One enormously helpful strategy for readers whose understanding breaks down easily is paired reading. Student partners sit next to each other with the book or text between them (or each with his or her own copy). Student A reads a paragraph or page aloud. Student B listens and follows along in the text. They stop and talk about what they understand so far. They raise questions; they point to what confuses them. Then they switch roles. Student B reads; they stop, talk, and perhaps jot down any remaining questions to ask the class. Both are minds-on and focused. Moreover, both have the opportunity to practice reading aloud without the pressure of the whole class listening, so they can build fluency. They also have the opportunity to stop when needed to ask a question or re-read a sentence that didn't quite make sense the first time. It's an excellent

activity to do especially with struggling learners just before a whole-class discussion.

Reciprocal Teaching. A more structured version of paired reading is called Reciprocal Teaching (Brown & Palincsar, 1986). For this strategy, students are taught to follow these steps:

Student A **reads** a section of the text.
Student A **clarifies** words and ideas.
Student A **asks** questions about the text.

surface level (who? what? when? where?)

and/or deeper (how? why?).

Student A **summarizes** what was read.
Student A **predicts** what comes next.
Switch roles and repeat steps with student B, using the next portion of text.

Paired reading, joint thinking.

Readers thus have multiple opportunities to make meaning: rereading, talking about the text, sharing insights and experiences, making connections, and grappling with the literary elements of the text. Eventually the readers internalize the process.

Think Alouds. With this technique, which is often presented by teachers but can be done by students as well, an experienced reader gives a play-by-play of how he or she is making sense of a text. Struggling readers are thus treated to all the strategies that get called upon while reading. First, the teacher selects a paragraph that is challenging for the typical student—something with some complexity to it or some demanding vocabulary. The teacher explains that he or she is literally going to think aloud for them, to show them the thought process involved in figuring out this tough paragraph. As the teacher reads a sentence or phrase aloud, he or she pauses periodically to reveal all the fleeting thoughts, questions, and hunches that occur during sustained silent reading.

This reporting helps students to develop their own internal dialogue while they read. Students begin to see that more than reading for plot or topic sentences, you read to understand what's

going on between the lines, and that to achieve this understanding, it's normal for your thoughts to be like a bunch of balls being juggled in the air. To comprehend, you make connections to your own experiences, you visualize a scene, predict what's going to happen next, infer what the author intends, and so on.

After the teacher finishes thinking aloud, a strong reader can think aloud the next paragraph, and so on. Then students can practice the strategy in pairs so that everyone has the experience. The goal is for this complex comprehension process to become internalized, as it is with proficient readers. We liken it to riding a bike; in many ways, once you internalize these moves, you're not really aware of using them, but you never forget how to get all these mental actions rolling.

Text Marks. Making text marks is another invaluable tool for struggling readers. Pam, a seventh-grade teacher, calls these "reader's marks." When we visited her class, she pinned a description of reader's marks underneath her Thoughtful Community sign and also gave a copy to every child for keeping.

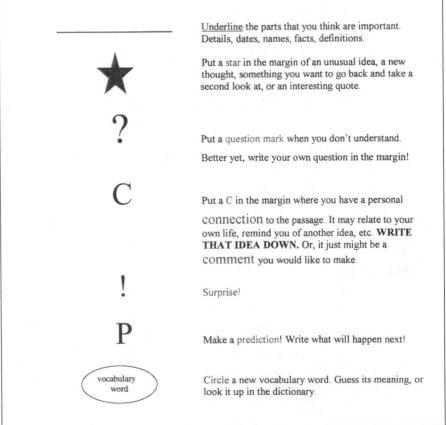

A Reader's Marks

Good readers actively think while they read. With the right equipment, a pencil or pen, you can master all you read. By making your thoughts visible you can: learn the basic facts, think beyond the passage, spot essential vocabulary, ask important questions, remember information, connect ideas, and gain confidence. You will see your ideas at work!

———————— Underline the parts that you think are important. Details, dates, names, facts, definitions.

★ Put a star in the margin of an unusual idea, a new thought, something you want to go back and take a second look at, or an interesting quote.

? Put a question mark when you don't understand. Better yet, write your own question in the margin!

C Put a C in the margin where you have a personal connection to the passage. It may relate to your own life, remind you of another idea, etc. **WRITE THAT IDEA DOWN.** Or, it just might be a comment you would like to make.

! Surprise!

P Make a prediction! Write what will happen next!

(vocabulary word) Circle a new vocabulary word. Guess its meaning, or look it up in the dictionary.

Text Marks: A constant companion at the beginning.

You'll find the reader's marks activity an engaging and effective tool for students of any reading level, but especially potent for struggling readers. As one student commented, when she was asked to underline important facts in a newspaper article, "I don't know what is important." Being allowed to take the time to mark the text with a fun code helps these students flag just where they struggle. They can then sort out the problem better when rereading or in subsequent class discussion or peer work. Of course, you and your students can invent your own series of helpful symbols. And when you're not reading a photocopy, students can write on sticky notes. A seventh grader told us that using sticky notes to make text marks while reading was beneficial for a number of reasons:

> I jot down questions, ideas and observations I have. This saves me a lot of time when journaling for class, because I don't have to go back and search for ideas; they are already there. I have learned to read not just for the plot but also real-world connections, symbolism and other observations. I find this enables me to enjoy the books more and not just read the words on the page.

A teacher put text marks at the bottom of each page to help her special-education students.

Critical Lens Cheat Sheet

<u>Comments</u>

@ Place an @ next to a sentence, quote, or passage that identifies tone. What words, feelings, and effects does the author use to create a mood for the piece?

T Put a *T* for any indication of theme. Is there a statement the author is trying to convey to the reader?

F Jot an *F* to mark examples of foreshadowing that the author may have placed. Maybe you can tie this with a prediction or inference.

= Place an = for the many types of conflict. What characters are struggling? Ask yourself who or what is triggering the action?

% Use a % sign to mark an area where the author has created point of view. Consider the author's choice. Is it active, passive, or shifting?

& Do you see examples of symbolism? If so, mark it with an *&*.

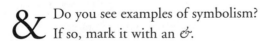

After students have become comfortable with text marks, a teacher raises the bar by extending student response into the fourth stance (see page 90). A prompt list such as this one helps students recognize and consider a text's literary devices and features of authors' craft.

Reading and Thinking about Poetry

The Runaway   *by Robert Frost*

[left margin handwritten annotations:]
Simile—
colt is like
a shadow
because the
roots like
a shadow

Well
his
mother
soon
noticed
is gone?

I am
surprised
he is afried
of snow!
It's just
white
cold
stuff!

C

In the
story
Call of the
Wild Buck
reacted toward
Snow to it.
ne ver saw it.

[poem text:]
Once when the snow of the year was beginning to fall,
We stopped by a mountain pasture to say, "Whose colt?"
A little Morgan had one forefoot on the wall,
The other curled at his breast. He dipped his head
And snorted at us. And then he had to bolt   5
We heard a miniature thunder where he fled,
And we saw him, or thought we saw him, dim and gray,
Like a shadow against the curtain of falling flakes.
"I think the little fellow is afraid of the snow.
He isn't winter broken. It isn't play   10
With the little fellow at all. He's running away.
I doubt if his mother could tell him, 'Sakes,
It's only weather.' He'd think she didn't know!
Where is his mother? He can't be out alone."
And now he comes again with the clatter of stone,   15
And mounts the wall again with whited eyes
And all his tail that isn't hair up straight.
He shudders his coat as if to throw off flies.
"Whoever it is that leaves him out so late,
When other creatures have gone to stall and bin,   20
Ought to be told to come out and take him in."

[right margin handwritten annotations:]
bolt—Runaway to charge
colt—Babby horse
forefoot—front leg
(hind leg)
Morgan—type of horse
used for pulling
very musclear

surprised.
he gestered
at them

Where
is
his mother
or
father?

C. In the story we just read
William thought his mom
didn't know anything about
homeless People

I wonder if
the colt is
afried of
any other kind
of weather?

Initial Understandings

1 What are your thoughts about the poem?
   • I thought the poem was really ween written. I can not believe the colt is afried of snow.
   • I also thought some parts of the poem was difficult to understand. The Author or the poet used strong writting.

2 What do you think the message of the poem is?
   • I think the message of the poem is to stay in the stall and whatch over you colt or neorse will wind up getting lost.
   • I also think the message is to be wise and think before you do something.

Multiple Perspectives

1 What do the people who stop by the mountain pasture witness?
   • The people who stop by the mountain witness a colt
   • The colt is afried of snow he isnt inside the stall like most animals

2 What are their thoughts?
   • Their thoughts are he is lost from his mother.
   • Their thoughts are he ought to be taken in.

A student marks up a text, making his thinking visible.

Some students happily used the text marks strategy throughout the year. For other students, the marks became a distraction and something they no longer needed, as they had internalized the idea. That's the beauty of scaffolding; when students no longer need the support, the scaffolding is removed.

In this chapter, we have focused on how to get started in building a dialogic classroom. We've suggested some strategies and corresponding tools for this beginning phase. In the next chapter, we look at some of the challenges and questions that may arise during the process.

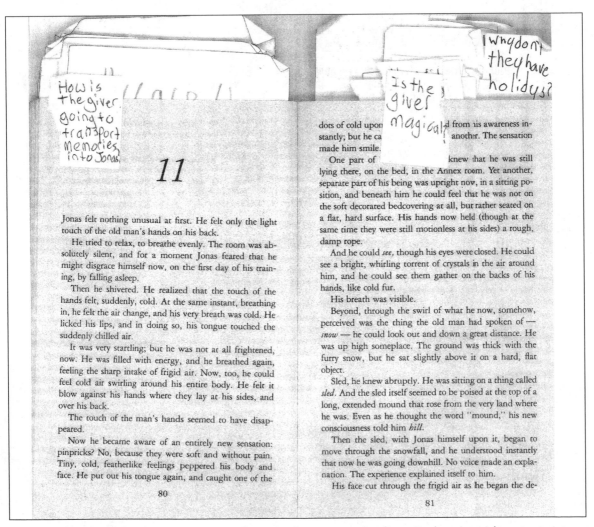

In this copy of *The Giver* by Lois Lowry, we see how a student prepares for discussion by using sticky notes to jot down authentic questions and ideas.

Chapter Three
Beginning Discussion

Reflection and troubleshooting

Now let's look at what really happens when the theory of dialogic interactions bumps up against the reality of middle school classrooms. This chapter and all the other troubleshooting chapters in this book are based on the real questions (and frustrations) that Partnership teachers experienced, so read on! We want you to feel supported every step of the way as you move from the basics to full-blown dialogic instruction.

In essence, as they implemented the strategies and tools outlined in the previous chapter, the Partnership teachers had questions about their role in this new kind of teaching and learning. Yes, they were excited to focus more of their curriculum and class time on students' ideas, questions, and diverse voices. They were becoming more adept at holding students accountable for participating, for producing a deeper understanding of the content. They wouldn't say every discussion was scintillating and successful, but things were progressing. And yet, they worried a lot that the shift in focus might be causing them to drop the ball on preparing students sufficiently. After all, students need to meet state standards and do well on the standardized tests at the end of the year. How do we do both? they all seemed to ask.

And so we focus this chapter's questions and answers on this issue. What is your function in a classroom that heavily relies on discussion as the engine of learning? Are you a facilitator? A subject matter expert? A guide? A coach?

Roberts & Langer (1991) analyzed a set of middle school discussions closely and found that teachers take on a number of different roles, depending on the needs of the students: "The teacher assumes the role of supporter of the process of understanding, through her involvement in the discussion as the *orchestrator* of the event, the *clarifier* of student meanings, and the *helper* and *supporter* of student attempts at more difficult tasks" (p. 37, emphasis added). *In this different kind of classroom, the teacher's role—as orchestrator, clarifier, helper, and supporter—is critically important, not because it provides the correct answer, but because it teaches students how to become participants in a conversation of their own making.*

Let's keep these varying roles in mind as we look at a number of common situations in which discussion wasn't completely successful.

Q: I tried the discussion and it was a complete bust. Students didn't seem to have anything to say. What do I do?

A: Don't give up. Students do have ideas to share. You may just need to try some different approaches. Here are some ideas:

Building Literacy Through Classroom Discussion

Revisit material before discussing it. You may be very familiar with the story, textbook chapter, or whatever it is you're discussing, but your students may not have looked at it since they read it, before the weekend or the big game. This is especially true for those on block schedules; a day or two may have passed since you last saw them. If you take a few minutes to review part of the text, perhaps doing a combination of brief reading aloud and some summarizing, students will be back in the mind-set you want them to be in, primed for discussion. Additionally, students who were absent will be able to catch enough of the content to follow the discussion and perhaps even participate.

Let students know you expect the world of them. We can't overemphasize how important it is to state your expectations for student thinking. Let students know that you want them to come prepared for a discussion, with ideas and questions to use as a starting point. Give them a few sticky notes so they can mark places that they want to talk about. Provide a few minutes before or during the discussion for students to review their notes or jot down some ideas to use as starting points. Then, begin by asking, "What do you want to talk about? Who has a question or comment to share with the group? What did your reading make you wonder about?" And remember, it's tough to overdo compliments—if they're honestly felt, that is. Refer back to insights and ideas of students that have stayed with you since previous discussions. This sends them the message that they are intellectual powerhouses, and that your goal is to build an ongoing conversation.

Give students the language for responding to each other. On the chalkboard, on a poster, and as a handout, provide students with phrases that work well to link to previous comments. Some phrases that work in most every discussion include
- At first I thought that . . .
- I agree with . . .
- I want to add to the comment about . . .
- I disagree with . . .
- I have more evidence for . . .
- I found that comment interesting because . . .
- I want to connect that comment to our earlier discussion of . . .
- I have a question about . . .
- I have an additional point to make . . .

Think of these sample phrases as ropes that students will use to loop their ideas onto those of the rest of the class. Without connecting phrases, their ideas will hang there, isolated, and dangle into oblivion. But hooked together, the students' words will create a great rope hammock that holds related ideas. Over time, your students will develop their own ways of phrasing.

> **Q: I tried the sample phrases, but students didn't use them to build on or comment on one another's ideas. They just kept adding new thoughts of their own. What do I do?**

A: Help students to listen carefully.

As we mentioned above, one of the most difficult challenges of a class discussion is helping students to actively listen so that when they add a comment, they stand a better chance of stitching it onto the content of what a classmate has just said. Some classes get into the swing of this with no difficulty at all, but most will take some time and practice. Some active-listening strategies that teachers have found to be effective include the following:

Periodically make overt connections between student comments. Here's an example from a seventh grade classroom discussion of a poem:

> TEACHER: Jenny, I'm going to draw a thread over here to Tom, because you two used the same word and I want to talk a little bit about it. The word is *popularity*. (*Long pause.*) Who deems whether you are popular or not? I'm wondering, perhaps, what is the definition of *popularity*? How does this phenomenon happen?

In this way, the teacher orchestrates the participants to listen to one another and build on the ideas they've already heard. The students in this class probably did not even realize that they were both talking about the concept of popularity. Because students typically are not skilled at this kind of conversation, you'll have to model this kind of support for quite a while.

Have students write about the discussion. In writing, students have an opportunity to absorb what they have learned from one another. Here's how a seventh-grade teacher explained the assignment to her class:

Building Literacy Through Classroom Discussion

I'd like you to write one, or two, or three sentences for me that you could bring to class tomorrow. I'd love to see a paragraph; I imagine I'll see many paragraphs. This is why I ask you: Many of you still had your hands up, so I want you to share your voice with me in writing. I'll still hear you. And when we come into class tomorrow, we'll use this as a springboard, to move back into the conversation. Here's your question: Tell me one comment that was powerful during today's discussion and why. One comment that you heard today. Do you agree? Do you want to disagree? Do you want to build on it?

By the end of the year, one of the students concluded that, "there is nothing to write about if you have not listened during class." Another commented, "I've discovered that when you listen to your peers, they can give you very good information, which may snag you and cause you to build upon or write about it in an essay or poem."

> **Q: I tried a discussion generated by students' questions. Their questions were okay, but they answered them really quickly and then went off on a tangent. How do I use the conversation to get at the important parts of the book?**

A: What kinds of questions stimulate discussion? Student questions, as you mentioned, are a great starting place. Yet when students begin asking questions, they often model them on what they've heard in previous classes. In other words, students at first may ask test-like questions, not ones designed to stimulate controversy or thinking. That's why the wonder questions described in Chapter 2 work so well; they're almost guaranteed to produce authentic inquiry because they're truly what adolescents are pondering.

As preparation, you'll want to have some backup questions prepared. What kinds of backup questions are helpful? Start with authentic questions (Nystrand, 1997). *Avoid questions to which there is only one answer, which you already know.* These are what we consider test questions. (Ramirez et al., 1991, call them "display" questions, because they are designed to get students to display their knowledge on a topic.)

Some good authentic questions that work with nearly every discussion include the following:
- What are your first impressions?
- What are you wondering about?
- What parts of the text or activity were especially powerful for you? Why?

- How did your understanding of _____ (a character, an event, a person, an idea, etc.) change over time?
- How can you relate what is going on (in this text or in an activity) to life outside of school?
- What texts, books, films, songs, or television shows does this (text or activity) remind you of? Tell us about the connection.

Some phrases/questions to use when a student makes an intriguing comment ripe for elaboration:

- You used the word _____. Let's think about that. Why do you think that word came to your mind as you were talking about this part of the story?
- Interesting. Tell us more about that.

We'll talk more about questioning techniques in Part 2. For now, know that you are going to do lots of modeling so that students can absorb the language and techniques of sharing thoughts and connecting them to the thoughts of others.

> **Q: My students talked, but they were tentative, looking at me for approval the whole time. How do I get them really motivated to explore a topic so that they're more independent of me?**

A: Be provocative.

A time-tested way to get students invested in the conversation is to ask them to wrestle with different, even contrasting points of view. Juxtaposing texts that speak to a compelling topic creates a thought-provoking environment in which students seek to elaborate on and support their ideas with evidence—skills that will serve them well on standardized tests and beyond. What are some ways to challenge students' thinking?

- **Use texts that approach an issue in different ways.** One way to do this is to find texts on the same topic, written in different genres. For example, students reading *The Watsons Go to Birmingham—1963* (published in 1995) could also read the 1963 *Washington Post* account of the bombing of the church in which four young girls died ("Six Dead After Church Bombing"). They could then examine the Norman Rockwell painting "The Problem We All Live With" (1964), which depicts an African American girl being escorted to a recently desegregated school. The difference in tone and focus between the newspaper account, the painting,

and the novel create a rich topic for discussion and analysis. Think back to that prism metaphor; if you can position topics so that they have these refracting properties, then the dialogue that ensues can more easily break into the various, bouncing hues of thought that successful conversations possess.

- **Provide students with a provocative quotation to which they can react.** Here are several, for instance, that teachers have successfully used with *The Giver* (but which apply to many young adult texts):

  - "When we lose the right to be different, we lose the privilege to be free."
    —Charles Evans Hughes

  - "Art upsets, science reassures." —Georges Brague

  - "Man himself has become our greatest hazard and our only hope."—John Steinbeck

  - "If people have to choose between freedom and sandwiches, they will take sandwiches."—Lord Boyd Orr

  - "I think of a hero as someone who understands the degree of responsibility that comes with his [or her] freedom." —Bob Dylan

- **Give students a couple of strong statements with which to agree or disagree.** For example, you might begin a discussion of John Steinbeck's *The Pearl* with the statement "Everyone is capable of greed and selfishness." Give students about five to ten minutes to take a position and write down some thoughts. Then let them go. If you've phrased your statement right, about half your students will agree, and half will disagree. Perfect. Get them talking, providing evidence,

---

<u>On My Honor – Who is to blame?</u>

Tony's death has left many questions in Joel's mind (and ours) regarding who is responsible, or whose fault it is that he died. Below, assign a number ranking to each person (1 – 4), which will signify who you think is most to blame for Tony's death.

1 = Most responsible
4 = Least responsible

Joel   _____
Tony   _____
Joel's dad   _____
Tony's parents   _____

In your assigned groups, come to a consensus, or agreement, about who is most at fault. You will be sharing your group's opinion with the rest of the class. Be prepared to justify your opinion, so, as a group, find reasons in the text to support what you decide.

Remember to follow our classroom rules for group work!

Names of my group members:

Group decision...

_____ is/are most responsible for Tony's death
because_____
_____
_____
_____.

Expressing their opinions on this handout helped a group of seventh grade struggling readers become engrossed in the discussion.

supporting their opinions, and listening to each other. Then, have that discussion again in light of the book.

- **Have students rank the degree of responsibility a person or character should take for his/her actions.** (See previous page for an assignment from *On My Honor,* by Marion Bauer.)
- **Select material with discussion possibilities.** What kinds of texts, activities, and writing assignments are good fodder for discussions? A key first test is to gauge your own interest level. If you find the text or topic boring, chances are your students will too. And who wants to discuss a boring text? A good second test is to look for texts/topics that incorporate *contrast* and *ambiguity.* Characters with more than one motivation, endings that are not clear-cut, processes that have more than one approach or answer, texts that present a different perspective than the norm—these are all types of material that should provoke lively thinking and discussion. See what happens when seventh graders sink their teeth into an ambiguous element in "Seventh Grade," a short story by Gary Soto:

JULIE: On the first page, in the second paragraph, it says, "She's going to be my girl." I don't see how he says that, because how's he supposed to know something like that?

TEACHER: Okay, why does he think he knows that; what does he mean by "she's going to be my girl"?

JULIE: I know what he means, but I don't see why he says it.

OSCAR: Okay, I have the answer to that. . . . Because he's gonna get her.

JULIE: You can't make someone be your girlfriend.

OSCAR: Yeah, if you do . . . if you impress her . . .

JULIE: That doesn't make her be your girlfriend . . .

OSCAR: What do you mean? If you impress her and stuff . . .

(Three other students have hands raised now.)

OSCAR: Wait, I'm talking to Julie, okay? You could impress a girl and then she might like you. And in this story she likes him because in the end it says something about, um, the teacher . . . he said something in French and then she was like, "I didn't know you knew French," and then he impressed her and stuff.

JULIE: But that wasn't *making* her like him.

OSCAR: How do you know? How do you know? The story didn't finish off.

CARL: Making her isn't . . . making her is—

TEACHER : Okay, okay, we might be just arguing about a word. . . . Obviously you can't make

anyone . . . but I think Oscar has a point that, that's how he's going about it, he's going to impress her. And that final scene in French class, that climax of the story, is really the height of him trying to impress her. Carl, what did you want to say?

CARL: I wanted to say that I don't think that he's saying he's going to make her be his girl-friend; I think he's saying "I just hope."

In this segment, students wrestle with the language of the text as well as with the concept of human nature: What does it mean to *make* someone like you? Is such a thing possible? Is impressing someone the same thing as making him or her like you? Doesn't the other person have some say in how they feel about you, independent of your actions? This conversation is possible because (a) the text does not definitively settle the issue of how Theresa and Victor feel about each other, (b) the teacher, comfortable with student disagreement, does not initially interrupt, and (c) once Oscar and Julie have made their points, the teacher intervenes by summarizing the situation, locating it specifically within the climax of the story, and then inviting a new student, Carl, to make his point. Although the facilitation is obviously very important in discussions, the text you choose is critical to stirring up a pleasantly heated discussion. See the sidebar on the next page for a list of texts that our teachers have found to work well.

Although texts and topics that are lush with contrast and ambiguity may not be found in a typical textbook, you can provide such depth by using the textbook to supplement longer works. For instance, the novel *The Giver* provides ample ambiguities. In journal entries, students often write such questions as "What about the Elders?" "How are they treated in this place?" "How come they have so much power?" This is an ambiguity because the social structure of *The Giver* is revealed only slowly over time, and because the structure is so different from what students know—so different from the way the elderly are treated (or mistreated) in today's society. You can contrast this view with shorter pieces from the textbook that offer different images of the elderly, such as those within a "Generations" theme. Students also might interview their own grandparents or other seniors in their community, so that it hits them full force that the elderly have so much know-how and wisdom, so many interesting stories, and yet have relatively little power in American culture. They might also look into the position of the elderly in other societies of the world, past and present.

So while your literature anthology may pale in comparison to whole texts, some of the selections will lend themselves to engaging discussions, especially if you pair them with a second text that addresses the same theme or issue. As we've said, inviting children to read across genres is excellent,

as it gets their synapses firing, and gets them to realize that an event or issue in a novel written today can be found in a lead story from a newspaper 40 years ago. They begin to connect concepts in a larger screen of understanding. We'll talk more about this in Part 3.

> **Q: A few times when I facilitated, students paused to listen to the question I asked, and then went right back to talking about the same issue as before. Why are they ignoring my question?**

A: This is a common phenomenon, in our experience. When students stop, look, and listen to your interjection, and then resume where they left on, they are signaling to you that your question *didn't take*—that is, either you chose a bad time to interrupt, or your question was too far removed from the topic at hand, or your students were simply more invested in the current idea. It's not personal—it's just a subconscious way of letting you know that they haven't really heard you. Wait a few minutes and consider the situation. Perhaps there is a better way of asking the question that will build off of the current topic in a more direct way. Or it may be that what you initially thought was a tangential topic is actually helping students to understand the text or activity. If students are absorbed in a discussion that you think has outlived its usefulness, try this

Texts that spark good discussions in middle school

Canyons, by Gary Paulsen. New York: Dell, 1991.

Esperanza Rising, by Pam Muñoz Ryan. New York: Scholastic Press, 2000.

Ironman, by Chris Crutcher. New York: Laurel Leaf Books, 1996.

Lyddie, by Katherine Paterson. New York: Puffin Books, 1992.

Money Hungry, by Sharon G. Flake. New York: Jump at the Sun/Hyperion Books for Children, 2001.

Nothing But the Truth, by Avi. New York: Avon, 1993.

145th Street: Short Stories, by Walter Dean Myers. New York: Delacorte Press, 2000.

Parvana's Journey, by Deborah Ellis. Toronto, ON: Douglas & McIntyre, 2002.

Shabanu, Daughter of the Wind, by Suzanne Fisher Staples. New York: Knopf, 1989.

Tangerine, by Edward Bloor. New York: Scholastic, 1997.

The Giver, by Lois Lowry. New York: Yearling Books, 1997.

The House on Mango Street, by Sandra Cisneros. New York: Vintage Books, 1991.

The Skin I'm In, by Sharon G. Flake. New York: Scholastic, 1998.

The Watsons Go to Birmingham—1963, by Christopher Paul Curtis. New York: Bantam Books, 1995.

Whirligig, by Paul Fleischman. New York: H. Holt, 1998.

Words by Heart, by Ouida Sebestyen. New York: Bantam Books, 1981.

approach: Jot a related question down on the board and have students write for three to five minutes on that question. Then ask for comments. Most of the time, writing helps students to collect their thoughts and refocus.

> **Q: I've noticed that even when students are facing each other and answering a question posed by one of their peers, they turn their heads to look at me. Why do they do this? And what can I do about it?**

A: Old habits die hard. Even when adults respond to a question posed by one of their peers, they make eye contact with the discussion leader—often completely ignoring the person who posed the question they are answering. We're all conditioned to answering authority. But that said, there are things you can do to try to change this engrained behavior. The gist is, you've got to change the rules of the game.

Clearly state your expectations. If you want students to respond directly to each other, tell them. Develop a nonverbal signal you can use when they fall back into their old habits and start to address all answers to you. Here are some that Partnership teachers used:

- Put your index finger up and sweep it in a quick circle, indicating the whole group.
- Tell students that you will be taking notes during the conversation. This strategy is effective in a number of ways (more about this later); one positive byproduct is that by keeping your attention focused on the page, it forces students to make eye contact with their peers.
- Use body language. Ask students to sit forward and lean in toward the speaker, to physically show their interest in the person's comment. Model this yourself, by sitting forward in your chair, looking intent, nodding when someone is speaking, and jotting down notes. Even students who aren't initially engaged will begin to look in that direction, just to find out what it is that is so darn interesting to you!
- When all else fails, draw a happy face on a big sheet of paper, and hold it up in front of your face during discussion, saying, "I'm not here right now. Talk to each other!"

Consider the pros and cons of hand-raising. If you are going to call on students and/or affirm responses in between each speaker, the conversation is more likely to run through you, which can interrupt and inhibit the flow of student ideas. Many teachers use the raised-hand sig-

nal effectively to maintain order and ensure that no one person dominates the conversation. However, if you have a class where behavior is less of an issue, you might try having students call on one another or simply speak in reply to one another. One teacher calls this mode of participation "discussion style." Her students knew that when she said "discussion style," they could speak without raising hands. They needed some practice and monitoring, and she reserved the right to call on specific students and interrupt arguments. She found that the "discussion style" technique moved the conversation forward more smoothly, helped students take ownership, and in the end got them genuinely talking to each other.

A student is eager to enter the discussion.

Q: I interrupted the discussion to pose a more complex question than the one students were discussing. Everyone stopped talking. What happened?

A: It's likely that your question was perceived as unrelated to what students were talking about, and so it threw them off track. They didn't know where to go with it. Collins (1982) coined the term *uptake* to describe what happens when a speaker incorporates a piece of the previous statement in his or her next question. It's a bit like an updraft, lifting a kite up higher, carrying it along. So as you get better and better at uptake, your discussions will seem more coherent, and you won't stop the show. Practicing uptake will increase the coherence of your discussions and give students a boost. As one teacher put it, "It makes the students feel validated in their opinions because you use their words when making a point." Uptake elevates their ideas powerfully. Uptake also assists in clarifying any confusion that may arise in the discussion, the teacher added.

Notice in the example that follows—from a conversation about "Seventh Grade" by Gary Soto—that you don't always have to wait for some astounding insight; simply repeating a student's language is effective.

PAUL: I was going to say that [Victor], he's not really...normal a lot of the time, he's not really acting like himself, so I don't know why she likes him.

TEACHER: So you're not sure why *Theresa likes him?*

PAUL: No.

TEACHER: Okay. How do we know Theresa likes him at the end? Andrew.

By incorporating Paul's phrase "likes him" into two subsequent questions, the teacher verifies what Paul is confused about. She also affirms that it's a reasonable thing to be confused about when she asks the class to consider the issue of Theresa's feelings for the main character, Victor. Make a conscious effort to use the uptake technique on a regular basis. There's no better way to help students to see the connection between what they are saying and where you want them to go.

> **Q: The discussion was lively, but later I realized that only a few students were actually speaking. How do I get more students to participate?**

A: Remember that speaking is not the only way of participating in a discussion, though it is the most obvious way. What about the body language of the other students? Were they sitting up, alert, listening, and watching the different speakers? If so, they were probably participating in their own minds, which means they were working through the questions, thinking of evidence, and agreeing or disagreeing with what others said. Consider doing a written evaluation of the discussion for homework, in which students write about what they learned from the discussion and who or what influenced their thinking. In this way all students can show you that they were participating in the discussion.

That said, it may be that something else is going on that is keeping some students from wanting to speak in front of others. Try keeping a seating chart near you during the discussion and discretely putting a little check mark next to students' names as they participate. After class, look over your chart. Are there any patterns to the lack of participation? One teacher, Sarah, noticed that one row was composed entirely of girls who had chosen to sit near each other. This row was almost entirely silent during discussions. The teacher reorganized the seating chart to put these girls next to others (students) who spoke more often. This had the effect of improving the social geography of the room so that discussion came from all areas. Students heard one another better and some felt more at ease in participating than when they had been seated in the "silent" block.

Try to use small groups for a while to see if that opens up quiet students. Also, think about the texts you're using—are they accessible? Are the characters, settings, authors, themes, genres, and reading levels varied enough to be inviting to students of diverse backgrounds and experiences?

Q: How do I prevent students from giving each other incorrect answers?

A: When wrong information is aired, the first reaction is to correct it, the sooner and more explicitly the better. Let's look at what happens when a teacher tries to correct a student's misinterpretation of the Elders in *The Giver:*

> **KENT:** The Elders are like the decision-making people; the old people. They make all the decisions in the community, except whenever they come by something hard. Since the Giver has all the memories, they ask him for his opinion and stuff.
>
> **STUDENTS:** (*commenting to one another*) Like the grandparents. I think the Elders are really controlling. It's the old.
>
> **TEACHER:** Careful, and I think what we are doing is we're confusing a couple of things.
>
> **KENT:** Was I wrong?

Kent's reaction is important to pay attention to—he's made a big investment in describing what the Elders do, he's gotten his classmates thinking about his ideas, and all of a sudden, with even a mild interruption from the teacher ("Careful"), his instant interpretation is that he is somehow wrong. Consequences: shut down, stop talking, avoid further mistakes. Right now, what's even more important than correct answers is allowing students the time to work through their interpretations of the material, which will likely begin with some wrong answers as they process the information along the way. Yet incorrect information has the potential to lead students astray and cause trouble if not corrected. In this case, the teacher may have helped some students from conflating the two terms. Here are a few other options for ways to handle misinformation:

* **Ask for evidence to support the assertions.** Students need to be able to back up their claims. "Let's explore Kent's idea. . . . Let's take a closer look to see if we can find an example of the role of the Elders in the book. Can anyone find a passage that tells us more about them?" You are guiding students into looking for textual evidence, a skill required by state standards and standardized tests. Students may be more motivated to do this than usual because *they're supporting their own ideas.*

Building Literacy Through Classroom Discussion

- **Ask for a different perspective.** "Thanks, Kent. Does anyone want to add to that? Or does anyone have a different understanding about the role of the Elders in the story?" Chances are a student will add a contrasting idea, which will provide Kent with an opening to comment again on the topic, clarifying his meaning and thereby avoiding "being wrong."

- **Tell students up front that you expect them to disagree with each other's assumptions.** So when a student gives a piece of inaccurate information, you can say, "Let's look at this idea. Does anyone agree with this idea? Does anyone respectfully disagree? Tell us about that." In our experience, students have a difficult time doing this, so it may take some time to develop.

- **When an idea, whether it's on target or off base, has been aired, allow some wait time for students to digest the information and think about how to respond.** An eighth-grade teacher, Andrea, kept an index card in front of her during each discussion, on which a single word—*wait*—was written in large red letters. Her students noticed the card and asked her what it meant. She explained, "It's my reminder that I'm going to wait for *you* to answer first." Other teachers take notes, drink from a cup of coffee, count to five, or do whatever they need to so that students are not immediately interrupted or corrected before they have a chance to think an idea through and perhaps correct it on their own.

- **If you feel the information hasn't been corrected and is important to clarify, do exactly that.** Say, "I want to clarify a couple of points" or "I have found a passage that presents a different idea than I'm hearing . . . . Let's take a look at it." Students rely on you for support and clarification, and they do want to know (before the exam!) when they've misinterpreted something.

- **You can always use journals, warm-ups, or homework to reinforce any clarifications.** Kent's teacher, for instance, could ask students to look carefully through the book for homework and make a list of two or three similarities and differences between the elderly and the Elders. This technique extends the conversation, deepens interest in the issue, and encourages practice in finding textual evidence.

> **Q: In a couple of my classes, students are resistant to discussion; they get into arguments easily; they start having side conversations. Are there some classes where discussion just doesn't work?**

A: There are definitely classes where discussion happens more smoothly than in others. However, even a difficult-to-manage class can engage in discussions. One teacher worked seventh graders who

were tracked two levels below grade level. Students were behaviorally and academically challenging. Yet discussion was possible. The teacher needed to use a lot of scaffolding with this group, much more than she needed to with other classes. Below is an excerpt from a discussion in this challenging class. At the end of each teacher turn, her role (orchestrate, clarify, help, or support) is indicated.

TEACHER: Take a guess. "A rose by any other name would smell as sweet."

LAFONDA: You copied this out of a book.

TEACHER: Yes I did. I took it right out of the story we're reading. Okay, let's go over this. "A rose by any other name would smell as sweet." Let's start with Chavonne, what do you think? (*Orchestrating, inviting participation.*)

CHAVONNE: I think, because it don't matter what kind of flower something is or what the name of it is, it's just how the scent of it is so you could pronounce it, and it'd be sweet.

TEACHER: So in other words you're saying that it doesn't matter what the flower is, the name that we call it, it's still going to smell the same? (*Clarifying, restating.*)

CHAVONNE: Yeah.

TEACHER : Let's go over to Jose next.

JOSE: (Inaudible)

TEACHER: Okay, so what Jose . . . I don't have all of your attention. So what Jose . . . what you're saying is it doesn't matter what name it is, it's still the same (*restating.*) So in other words, we can change Sylvia's name to Viviana, but is she still Sylvia? Is she still who she is? (*Extending.*)

STUDENTS: Yes.

TEACHER: So it doesn't matter what we call her because it's what's inside that matters? Althea, what do you think? (*Orchestrating, inviting participation.*)

ALTHEA: (Inaudible)

TEACHER : Okay, so you think it *does* matter what people call you (*Clarifying, restating*).

ALTHEA: Yes.

TEACHER: And why do you say that? Why *does* it matter what people call you? Why *does* it matter if I call you Althea or if I call you Rebecca? (*Supporting, upping the ante on students' thinking.*)

ANGEL: Because your name describes you.

DAMIEN: That's why . . . it doesn't mean what you think it would mean.

TEACHER: Okay, so names have a meaning to them? Is that what you're saying? That if your mom named you that, it's there for a reason? (*Helping, expanding students' response.*)

LaFONDA : Yeah.

TEACHER: Okay, so Chavonne, what do you think? (*Orchestrating, inviting participation.*)

CHAVONNE: Your name just plain describes you. You have a name for each part of a person. Could be your personality or . . . what you like or what you dislike and stuff.

TEACHER: Exactly! What does Jose think? (*Orchestrating, affirming, inviting participation.*)

JOSE: I don't know why we really have names.

TEACHER: Why do we have names? (*Clarifying, restating the question.*)

JOSE: Yeah.

TEACHER: That's a good question. Why do we have names? What's the meaning of even having a name? (*Lots of calling out.*) Raise your hand, raise your hand. Listen. (*Orchestrating, uptake, reminding of class rules.*)

SAMMY: So people can tell you apart.

TEACHER: Okay. One, it tells people apart. (*Clarifying, restating.*)

TOM: It tells you like if you need something, where, if you need an application, it tells your last name and everything.

TEACHER: So are you saying it gives us information? (*Helping, summarizing.*)

TOM: Yeah, it gives us information.

The key to a successful discussion with this class was the teacher's careful, patient facilitation and use of authentic questions and uptake. Consequently, students became involved in sharing their thoughts about the quotation, and in the process learned more about how to talk and think about literature (for more on this class, particularly the teacher's own words about her process, see Anderson, Adler, & Morrill, 2002). Here are some other suggestions for challenging classes:

Don't neglect the ground rules. Chapter 2 provided some ideas for setting ground rules prior to beginning a conversation. Review these briefly before each discussion. Many teachers post ground rules prominently in the classroom.

One teacher was grateful to have the ground rules in place when a student blurted out, "It doesn't make any sense! I have no idea what she said." The teacher looked at the student and said, "I am very disappointed in you. Remember, we can disagree with the statement or ask for more

information, but we do not insult the person. Can you phrase that in a more appropriate way?" He did so and after a time felt comfortable enough to continue participating. Having the ground rules in hand helped the teacher and students to deal with a difficult situation quickly and efficiently.

Change the chemistry, if you can. Sometimes you may have a class where nothing seems to work; students just don't seem to get along with one another. Appoint a couple of students to be your note takers. Explain to the class that these students are going to jot down ideas that are offered in class, and that these notes will help everyone to see how each student contributed to the overall learning. When the discussion is finished, invite the note takers to summarize the conversation for the class. These summaries will help students to listen again to the conversation, highlighting important contributions. By rotating the job of note taker, you can give a number of students the experience of listening carefully to their peers (as well as practice in the important skills of note taking and summarizing). A variation on this activity is to have a pair of students keep tallies on participation in general, so that you can see patterns of who spoke too much, just enough, and not at all.

And as we said earlier, look at the seating arrangement. Is the organization awkward in terms of the social relationships between students? You may want to separate students who have strong feelings for one another, either through friendship or discord. One teacher we know has students move seats in a circle when they are discussing, seating themselves in a boy-girl-boy-girl pattern. Another seats students by first name in alphabetical order. These strategies can draw attention away from any awkwardness among friends or foes, and students can relax and participate.

> **Q: The discussion went by so fast and I had so many thoughts in my mind, that I had a hard time remembering what the students actually said! How do I keep track of their ideas and still monitor the discussion?**

A: In time, you'll find a strategy that works for you; here are some ideas to try. Some teachers we know like to keep a journal just for discussions, in which they jot down the student's first name and a quick phrase capturing what he or she said. For others, a visual map in which they jot down a word or two next to the student's name is helpful.

Another effective technique is to appoint a student to keep a list of questions/topics and speakers.

Perhaps the most powerful way to have perspective on a discussion you've facilitated is to videotape it and then watch it. It's a tremendous way to see who is talking, who isn't, all the non-verbal communication that goes on, and to evaluate the quality of the contributions. We've asked the teachers we've worked with to select a five- to ten-minute segment that they'd like to share with colleagues. With each viewing, teachers picked up on comments and behaviors that they had missed before. Often teachers who initially thought poorly of the conversation changed their minds completely when they could sit back and watch it on videotape! One facilitator, Eileen Kaiser, reported that teachers found it useful to show the videotape to their classes so that the students could comment and reflect on the discussion.

All of these techniques help to tune the ears so that you discern and remember the topics that arise. Your scaffolding can be more immediate—in other words, while you are "with" the students in the conversation, hearing their words, you are *also* thinking and processing the next direction in

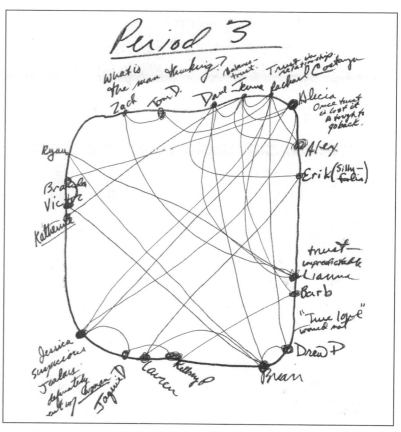

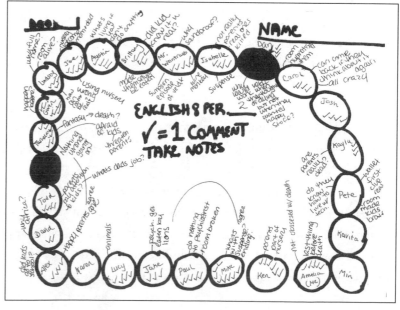

Ways to map the conversation—for teachers (top) and students (bottom).

which to go. With practice, you eventually get to a place where you can really use the discussion as a tool to see what students are thinking. Once you can see this, you can design written and oral assignments to lead into or extend out of the discussions, to help push thinking forward in more sophisticated ways (more about this in Part 3).

Q: One of my nonreaders really got into the discussion and wanted to participate. Should I be encouraging her to speak when she hasn't read the book?

A: Some teachers are reluctant to allow nonreaders to participate in the discussion, even as listeners, but would rather have them use the time to read, say, in the library. If students are not already reading, though, then sending them somewhere else to read is probably not going to help build their literacy skills. However, becoming actively involved in a good discussion of the book just might do the trick. If this student participates, she is increasing her motivation for reading—she has learned that she will have occasion to talk publicly about the text. She also might be curious enough about the text that she will read it after the discussion, having heard enough information to form a scaffold to help her with the difficult parts. The downside of allowing participation, possibly, is that she will not be able to support her opinion with enough specifics from the text. Other students can help with this for the time being, and you can let her know privately that she needs to start supporting her ideas with examples from the text. At that point, you've established motivation and a positive relationship with the text (something unusual for nonreaders); perhaps at this point it will be possible to work one-on-one to address some of the deeper issues that surround her inability or refusal to read.

Q: The discussion was good yesterday, but we didn't get as far as I'd wanted and now I need to move on in the book. What do I do?

A: In our experience, a good, sustained whole-class discussion in middle school ranges anywhere from 20 to 50 minutes. (Teachers who can get students quickly focused on their wonder questions have more time for discussion of ideas.) This means that you cannot possibly do discussions every day, nor would you want to. Save discussions for times when there is something to talk about. Some of the best times to have a discussion include:

Building Literacy Through Classroom Discussion

- when something controversial, perplexing, or confusing has happened (in real life experience, in an activity, or in a text),

- just before the climax of a text or just after foreshadowing,

- after finishing a poem, short story, or newspaper article,

- at the end of a book or other text (use as prewriting before papers or exams!),

- after reading a second or third piece on a similar issue with a different perspective, to reflect on what was learned and what questions still remain.

Writing to Extend Conversation

If it *is* a good time to have or continue a discussion, you might see if there is a way to move something around to allow it to happen. If this isn't possible, you can always do a *written* version of a conversation (Rougle, 1999):

- Have students write letters to one another for homework, then trade in class and write a letter in response for homework the next night, or

- have students write for ten minutes in their journals, then trade, respond to one another, then trade back and write a final reflection, or

- take 15 minutes to have students pair up and pass a note paper back and forth; on the paper they are to take turns speculating on a "big" question (yours or theirs) about the text or activity. It's note passing, so no talking is allowed.

For any of these assignments, you can simply collect the papers/journals, read them, and give a participation grade. The benefit to you is that you can quickly see where students are in their thinking—from there you can determine whether you will stay longer in the text, move on, or find another text with a contrasting point of view. The benefit to students is that they gain a second person's perspective, and they are actively working with and manipulating the text in ways that will help them remember and explore the ideas within it.

Q: How do I assess a discussion?

A: This question came up a lot as teachers worked with us to figure out the issue of assessment as related to discussions. Should discussions be graded? How? How often? How do you grade silent participants?

One of our teachers developed a rubric that she titled "Rubric for a Good Conversation." Here

are some criteria that went into it, and that you could adapt for your own needs:

- The students are engaged and actively listening.
- The students' body language conveys participation (they nod their heads, sit in attentive postures, etc.).
- The students contribute to the conversation (frequently/sometimes/seldom/never).
- In written work about the discussion, the students' "voice on paper" is evident.
- The students build on what others say (using uptake, scaffolding).
- The students raise questions.
- The students probe what is being discussed.
- The students can respectfully disagree—thus providing other perspectives.
- The students use examples as evidence to support their thinking.

A rubric like this could be used in a number of ways: to be completed as a self-evaluation by each student for homework; to be used by the teacher as a diagnostic tool to monitor discussions in general; to be reviewed orally with the class immediately following the discussion, as a means of improving group participation. A teacher *could* create an individual rubric and use it to score students on their participation, though it would be time consuming to complete for each student during a discussion. Rather than focusing on evaluating individuals, it may be more productive for teachers and students to have criteria in mind that describe a good conversation and to periodically return to the criteria for reinforcement.

The issue of assessment is an important one, though, particularly in the minds of students. If they are being asked to participate in discussions, but their participation isn't noted, and the discussions do not have anything to do with other graded class material (tests, quizzes, papers, projects), then they may not see the connection between participation in the conversation and success in the class. In Part Three we will look more closely at connecting discussions to written assignments and other parts of the curriculum; we'll explore assessment ideas further then.

> **Q: Is there a way to easily incorporate more dialogue in other parts of my curriculum?**

A: It's an important question. How can you give students regular discussion practice, when you simply do not have the instructional time to have formal whole-class discussions as often as you

Building Literacy Through Classroom Discussion

would like? The solution is to use dialogic approaches in your daily practice, and save more-formal discussions for times when you have a rich text or topic that will benefit from sustained focus. Here are some ideas for ways to incorporate dialogic methods into your regular instruction:

Invite student questions and comments. Whether you're teaching the difference between similes and metaphors, or the finer points of oral presentations, you can make your presentation more dialogic by inviting students to ask questions and to make sustained comments. Here are some phrases that you can use during almost any activity to open it up to student inquiry and learning:

- What questions are on your mind about this?
- What part of this lesson is still a little muddy for you?
- What surprised you about what we just did?
- Who can add to this idea with an example?
- Tell us how you think you'll use this information.

Note that most of these questions will work as prompts for quick written responses (like a "ticket out" on page 133).

Use questions and comments as an opportunity to invite more participation. As the subject matter expert, you are used to answering questions, to explaining the differences between concepts, and clarifying information about texts. But see what happens when you "hand over the mike" to students. Try deflecting a student's question by restating it and bouncing it back to other students to answer. When a student makes a comment, ask other students to speak up, to connect to it. For example, when a student asks during a grammar lesson if all -*ly* words are adverbs, pause and then say: "Sara wants to know if all -*ly* words are adverbs. What do you think? Can someone respond to Sara?" By doing this, you enliven the atmosphere in the room. Students have more incentive to wake up and take notice, because you are taking notice of them. You are implicitly and explicitly letting them know that you value what they know, and that they have a duty to share that knowledge with their peers.

Try a dialogic test review(!) In our experience, teachers returned to monologic classroom discourse most often when they were helping students prepare for an exam. And it is indeed an effective way to review a lot of information and understandings quickly. See if you can mix up the monologic approach a bit, however, by having students pair up to discuss an important question and find textual evidence to support their answers. Then ask the pairs to share some possible

answers with the group. By orchestrating their responses (with such questions as "Who would like to add to that?" "Who disagrees?" "Why?" "What evidence can you find to support that?" "What questions do you have about what Tom just said?"), you can effectively review for the test but also keep students in a "wide-awake" learning stance by given them a way to interact with the material and the discourse.

One teacher, Annie, had given a multiple choice test on the short story "Rikki Tikki Tavi" by Rudyard Kipling. Students did okay on the test, but she wanted them to go over their answers and become more proficient at distinguishing the "best" answer from "possible" answers. She brought her students into a discussion circle and had them look at each question and evaluate the answers they had given. She told them that they were free to argue an answer if they could provide sufficient evidence directly from the text that it was the *best* possible answer. As students began to talk, Annie orchestrated with comments such as, "Can you build on his argument?" or "You need to find supporting evidence for that idea." Students talked, agreed, disagreed, persuaded, and generally explored both the test construct and the original story, looking for support for the questions that were argued. Annie was surprised to hear how sophisticated her students sounded as they raised their hands and said, "Okay. I have an argument for the best answer." On one question they were actually successful in persuading her that there were two best answers! Moreover, students were engaged, were learning how to interpret test directions and multiple choice items, and were paying particular attention to wording and evidence. Although it took some time, the intellectual payoff was worth it. The critical-thinking skills the students honed are transferable to virtually any endeavor.

Incorporate questions-and-answers after presentations. Oral presentations and speeches are a staple in middle school. For the presenters, the assignment sharpens their use of rhetoric and evidence, not to mention their public speaking skills. For the listeners, it can be an opportunity to learn about an unfamiliar topic. But in reality, sometimes everyone walks away unmoved. The presenter may get little or no response to his or her efforts, and the audience may feel disengaged. To increase interaction with the material, try having students write silently for two minutes after each speaker. Then ask them to share any questions or comments with the speaker, for a pre-specified time limit. Altogether, this may add one additional day of class time to your presentations, but the increased attention to listening and inquiry may make the extra time very worthwhile.

Final Thoughts

The process takes time

One teacher, Samantha, moved her chairs into a circle, spent a lot of time going over the ground rules, and encouraged student questions. However, when students didn't quickly come up with the answers she wanted, she became frustrated and started to explain to students where the information was that she wanted them to know. She did this in a question-and-answer format, so that it seemed like a discussion, but it was very clear that there was a single, pointed (short) answer to each question. Students returned to their old habits of responding minimally, directly to her. She had overtly stressed participation, but tacitly shown them that she wanted limited and correct answers to her questions.

In principle, Samantha knew the importance of student talk, but in practice, she had difficulty truly embracing the belief that through discussion, students really could wade through the murk of an ambiguous text or complex issue and arrive at clear and comprehensive insights and understandings. She worried that her students wouldn't learn enough of what she felt they needed to learn.

We share Samantha's story as a way of underscoring: *This process cannot compete with the amount of information you could provide to students through direct instruction.* But providing information does not mean that students have learned it. The dialogic process produces a depth of knowledge because students have worked through an understanding of the material. Moreover, students gain the opportunity to observe the techniques that good readers use (prediction, summarizing, questioning, inferring) by watching their classmates make sense of the text (Greenleaf, Schoenbach, Cziko, & Mueller, 2001).

Completing a shift to a dialogue-based classroom can take weeks, months even. (And as is true of all teaching, you refine your practice each year.) So be patient with yourself and your students, because at this point in the journey, the really interesting work begins.

In Part 2 of this book, we explore some of the moves you'll make to raise the level of discussion. Specifically, we look at how to sustain and deepen a conversation, especially with regard to literature. In Chapter 4, we step back for a moment to look specifically at some of the research on the process of making meaning from literature. Then in chapters 5 and 6 we will return to the discussion process to focus on ways to extend conversations across the curriculum.

Part Two

Sustaining Discussion

Chapter Four

Deepening the Intellectual Exchange

Using envisionment building as a framework for orchestrating discussion

Imagine that you are wading into the ocean for a swim, when all of a sudden you find that the ground that had been solid beneath your feet drops away, and you're in deep water. You may flail your arms a bit as you regain your balance, but then you go for it—you swim. You may have a similar moment of disequilibrium as you wade further into dialogue-based teaching. Ellen, a teacher in upstate New York, lost her footing a bit when discussing *The Adventures of Huckleberry Finn*, by Mark Twain, with her eighth graders. She observed that her students were not engaged with the book. When we asked her, "What do you think students will want to talk about in this part of the book?" she answered, "They should know it's a satire" (Adler et al., 2003/2004). With her answer, she revealed to us exactly why her discussion hadn't worked. She'd run into the central challenge teachers face as they learn to orchestrate dialogue.

Ellen's desire to have the students know more about the genre of the work is important, and we don't mean it should be abandoned. However, it had become the *overriding* goal. Ellen, like many teachers, was so driven to cover the curriculum that it was difficult for her to trust that it was okay to focus on students' own thinking.

A question to consider: *When are you building on students' understandings, and when are they supporting yours?* Or let's frame it a little differently: *In discussions, how often are you awakening and pursuing students' curiosity, and how often are you attending to your own teacher interests?* We pose these questions with deep understanding of the pressure teachers are under to cover the curriculum. We pose them gently to nudge you to toward a different paradigm, one in which the weight of imparting the curriculum is no longer on your shoulders alone. Rather, we assume that middle school students are capable of making meaning—with assistance—and are not simply repositories of information that the teacher deposits. Or, in the famous words of Freire (1970/2000), a teacher no longer needs to "'fill' the students with the contents of his narration" (p. 71). Consequently, the questions we ask assume that teachers use their knowledge selectively to structure learning opportunities in which students construct meaning for themselves and one another.

In Part 1, we began describing a way to structure a minds-on learning environment in which students are meaning makers. In this kind of classroom, the teacher invites students to talk to one another, helping them to become thinkers who know how to share their ideas, questions, and thoughts with one another. Students have learned how to discuss—how to have comments, questions, and ideas, and how to bring them to the floor. They've worked on appropriate classroom rules for listening and speaking; they've begun to respond to one another, to agree or disagree, and perhaps they've brought an alternative perspective in now and then. They may have even shared some surprising ideas or experiences.

At this point, it is likely that conversations have stayed at the level of sharing personal experiences, character likes and dislikes, and predictions. For instance, you may have had quite a few students who were able to articulate something like, "This reminds me of a time when . . ." or "I saw a movie the other day about this kind of thing" or "I think Sam's father is not going to come back from the war" or "I wonder if someone will steal the pearl from Kino." This potpourri of comments, while good for beginning the conversation, tends to stay somewhat undeveloped and disconnected from larger themes. It is as if the conversation were hovering over the text, close to the text but not delving in deeply. While students may connect with one another's ideas, they often do so in a superficial, associative, and serendipitous manner.

Your students need your expertise to help them move to a higher level of thinking and understanding of texts and experiences. And this is where we bump into that same conundrum we opened this chapter with: How do you balance your purposes for the activity with students' need to explore on their own and participate in the class dialogue? How do you get students talking about the genre of satire when they want to talk about Jim's strange superstitions? Moreover, how do you value and stay open to students' contributions and alternate perspectives without relinquishing your own or the dominant interpretation of the text? In a sense, what we are talking about is how you maintain your teacher voice.

In the next three chapters, we focus on how you can orchestrate discussions and writing assignments so that students arrive at their own well-supported interpretations, aware of the dominant views but not overpowered by them.

A good conversation is a place for students to find their voice and grow academically.

Envisionment Building, Scaffolding, and High Literacy

So what is a rich, literary discussion? We've talked about a multiplicity of voices and viewpoints refracting like a prism, but when you're gathered in a circle with a bunch of middle school students giving you that "So what's next?" look, you're going to need more than metaphors! Your students need: 1) a *developing awareness* of what it means to read well and discuss ideas well; 2) a *framework* for putting these processes of thought into action; and 3) your *support* as they climb up to high literacy, discussion by discussion.

Envisionment Building: A Way of Talking About Our Thinking

All three of the core things your students need at this juncture spring from a concept called envisionment building, which is both a way of looking at the reading process and a method for discussing a text (or analyzing a movie, a painting, or virtually anything). As a discussion tool, envisionment building can help you to orchestrate rigorous discussions where students explore all facets of the text, including literary analysis and the author's craft.

In *Envisioning Literature*, Judith Langer (1995) explains the concept of envisionment:

> I use the word envisionment to refer to the world of understanding a person has at any point in time. Envisionments are text-worlds in the mind, and they differ from individual to individual.... Envisionments are dynamic sets of related ideas, images, questions, disagreements, anticipations, arguments, and hunches that fill the mind during every reading, writing, speaking, or other experience when one gains, expresses, and shares thoughts and understandings (p. 9).

Envisionment is what we see and understand in our mind's eye as we interact with the world. It's a great Technicolor movie composed of image and color, thoughts and memories, information and interpretation that rolls when we read a book or watch a film or listen to a friend. In the context of the classroom, when we help students to build envisionments, it's as though we are outfitting them with lots of different camera angles and techniques so they can direct their movie rather than simply watch it.

Characteristics of Envisionment Building

Envisionment building is:	Envisionment building is seldom:
The way your mind works to come to an understanding about a text or experience at any point in time	Closure on a text or topic
Fluid, flexible, tentative, open-ended	Fixed, singular, defined, and targeted
Recursive, nonlinear	A straightforward process that moves from the beginning of the text in linear fashion to the end
Speculative, using hunches and questions about the possibilities that are to come	Definite, looking for prespecified answers
Local and global. (Local envisionments grow and change as you move through a piece. Global envisionments are the understanding of the whole that develops out of the sum of these local envisionments.)	Point of reference reading. (Any new understanding creates a more cohesive understanding of a fixed topic. Evidence that potentially contradicts this or creates tensions in this thesis is irrelevant because it does not push forward to the final destination.)
A process of dropping details out of the larger understanding when they are no longer relevant to the big picture	Mining the text for the meaning of specific details
Constructing meaning out of our knowledge and the text interacting	Meaning being constructed by the teacher and transmitted to the student
Developing meaning from the connections between the text, the individual's life and educational experience, and the individual's relationship and history with the larger society	Contained within the text; rather, it needs to be uncovered by the reader

So with this concept, we say good-bye to the notion that curriculum content is a locked box of precious information that we crack open for our students each year, thought-jewels for them to stash

away and then unwrap during exams and college interviews. Instead, we say hello to the idea that curriculum is conversation, and our students are participants, shaping the content. Each of our middle schoolers brings to any text and discussion his or her thoughts, experiences, a unique cultural history, and a finger on the pulse of the current culture. These sources of insight are the special lenses students wear as they develop their perception of any text.

A class discussion represents one of the most natural arenas in which students can build their envisionments and share them, because we are so explicitly inviting them to speak their minds—to tell us how they see things. Using the tools of dialogic discussion, we teach and re-teach them how to defend an idea, build it, and ride out the sometimes choppy waves when others disagree with what we have to say. We teach them that a difference of opinion is collaborative not adversarial, and that it's okay and even expected to change one's interpretations over time.

Students' diverse backgrounds and experiences enrich classroom discussions.

And together, we and our students begin to notice a pattern: What we perceive—and in turn what we converse about—continually runs up and down a scale of connections, from the local level to the global level and back again, from self to world, from single (a comment about a single word, a connection to a single personal experience) to plural (a question aimed at larger ideas, histories, and collective experiences).

The Four Stances

For Judith Langer, this "scale" of perceptions comprises four major chords. In researching what readers do, she asked participants in her study to verbalize their internal thinking as they read using the Think Aloud process. She noticed that the readers were doing four things consistently. Langer (1995) calls these four behaviors *stances*, or ways to build envisionments of the text. Below, we

define these stances in the context of literature, though they can also be extended to the process we use to make interpretations of any text or experience. These stances represent different options, or angles of understanding, that readers can adopt as they progress through a text:

- **Initial understanding:** This stance refers to the individual's thoughts and feelings that occur very early in the interpretation process, such as the first moments after the film ends or the passage is finished; they may be as simple as a connection to something in one's own life, either a personal experience or an event. These connections help the reader to step into the text.

- **Developing ideas:** In this stance, the reader is moving through the text, building an understanding of the evolving whole. He or she is trying to answer the basic question, "What is this story about?"

- **Learning from the text:** In this stance, the reader steps outside the text, using it to reconsider or rethink what he or she knows of the world in light of that information. For example, after reading Shakespeare's *Romeo and Juliet*, the reader may think differently about how contemporary family pressures affect teenage relationships and dating.

- **Taking a critical stance:** At any point in reading, the reader may become aware of the writing, the structure, or some other literary quality and temporarily disengage from the story to comment on the author's craft.

These four stances together represent a complex act of interpretation. The stances are not distinct in a reader's thought process, but isolating them helps us to know what proficient reading is all about. We can then use the definitions as a kind of menu we can offer students, each stance a different course of thought that will help them think about texts—and talk about texts—in a manner that yields rich understandings. In so doing, we are applying what Langer discovered about the interpretation process, using the stances as an instructional tool. "Taking a Stance," as shown on the next page, is designed to be used in the classroom as a quick reference guide for the four stances. It provides a short description of each stance and how it supports student thinking. Following each stance are two prompts that you can use to ensure that students express their ideas in a variety of ways. Teachers who have used this information have said that it helped them to deepen the level of the conversation.

Taking a Stance: A Framework for Guiding Discussion After Reading a Text

Initial understanding*: Here your students use their background knowledge and experience to step into a text. They begin to make a mental picture of the text world.

    Questions that provoke students' thinking:
- What are your first impressions? What are you wondering about?
- What questions do you think we might discuss?

Developing ideas: Here your students move through the text and explore possibilities. They fill in the pictures in their mind, connecting relevant details to build a more cohesive text world.

    Questions that provoke students' thinking:
- How did your understanding of the characters change as you read?
- What did you think of the ending of the story? How does it relate to the beginning?

Learning from the text: Here your students step out of the text and use it to think differently about their own lives and the world they live in.

    Questions that provoke students' thinking:
- How does what happened in the story make you think differently about _____?
- What did you learn about history, relationships, or human nature by reading this story?

Taking a critical stance**: Here your students step out of the text to critically and objectively examine the effect of the text on the reader.

    Questions that provoke students thinking:
- What parts of the text (phrases, sentences, images) were especially powerful for you? Why?
- What other pieces does this text remind you of? How?

*   For instructional purposes, we always start the discussion by posing questions that awaken this stance, but in actuality, the mind moves through the stances in no particular order.

**   If you can discern which stance a student is responding from, you can tap unexplored stances to enrich interpretation and deepen understanding.

"Taking a Stance" in Action with *The Giver*

Now let's look at some excerpts from discussions of *The Giver*, so you have an idea of what student responses are like in relation to envisionment building. In the original transcripts, of course, stu-

students didn't speak from the four stances in a neat sequence from initial to complex thinking. Rather, students and their teachers shifted back and forth among the stances as they built their envisionments.

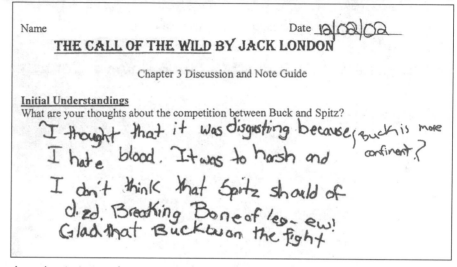

Name _____   Date 12/02/02

THE CALL OF THE WILD BY JACK LONDON

Chapter 3 Discussion and Note Guide

Initial Understandings
What are your thoughts about the competition between Buck and Spitz?

I thought that it was disgusting because Buck is more confinent? I hate blood. It was to harsh and I don't think that Spitz should of died. Breaking Bone of leg- ew! Glad that Buck won the fight

A teacher invites students to write their initial thoughts about an important event in *The Call of the Wild*.

Initial Understanding

LAKISHIA: I like how they share their dreams in the morning.

TEACHER: How many of you have shared dreams with parents before?

Developing Ideas

LAURA: If they didn't want to talk about it, couldn't they just lie and say they had dreams about something else?

TEACHER: Laura's point was . . . couldn't they just lie? Let's think about their society.

Learning from the Text

JASMINE: They didn't have a choice. They didn't want to [reveal their dreams] then they wouldn't have to. Because like sometimes, you can have a personal thing that you don't want [your parents] to know about, but then other times you could like have nightmares that you want your parents to know about. . . . You might want to share that.

ALLYSON: Well you see . . . I would like . . . can I connect?

TEACHER: By all means.

ALLYSON: Well, you see . . . if I ever like had a dream about this boy I really, really liked, I would not tell my parents. I would tell a friend more than my parents because if I ever told my parents something I did during my dream, I think they would like kind of freak out. With a friend they'll probably think, oh yeah, that's cool.

TEACHER: You're saying probably your friends will understand . . .

ALLYSON: (*at the same time*): understand . . .

TEACHER: because they're the same age, where your parents might get a little judgmental?

Taking a Critical Stance

NATHAN: I think in the beginning there were so many things . . . that I couldn't figure out what was important.

PATRICK: Like every book I read, every time I stop, I want to keep reading, because I just want to know what happens next. But this book, even though I don't really like it that much . . . I only like the last two chapters we read. That was it.

TERRAH: I find that in the beginning of the story, the author like, buries you with too many unimportant details in the beginning of the story, and you don't get the main idea of the story.

Note that in the third and fourth stances, students speak from a position outside of the text. In Learning from the Text, students step out of their immersion in the story and use the narrative to venture some new guesses about society at large, and perhaps the society of their own family. For example, students take the idea of sharing dreams from the story and extend it to their personal lives, thinking about whether they would be willing to do such a thing with their own family. In Taking a Critical Stance, students see the text through the lens of critic/reader and use their experience with other texts or genres to help them consider the story's structure, themes, or language use. For example, Terrah is critical of the amount of detail used early in the story, finding that it serves as a barrier to the reader who is trying to get a sense of the plot.

In Chapter 5 we'll explore the envisionment-building process again, delving further into how to use it to generate questions that scaffold students to high literacy. We'll look at how to use this guide at many stages of teaching and learning, including planning curriculum, assigning writing in response to reading, orchestrating discussions, and designing assessments.

Scaffolding: Teaching at the Tipping Point

Scaffolding has been widely written about in the literature of constructivist pedagogy (Hillocks, 1995; Langer & Applebee, 1987; Wood, Bruner, & Ross, 1976). We look at it now because it's so central to fostering higher-order thinking before, during, and after discussion.

Scaffolding, or instructional help, is pivotal to effective teaching. The teacher assesses where the learner is in his or her process of understanding a concept, a skill, a narrative, and so on. The teacher continually asks herself or himself questions such as, How can I help my students to grasp this concept? Where are they now in their understanding and what do they need to know to accomplish the task? How can I step in and model more complex ways to help the student do the task with more sophistication than before?

In other words, an effective scaffold grows out

> ### Defining Our Terms
>
> Envisionment-building guides are quite different from most study guides. They're designed to open up conversation, to stimulate thinking, to generate different perspectives on a topic or topics. Study guides, in contrast, are generally designed to help students consolidate information in a succinct way. Consequently, they tend to close down conversation. In Chapter 6 we look at how you can adapt the envisionment-building concept into a study guide format so that students can use these more open-ended questions throughout a longer work.

of a student's current cognitive needs. Vygotsky (1978) describes this process as one of assisted learning within a zone of proximal development (targeting the space between what a student can do independently and what he or she can do with help from others). Teachers orient their instruction with students' *developing* skills and abilities in mind; they focus on each student's "budding" knowledge. Scaffolding is forward thinking, teaching at the tipping point between what the student could accomplish yesterday and what she or he will achieve tomorrow. In other words, it is not teaching in the safe zone of already mastered abilities.

Scaffolding Within a Discussion

Now let's look at scaffolding within a discussion. As we see it, there are at least three ways you can offer this support.

- **Pose an open-ended question or two that unearths students' current understandings.** Teachers often have students answer questions in writing prior to a discussion, but many variations are possible. The payoff is twofold: First, students express their initial impressions and questions, and thus begin to articulate their interpretations. And second you get the lay of the land so that you can scaffold more effectively. You'll discover the answers to such questions as, What are they thinking? What topics for discussions are emerging? Where does there seem to be consensus, divergence, confusion? What do they know about the context of this text (concept, etc.)? What ideas and information might you need to teach them now so they won't struggle too much with the text?

A quickwrite before discussion helps students find something to say.

- **Use students' responses to launch your moment-to-moment orchestration.** From this point on, you'll need to engage in that fast dance of taking in what students are saying and leaping ahead in your mind to anticipate where the comments might lead. It's a skill you'll get better and better at. This is scaffolding in action. Roberts and Langer (1991) call it *orchestration*, another term we like. Whatever you call it, think of it as your intuitive sense of when to interject, when to clarify, when to keep silent and let another student respond, when to bring another perspective, when to ask for evidence, and so forth. In the next chapter we'll look at the art of orchestration in more detail.

- **Use Langer's four stances to move the discussion toward deeper levels of thinking.** You may wish to prepare an envisionment-building guide prior to the discussion (see pages 105–107). This will give you thought-provoking questions at a glance—the guide reminds you of aspects you want your students to examine. In our experience, the stances most often neglected are stances three and four: learning from the text and taking a critical stance. You want to be sure your students take them on, as these are the stances that most

Building Literacy Through Classroom Discussion

require higher-order thinking. Students identify and apply a text's themes in a wider context; they infer; they try to tease apart an author's belief from a narrator's point of view, and so on. In short, students' work all falls under the umbrella of analytical thinking, the key to developing a literate mind. It's also a critical skill to have for the high-stakes tests and any other academic task.

Enthusiasm and tuning in to students' responses are key for facilitation.

Teaching at the Edge of Higher-Order Thinking

As you may recall, Bloom's taxonomy (Bloom, Mesia, & Krathwohl, 1964) is typically used to show how higher-order thinking works; it implies a progression from lower to higher levels. Knowledge comes first, then comprehension, then analysis and application, and finally synthesis and evaluation. By this logic, students must be able to recall simple information and to summarize it *before* moving to analysis or evaluation. We'd like to shift the emphasis toward the upper echelons of Bloom's taxonomy, and here's why: Think about how you respond to a book or a movie or a lecture. Do you proceed from simple to complex in a neat series of thoughts? It's not a stretch to say that adolescents exiting a popular film can easily move into evaluation without having to first take the time to recall for one another what happened. In fact, the skills move in tandem with one another: "That was a terrible movie. Did you see the scene where that happened? It wasn't realistic." In this manner, we all move back to lower levels of the taxonomy when we need evidence to provide a logical consistency to our analysis.

So let's not have our instruction linger at lower levels of thinking; let's invite students to interact with interesting, higher-level questions from the get-go. Scaffolding allows you to accomplish this acceleration while keeping your students' wheels on the road, because you are in a sense riding shotgun and can aid them in their journey whenever there are bends in the road. You aim each question,

comment, glance, follow-up, writing assignment, and so forth to anticipate the upcoming curves—the stretch between what students can already do independently and where they are ready to go next.

The learning that results from this effort will be qualitatively different, and better, than the thinking engendered by the common stepwise approach to Bloom's taxonomy. Often, when students are given the chance to share their initial impressions of a piece, their thinking races to the highest level in Bloom's taxonomy. "I think in the beginning there were so many things . . . that I couldn't figure out what was important," Nathan said of the first part of *The Giver*. Nathan thus raises an evaluative issue and invites his peers to help analyze it with them. Terrah takes up the issue and builds on his and others' thinking, asserting, "The author like, buries you with too many unimportant details in the beginning of the story."

If Nathan and Terrah's minds had been busy with a more traditional assignment of, say, summarizing the first chapter, or retracing the plot, they might not have had the time or inclination to take a critical stance on the text itself. Calling a published author into question is a pretty bold thing to do. It bespeaks an intellectual engagement and confidence that is just what we want from our students. Nathan and Terrah's comments are valuable because they ask everyone to immediately engage in evaluative/analytical thinking and to support their assertions by looking closely at the text structure and content. This kind of analysis can lead to fresh, deep insights that link observations about the author's craft with understandings about its effect on the reader.

Students will need to return to lower levels of the hierarchy to search for specific information: to review plot points in order to back up their claim that the events are not realistic; to recall what a character says in order to support a statement that he is a phony; or to reexamine a matter of style they have taken a critical stance on. For example, Terrah and Nathan will need to support their assertions by looking carefully at the beginning of *The Giver* to find what they consider extraneous details. This could trigger an opportunity for the teacher to orchestrate a discussion about authorial technique. For example, upon further examination, the class might consider whether the many details Lowry provides in the opening chapters are essential to establishing the utopian (or dystopian) society in which her characters live, one that is so different from our own. After all, this emphasis on the details of the setting is a common trait in the fantasy and science fiction genre. In other words, an experienced orchestrator can take even a dismissive student comment—*the first chapter was boring*—and run with it in a great direction.

In sum, skills such as recall, summarization, and identification are used *in the service of* critical-thinking skills such as analysis, synthesis, and evaluation. They do not in and of themselves suffice to build complex envisionments of a text or experience.

High Literacy: Possessing the Attributes of Highly Literate Thinkers

When we talk about higher-order thinking in the context of sustaining discussions, we are really talking about high literacy (Bereiter & Scardamalia, 1987; Langer, 1999). What do we mean by high literacy? The following attributes characterize what a highly literate thinker should be able to do:

- pose questions
- develop logical reasoning
- consider an issue from multiple perspectives
- cope with ambiguity and conflicting ideas/tensions
- seek complexity rather than simple answers
- challenge another's opinion or viewpoint
- think flexibly rather than rigidly
- look for the marginalized or silenced voices in and out of the text

Ivana Markova (1982), a psychologist interested in dialogue and communication, describes complex thinking in a similar way. People who think in this way are "more flexible in their attitudes toward others, they seek out a variety of information when solving problems, interpret the same information differently in different contexts, and make finer differentiations among people and events" (p. 165). As Judith Langer (2004) puts it, the literate mind "involves the ability to use language and thought to gain knowledge, share it, and reason with it" (p. 1).

The attributes of a literate mind are valuable both in and out of school. But be careful to not emphasize only the short-term payoff, e.g., "You need to learn this because it will be on the test." Rather, with discussion, we help students to succeed both in school and in life. Sure, this experience will help them succeed on high-stakes exams. But we're really providing authentic opportunities to develop essential, life-long thinking and reasoning skills. The message we want to give our students with our teaching is: "You need to learn this because you will want to know what's going on in the world around you and to have some power to change things when they need changing."

Au (1993) reminds us that there is an additional attribute to literacy that many overlook—the willingness to use it. As she puts it, "Literacy is not just a matter of skill or cognitive strategies, it is also a matter of will or feelings and emotions" (reference to Winograd & Paris, 1988, in Au, 1993, p. 21). Skills and strategies are of no use if the student has been given the message that his or her abilities are not valued in the school setting. Fortunately, discussions, and envisionment building in particular, are effective in motivating students to bring their knowledge to bear on the conversation.

Many students in the Partnership project came to look forward to the opportunity to discuss their perspectives, to ask questions, and to hear from their classmates. Anecdotally, we heard from teachers in the second year of the project who reported that students from the first year came to class expecting to participate in discussions, even with a new teacher. One teacher told us about a time that her seventh graders became so heatedly involved in a literature discussion at lunchtime that the cafeteria aide came to get her so she could "calm them down"! While this was a rare occurrence, conversations in many classes did continue beyond the classroom door, spilling out into the school corridors, at students' home dinner tables, and again in subsequent class discussions.

The body language of an active listener in a discussion circle.

How Discussion Helps You Meet the Standards

The richness, literary quality, and critical thinking inherent in high-level discussions can promote student achievement as measured both by our definition of literacy and by tests of achievement in English language arts (Applebee et al., 2003). Because sustained discussion through envisionment building relies on higher-order thinking that is supported by evidence, students gain authentic practice with reading comprehension skills. Moreover, teachers can focus on a variety of skills within a single conversation, orchestrating a discussion in which students are required to supply textual evidence, predict, discriminate between fact and opinion, and look carefully at word meanings and figurative language.

To illustrate the relationship between envisionment building and standardized tests, we have compared the envisionment-building stances with the state standards for English language arts for both New York and California, on which many high-stakes tests are based. On the next page, we look specifically at California standards for grade eight.

Envisionment Building Stances	California English Language Arts Standards for Grade 8 that may be met through the use of envisionment-building stances (R=Reading; W=Writing; LS=Listening and Speaking)

Initial Understanding	1.0 (LS) Students write and speak with a command of Standard English conventions appropriate to this grade level.
	
	1.2 (LS) Paraphrase a speaker's purpose and point of view and ask relevant questions concerning the speaker's content, delivery, and purpose.
	
	2.1 (W) Write biographies, autobiographies, short stories, or narratives:
	  a. Relate a clear, coherent incident, event, or situation by using well-chosen details.
	  b. Reveal the significance of, or the writer's attitude about, the subject.

Developing Understanding	1.1 (LS) Analyze oral interpretations of literature, including language choice and delivery, and the effect of the interpretations on the listener. 1.1 (R) Analyze idioms, analogies, metaphors, and similes to infer the literal and figurative meanings of phrases. 1.3 (R) Use word meanings within the appropriate context and show ability to verify those meanings by definition, restatement, example, comparison, or contrast. 3.2 (R) Evaluate the structural elements of the plot (e.g., subplots, parallel episodes, climax), the plot's development, and the way in which conflicts are (or are not) addressed and resolved. a. 2.4 (W) Present detailed evidence, examples, and reasoning to support arguments, differentiating between facts and opinion.
Learning from the Text	3.0 (R) Students read and respond to historically or culturally significant works of literature that reflect and enhance their studies of history and social science. 3.5 (R) Identify and analyze recurring themes (e.g., good versus evil), across traditional and contemporary works.

continued on page 102

Taking a Critical Stance	2.0 (R) Students read and understand grade-level-appropriate material. They describe and connect the essential ideas, arguments, and perspectives of the text by using their knowledge of text structure, organization, and purpose.
	2.3 (R) Find similarities and differences between texts in the treatment, scope, or organization of ideas.
	2.7 (R) Evaluate the unity, coherence, logic, internal consistency, and structural patterns of text.
	3.3 (R) Compare and contrast motivations and reactions of literary characters from different historical eras confronting similar situations or conflicts.
	3.4 (R) Analyze the relevance of the setting (e.g., place, time, customs), to the mood, tone, and meaning of the text.
	3.6 (R) Identify significant literary devices (e.g., metaphor, symbolism, dialect, irony), that define a writer's style and use those elements to interpret the work.
	3.7 (R) Analyze a work of literature, showing how it reflects the heritage, traditions, attitudes, and beliefs of its author. (Biographical approach)
	2.2 (LS and W) Deliver oral and written responses to literature:
	a. Exhibit careful reading and insight in their interpretations.
	b. Connect the student's own responses to the writer's techniques and to specific textual references.
	c. Draw supported inferences about the effects of a literary work on its audience.
	d. Support judgments through references to the text, other works, other authors, or to personal knowledge.

The chart above shows how, by using typical questions used in envisionment-building discussions, identified by stances, teachers can satisfy a number of standards requirements holistically through authentic discussion. You may notice that EB questions are qualitatively different from the standards, though they do support one another. This is because the questions are driven by the need to support students' thinking, as opposed to the standards, which primarily reflect the domain of what is important to know about the discipline. Consequently, the envisionment-building questions tap into acts of learning and teaching about texts and experiences. Within these comprehensive, interactive discussions, specific skills are addressed, meeting the standards while involving students actively in the teacher's unique curriculum.

Chapter Five

Using Discussion to Further Develop Students' Literacy Achievement

Ways to help students to reason, challenge a viewpoint, consider an issue from multiple perspectives, and develop other habits of literate thinking

B y now, you've accomplished the impressive feat of getting your students talking and listening to one another, you've reviewed the attributes of high literacy, and you've begun to use the envisionment building framework to help you orchestrate discussions. Now we're going to take a look at excerpts from actual literature discussions, so we can give you more strategies and tools for facilitating discussions. We'll address questions such as how to prepare, what to focus on, when to respond, and what kinds of oral and written responses will produce higher-order thinking.

STRATEGY: Starting the discussion on a high plane
TOOLS: Prepare an envisionment-building guide before discussion

Now we're ready to look at how to help you use Langer's four stances to create your own envisionment-building guide, or EB guide, as we came to call it. In short, it's the smartest "cheat sheet" around. Prepare it in advance of a discussion, and it will provide you with excellent options for guiding the discussion with skill and ease. As you can see in the sample on pages 106–107, the EB guide is a set of open-ended questions aligned with reading stances. The questions can stimulate your own thinking in the midst of a discussion, helping you to anticipate the hunches, disagreements, comments, and questions that are likely to arise. Most importantly, the guide gives you the language to connect student comments and questions to critical issues in the text.

Taking a Stance

INITIAL UNDERSTANDING*: *Here your students use their background knowledge and experience to step into a new text. They begin to make a mental picture of the text world.*

Questions to tap this after reading:

- What are your first impressions? What are you wondering about?

- What questions do you think we might discuss?

DEVELOPING IDEAS: *Here your students move through the text and explore possibilities. They fill in the pictures in their mind, connecting relevant details to build a more cohesive text world.*

Questions to tap this:

- How did your understanding of the characters change as you read?

- What did you think of the ending of the story? How does it relate to the beginning?

*We always start with the first stance, but the mind moves through the stances in no particular order.

LEARNING FROM THE TEXT: *Here your students step out of the text and use it to think differently about their own lives and the world they live in.*

T A K I N G A S T A N C E

Questions to tap this:
- How does what happened in the story make you think differently about _____?
- What did you learn about history, relationships, or human nature by reading this story?

TAKING A CRITICAL STANCE:** *Here your students step out of the text and the experience to critically and objectively examine the effect of the text on the reader.*

Questions to tap this:
- What parts of the text (phrases, sentences, images) were especially powerful for you? Why?
- What other pieces does this text remind you of? How?

> ** *If you can see which stance your students are responding from, you can tap unused stances to enrich interpretation and deepen understanding.*

CELA Partnership for Literacy, 2002

A general EB Guide like this can be laminated and used as a bookmark; pull it out as a reference during any discussion when needed.

Building Literacy Through Classroom Discussion

Many Partnership teachers began by using generic questions for each of the four stances—questions that will work with just about any text. They printed them on a wide slip of paper, which they came to call the bookmark. Some teachers laminated the bookmark and kept it close by between the pages of a book, while others taped it on their desks or pinned it on a wall.

However, you will get a finer tool when you create your own authentic questions that grow out of a text you are about to discuss with your students. Use the general questions on the bookmark as a starting point. Ask yourself: In light of this text, how would you answer them? Jot down ideas. It's in these responses that you have the seeds of your own authentic questions. Make your own bookmark with the questions that resonate for you. They are probably ones that will intrigue students, and the ones that are most effective in helping students tackle a text's complexities. For example, when we created an EB guide for "Thank You Ma'am," by Langston Hughes, we came up with this question: "What other social issues does this story make you think about? (Issues of underage crime? Latch-key children? Poverty?)" Suddenly the story took on a new relevance in our minds. Developing the questions had helped us to think about the story and to ponder several possibilities in order to make sense of it.

Over time, generating envisionment-building questions becomes a natural part of the planning process; your questions may not even need to be written down in advance of class discussion. The class can even create their own envisionment-building questions after you have modeled the procedure. Students will appropriate and try on the kinds of questions asked during typical discussions. When students apply this approach to other texts they encounter, they are able to ask similar questions in their own minds, and their thinking improves.

How to Develop an EB Guide

Envisionment-building guides have four sections that correspond to the stances that effective readers take as they read texts: initial understanding (stepping in), developing ideas (moving through), learning from the text (stepping out), and taking a critical stance (stepping out and thinking critically). In the sample guide for "Thank You Ma'am," on the next page, you can see how the focus of the questions—and the purpose behind them—is different in each stance.

"Thank You Ma'am" by Langston Hughes Envisionment-Building Guide

Part of a larger conversation on:

This signals that we plan to connect these discussions with other discussions, within literature, across content areas, and beyond.

Initial understanding:

- What are your first thoughts or feelings about the piece?
- What did you notice? What is this story about?
- Does the piece evoke any childhood memories in you?
- What questions came to your mind?

These are designed to help readers articulate their first take on the story, from plot understandings to connections they make to their own experiences.

Developing ideas:

- What kind of person is Mrs. Luella Bates Washington Jones? How do you know?
- Why do you think Mrs. Jones leaves the door open and her purse on the bed, once they are in her house?
- What do you think it means that Roger "did not trust the woman not to trust him"?
- How do you notice Roger changing as you read the story?
- Should Roger have been punished for what he did? (Did Mrs. Jones do the right thing by helping him?)
- Why do you think Roger can only say thank you at the end of the story? How does that tie in with the title?

Here, we want students to develop their ideas about the story world. Readers will drop irrelevant ideas from their understanding in order to make room for new and more important information (Langer, 1995), so it's important not to dwell on insignificant details, but rather to help them think about larger issues of what is happening, why it's happening, and why and how characters act and do things.

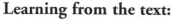

Learning from the text:

- Do you think this story is realistic in terms of what you know about how people act toward others in our society today? Explain.
- What other social issues does this story make you think about? (Issues of underage crime? Latch-key children? Poverty?) In what way does it confirm or change your thinking about these issues?

Here readers step outside the story world to apply its lessons to today's world in some way. These questions help readers to think about why the text is significant—how does it change the way we think about our lives, our families, our communities, our culture, our educational system, and our larger society?

Taking a critical stance:

- What did the author do in this story to create tension for you as the reader? Why do you think he did that?
- Do you think the use of humor is appropriate in this story? Explain.
- Why do you think Hughes chose to tell this story in third-person point of view? What would change if Roger or Mrs. Jones told it?
- What effect did the dialogue have on you, as a reader? Do you think the author should have used standard English? Why or why not?
- What lines were especially powerful for you? Why? How did they add to your understanding of the piece?
- Have you read other works by Langston Hughes (such as "Mother to Son")? How is this piece similar/different to them, or to other stories you've read?

Now, we look critically at a text's construction, its language, its effect on the reader, its connections to other texts, ideas, and historical context. We want students to entertain questions about perspective, about a writer's choices, and about powerful language or metaphors.

The best way we know to develop effective EB guides is to use a completed one as a model. In the next section, we explore how a teacher uses the EB guide to orchestrate a productive, sustained discussion.

STRATEGY: Sustaining the discussion on a high plane
TOOL: Use an EB guide during conversation

The process of preparing for discussion helps breathe life into a text. It also sparks your curiosity about how students might respond. Whether working with newly created text-specific questions or simply practicing by using a bookmark (see page 104), you are mentally prepared. During the actual discussion, you may only occasionally need to consult the guide, because new or similar questions will naturally arise. At this point, facilitation takes over and comes into its own.

In a study of classroom interactions between a middle-school English teacher and her students, Roberts and Langer (1991) found that what participants said during a discussion varied according to their purposes. Some of these purposes related to the discussion process, such as calling on a speaker, inviting someone to participate, or presenting a new topic for others to take up. Others related to the content of what was said, such as challenging someone's point, disagreeing, expanding on an idea, or "upping the ante"—raising the bar to pursue a higher level of thinking on a particular topic. Still others related to helping participants to build on one another's ideas more effectively. Help included focusing, modifying or shaping information, summarizing ideas or responses, and stating facts or information (pp. 10–11).

Teachers who orchestrate effective conversations are constantly engaged in the kinds of interactions that Roberts and Langer (1991) describe. They operate on at least three levels at any one time—first, helping participants to learn appropriate ways to discuss, listen, and participate; second, developing student understandings about the text in deeper ways; and third, guiding the conversation so that comments build upon one another and collectively produce deeper thinking than any one individual could on his or her own. At first this process can be overwhelming. (That is why the EB Guide is helpful to do in advance as preparation.) However, over time, students can begin to take over some of the facilitation, and the teacher will have the opportunity to say less and listen more.

One way to understand what a teacher does during a discussion is simply to look closely at student-teacher interactions and pay attention to who is speaking and what they say. For this reason, we asked Partnership teachers to view videotapes of class discussions from their own classrooms. Teachers could watch them privately at home and then select a clip to bring in during a group meeting. During our meetings, we watched the clips and took notes on what the teacher and students did and said. Sometimes a video of a class that a teacher thought was a miserable failure turned out to have some pretty interesting learning going on. And sometimes a video that was successful on the surface revealed new places to focus the teacher's and students' energy.

In the pages that follow, we will approximate a video by showing you a transcript of an eighth-grade class discussion and analyzing it to learn about what participants did and said. This transcript comes from field notes taken in Liz's class, a heterogeneously grouped, classroom. Students range from special-education to gifted. They have the advantage of having had this teacher the previous year and have become used to classroom discussion over time. Consequently, the students are comfortable talking to one another. The teacher takes the role of facilitator of thinking, using the different stances to scaffold student ideas. Let's watch what happens as they begin a discussion of *Nothing But the Truth*, by Avi, a nontraditional narrative in which a teenage boy tries to get out of his English class by bending the truth about a school rule regarding the national anthem. As we jump into the discussion, students have begun comparing this text to a previously read novel, *The Pearl*, by John Steinbeck. Liz takes this as an opportunity to connect students to the critical stance by having them think about the structure of the book and the effect that a nontraditional format has on them as readers. Let's listen:

JOHN: This is a newer book. It's more exciting than *The Pearl*.

TEACHER: *The Pearl* wasn't exciting? ....➤ Clarify

JOHN: Well, the last chapter was.

MATT: It's an easier format to read. It's more conversational.

TEACHER: Keep that in mind. Did the style of the narrative make it eas- .....➤ Uptake, expand to
ier to read? critical stance

STUDENTS: Yes.

TEACHER: Could this story be told in a regular prose format? ....➤ Up the ante

JASON: The scene where Allison's talking with her friend would be con- .....➤ Stepping out and
fusing if it wasn't in dialogue. taking a critical
stance

CRYSTAL: Too much dialogue wouldn't work well in a regular prose format.

FRANK: I think it would be better if it wasn't just the dialogue. In a regular book you can picture it in your mind better. With just the dialogue you don't have a picture of it in your mind.

TEACHER: That's interesting, that details help you to envision the ....➤ Restate,
story. What do you [the class] think about that? orchestrate

JOHN: That's true, but it also lets you picture it yourself based on your
own imagination rather than the author's imagination.

CRYSTAL: I agree with John. It's up to you to decide. I don't think the
story would be as enjoyable in prose format.

PATRICK: I like that it's written in dialogue because it gives the point of view → Expands, builds on John's idea
of the characters more. You can see where they stand more easily.

TEACHER: So would you say that it gives the inner thoughts of the → Restate, modify
characters more than with a third person omniscient point of view?

STUDENTS: Yes.

TEACHER: Do you remember what omniscient point of view is? → Check understanding, explains

BETH: It gets me confused because there's not enough of Philip's jour-
nals in there to really get a picture of what he's thinking. → Back in second stance, moving through the text, developing ideas

JILL: I agree, because at first I was on Philip's side and then I started
changing my mind as I read other parts.

MATT: A lot of times with normal books it starts with scenery, but this → Critical stance again
time it starts just with what happens. It just starts quicker.

TEACHER: Yes—it starts right with the action, the plot. → Uptake, restate

MATT: Right.

By hooking her fourth-stance question, "Could this be told in a regular prose format?" onto the discussion students had already started about *The Pearl*, Liz was able to orchestrate a discussion in which students pulled back from the action in the book and looked at its structure compared with those of more traditional texts. She also restated student comments at times, modeling more appropriate language for students. Instead of "It just starts quicker," students now know that they can say, "It starts right with the action, the plot." In this way students can see how to use elements of literature the way that experts in the field use them—in practice, in discussion, rather than isolated in worksheets or tests. There's a danger, of course, of overdoing this kind of thing, resulting in the teacher taking over the discussion. However, Matt accepts her restatement as a clarification, saying, "Right."

Perhaps sensing that students had exhausted the issue, Liz then introduced a new topic. This can be a good time to ask students what other questions they have, to help them continue exploring issues that concern them. Teachers who are familiar with students' typical reaction to this book, though, will tell you that many students sympathize with Philip; some do not even see anything wrong with the lies he tells that eventually affect his teacher's job. Liz broached this topic with her students next by introducing her own discomfort with the character:

TEACHER: I have to tell you, I'm bothered. I'm truly bothered by Philip. → Present a new topic
He's driving me nuts.

JOHN: He's just standing up for what he believes in.

TEACHER: But is he? .... Challenge, up the ante

ANGIE: He's just trying to get Miss Narwin in trouble. He really doesn't ..... In second stance again,
care about her or anything. He just wants to get out of her class.   developing ideas

JASON: I don't know. I'm still on Philip's side. There doesn't seem that
much evidence that he's obnoxious.

FRANK: I do think there's some evidence that he's distorting the truth. ..... Challenge

JILL: Can we just finish reading it and then discuss what happens?

MATT: I have a question. I don't know if it matters in the story, but is ..... Asks a question
she [Miss Narwin] British?

TEACHER: Yes. .... Tell

STUDENTS: What?

TEACHER: She writes a letter to her sister in England. .... Tell

ANGIE: I think Philip is obnoxious. When he's talking to his family at dinner, he leaves information out to make himself look better. .... Recycling earlier topic

JOHN: Yes! Doesn't this go back to what we were talking about last
week about lying by omission?

ANGIE: He leaves out that it was a rule not to hum the "Star Spangled
Banner."

JOHN: No. He says that to them. He says it's a rule. .... Disagree

TEACHER: Find it. Show us textual evidence. .... Up the ante

JOHN: I'll find you textual evidence! (Reads from the scene at the din- ..... Supports opinion with
ner table).   evidence

LINDA: He said it was a rule to sing the "Star Spangled Banner" but ...... Clarifies
actually it was a rule to be silent during that.

JOHN: I have to say I'm pro-Philip!

BOYS: Yeah!

CRYSTAL: I'm surprised there are some bad words in here. .... Presents a new topic

TEACHER: The "B" word. .... Uptake

STUDENTS: And his parents don't even care!

TEACHER: Let me ask you this. The author puts in a few bad words here ..... Up the ante; extends
and there, I agree. Let me ask, why?   to critical stance

Liz's students take up the topic she has introduced. Fortunately, students have varying opinions about Philip's actions and are willing to say so. Liz's role is to raise the bar for her students, asking them to present evidence to support their lively difference of opinion. Having done so, students move on to a new topic—the author's use of "bad words." Typically, Liz takes this as another opportunity to up the ante, asking the group to think about why Avi might have chosen to use such language in a book meant for teenagers. And they go on. Interestingly, a digression in the middle of this—Matt's question about whether Miss Narwin is British—does not sidetrack the discussion, possibly because Liz quickly gives Matt the information he asked for, and then they return to the previous topic. Had his question been more substantial, Liz might have chosen to remain silent and allow other students to respond, starting a new thread.

Throughout the discussion, students' comments are listened to and often form the basis for the subsequent question or remark (again, this is uptake, associated with higher achievement (Nystrand, 1997)). Student-to-student address is common; students have the opportunity to say what's on their minds while at the same time being challenged by their teacher to think more deeply and to offer support.

Developing Students' Thinking With Writing Assignments

In addition to providing stance-related questions during a discussion, the EB guide can also be used to develop writing assignments, before or after discussion. We lace writing assignment ideas throughout this chapter, particularly pages 126 to 133 and again in Chapter 7, pages 163 to 165.

Let's look at how Lani, a seventh-grade teacher, connected writing to a discussion of Yoshiko Uchida's "Prisoner of My Country," a short story about Japanese internment camps. Having written out some EB questions ahead of time, Lani was excited when a student, Maria, asked a question similar to one she had posed on the guide: "If they were

Writing assignments can be used before, during, and after discussion.

supposed to be doing it for the Japanese Americans' own good, what's the point of taking someone's whole life away instead of just punishing the bad guys?" Lani wanted students to think more about this complicated issue. So on the spot, she orchestrated a written assignment—a journal jot—that hooked an envisionment-building question onto Maria's point:

> Great question!! I'm going to have you write about that in your journals, now. Here's the question: Do you believe that the Japanese Americans were interned for their own good? Was this in their best interests? Or could there have been another way, as Maria suggested? Give me details from the book to support your opinion.

Other teachers have also found that writing is an effective way to extend discussion, sometimes finding prompts in unused envisionment-building questions.

Preparing for a discussion and orchestrating it effectively are two of the most essential strategies to develop students' thinking over time and increase their ability to develop deeper understandings about the texts they read. At this point students are actively involved in developing the kinds of sophisticated literacy skills that will help them to be successful in college- and high-school-level reading and writing tasks. These necessary literacy skills are embedded in the three goals we focus on next:

- the ability to consider *multiple perspectives*;
- to regularly use *textual evidence*;
- and to develop *new understandings* that grow over time.

On the next page is a graphic representation of the relationship between these larger goals and the strategies and tools that we discuss in the following sections.

> What questions would you like the author to answer if you could speak to him?
>
> • Why did you want to write about a dog in the frozen tundra?
> • What does survival mean to you?
> • do you like killing or something?
>
> Any advice for Buck?
>
> Stay out of other people's business and don't fight no matter what.

Quick jots and questions serve as a take-off place for discussion.

Qualities of Successful Literacy Achievement

Goal	Consider multiple perspectives	Use textual evidence	Develop new understandings over time
	↓	↓	↓
Strategy	Invite diverse voices (students, texts, genres, authors)	Necessitate verbal and written support for ideas	Create constant opportunities for reflection and exploration
	↓	↓	↓
Technique	• Critical stance • Stand and Deliver • Anticipation Guide • Open Mind • Cross-genre conversations	• Upping the ante • Model phrases • Anticipation Guide • Connection to writing assignments	• Pre and post T-charts • Journal jots • Note taking • Written reflection on the discussion

STRATEGY: Invite diverse voices (of students, texts, genres, authors) as a way to develop an understanding of multiple perspectives

TOOLS: Critical stance, Stand and Deliver, Anticipation Guide, the Open Mind, peer-led discussion, cross-genre conversations

Considering multiple perspectives is essential in a literature discussion. When supported, these perspectives can open a window into a new interpretation or provide a critique of the text. For instance, in a discussion of *Lyddie* by Katherine Paterson, a boy asked, "Where is the father?" Later on, another student asked, "Where can we read about positive male role models?" It was an apt question, because the main character's father has abandoned the family, forcing Lyddie to work in the mills to make ends meet. Edelsky (1999) encourages us to always ask this simple question: Whose voice is not present/heard?

When students have built fairly strong envisionments of a longer text, you may want to up the ante and help students to think about the text through a critical lens. You can choose to focus on one part of the envisionment-building guide, as Carla, a Partnership teacher did. Carla's students were used to literature discussions. In April, during our second project year, Carla and her seventh graders were reading *My Brother Sam Is Dead*, a novel of the Revolutionary War. The class had been studying the colonial period in social studies. Carla wanted her students to take a critical stance on what they were reading. On the chalkboard, she had written questions from her envisionment-building guide to make a group assignment for her students:

THEME
What are the underlying themes that you see developing in the story?
- **What might others think about this novel?**
- **How might this story be different from the colonists' point of view? The politicians' of the day? The Loyalists'?**
- **Is the novel one-sided? Does it seem historically accurate?**

Students were eager to discuss these questions. Afterward they recorded their group thinking on a posterboard, which they later presented to the class. As homework, students pondered this question:

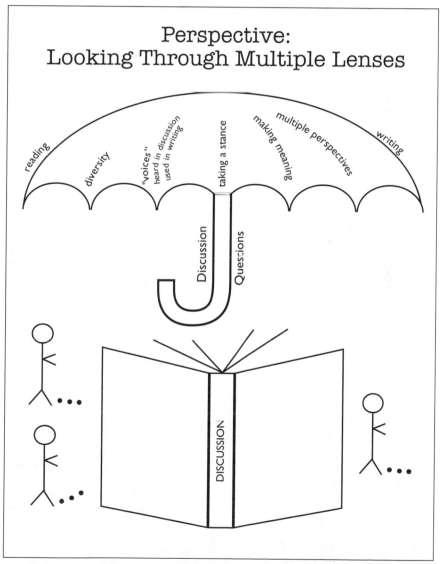

Partnership teachers developed these graphics to represent their conception of discussion.

"How might someone's point of view affect how they think about events in the past?" They wrote their answers in their journals, which served as a springboard for the next day's lesson in the classroom. Through these different questions Carla engaged students in thinking about the novel in a number of ways, from different angles and perspectives.

Toward the end of our Summer Institute week the teachers were asked to think about a metaphor to capture their vision for the Partnership collaboration. One group of teachers created the picture on the previous page.

These teachers recognized the importance of diversity and student voices in creating multiple per-spectives in the classroom. Let's look at some of the tools that teachers can gather together under their "book discussion umbrella."

The Open Mind

One tool, the Open Mind (Tompkins, 1998) is a visual aid that helps students to step inside another person's mind. Students brainstorm ideas that they attribute to a fictional character or person and fill the Open Mind diagram with pictures, symbols, images, words or phrases. In our experience, all students like this activity; even those who struggle with writing can draw their ideas using symbols. When shared, completed diagrams show rich diversity in students' ideas and opinions.

Character Analysis: An Open Mind

An Open Mind diagram is a way of getting inside a character's head to see what the character might be thinking or feeling. Imagine that this character thinks in *pictures, symbols, images, words, or phrases.* Use these in the head below to show what the character is thinking and feeling. On the other side, explain what this Open Mind helped you to realize about the character in the story. Underline one or two ideas that you want to bring to class discussion.

Adapted from: *Book Clubs: A Practical Handbook of Models and Activites for the K-College Classroom (UCIWP)*

A rich coming-together of images, quotations, and words in two languages shows a student's careful thinking and insight into a character.

They can be used at any point during the lesson: at the beginning to tap into prior knowledge students have in their own heads; during a reading to give shape to developing understandings about character motivation; and/or at the end of a reading and discussion to capture what has changed in students' ideas about the character or individual. The Open Mind helps students who struggle with words but think well visually in pictures, and thus it works as a scaffold for multiple intelligences (Gardner, 1993). Moreover, it helps students develop a sense of empathy by walking for a bit in someone else's shoes.

For instance, when eighth graders had finished reading a biography of United Farm Workers cofounder Dolores Huerta in their textbook, they filled their Open Minds with myriad images, words and symbols. Since every head looked different, students could draw from a variety of ideas as they started to discuss Huerta's life. The assignment helped one student, Marcos, to envision the story in a different way. Underneath his Open Mind, he wrote, "I learned how unfairly migrant workers are treated. I learned that if you have a cause worth fighting for you should never give up."

Stand and Deliver

Carla proudly states that her students come to class with an active curiosity. "What are we going to do in her class? What is she going to pull on us today?" they wonder. Stand and Deliver, a tool that Carla often relies on to get the adolescents in her classroom interested and involved, helps produce this excitement. Gloria Ladson-Billings introduced this activity to us at the Partnership Summer Institute of 2001. Provocative statements on a the-

Students entertain multiple points of view during a Stand and Deliver activity.

matic issue are listed alongside a scale from 1 (strongly agree) to 5 (strongly disagree). Privately, participants individually decide on where they stand on the statement.

Then, numbers from 1 to 5 are placed around the room. Participants move to the number

A girl changes her mind about an issue during a Stand and Deliver activity.

that corresponds to their ranking. They explain why they chose that particular position—hence "delivering" their opinion to the group. They support their thinking, for instance, by making a reference to the text. Others listen to the different arguments, ask questions, and may even change positions as a result of listening to one another. The opportunity to see the diversity of opinion in the room, hear multiple perspectives on issues, and have an equal opportunity to develop one's own stand (even a dissenting one) may be what living democracy "looks like . . . sounds like . . . and feels like," according to Carole Edelsky (2004, p. 10).

Many Partnership teachers adopted the Stand and Deliver activity and shaped it to work for them. (It is natural that teachers will modify and leave their own distinctive mark on different teaching techniques, including those we suggest. As with any tool, they are shaped by the hand—in this case, the mind—with purpose.)

Rave Reviews

"Students really like Stand and Deliver, because they generate the conversation," says Carla. "They can agree and disagree. It fosters great conversation, good thinking, good speaking, good listening, within respectful environments. They gain confidence; they understand their individuality; they support each other. It's just a really neat exercise for them to put their best foot forward and appreciate each other in a confirming environment. It gets them to really take a look and listen to others, to consider new perspectives that they might not have brought to the table themselves."

Building Literacy Through Classroom Discussion

Sometimes, Stand and Deliver was an effective way to develop a deeper understanding about the story, such as the characters' motivations or conclusions. Social studies teachers in particular have found it useful as a way to help students articulate their ideas prior to writing an essay. At other times, it provides a way to help students work with larger ideas that would be part of the thematic unit of study. For instance, before reading *The Giver*, a class took a stand on the statement, "Diversity makes life complicated."

Taking a Stand

Pam, an urban seventh-grade teacher, had just assigned students to read "The Scholarship Jacket," an anthologized story by Marta Salinas about a young Chicana who is prevented from winning the prize that she rightfully earned. Pam's students, many of whom were reading below grade level, used paired reading and reader's marks to help make sense of the text. Pam decided that she wanted them to think more deeply about the story by having them consider a variety of perspectives. She created an activity she called Taking a Stand: "The Scholarship Jacket," with provocative statements such as these:

1. Because Marta is a smart girl, she must have high esteem.
2. Schools should not publicly recognize academic achievement, only athletic achievement.
3. Life is expensive, so the fifteen-dollar charge in this story is fair.
4. Differences in power, money, culture, race, gender, age, style, religion, and abilities often cloud our thinking.
5. Grandfather gave good advice.
6. The principal was a follower.

Pam asked students to pick a position on each statement (strongly agree, agree, unsure, disagree, or strongly disagree), and give their reasons. These seventh graders debated back and forth, finding the second statement especially compelling. They used examples from the story and their own lives to back up their differing views. Although students had time to discuss only a couple of the statements, they brought multiple and diverse opinions to the floor. Pam's students learned to listen both to their peers' supportive and contrary comments on the issues.

Later on, when her students were in the midst of the novel *Lyddie*, Pam used students' experiences with the Taking a Stand activity as a scaffold. She gave them these instructions: "In class we have been practicing Taking a Stand, a thinking/speaking activity. Now get ready to think and to write. Write down your position and provide as much backup as possible." In this way students were able to transfer skills from the verbal activity into their writing. In one student's written response, we can see her developing skill in anticipating other perspectives and in supporting her own opinion with evidence from the text (see sample, right).

Pam responded to this student by writing comments such as "powerful conclusions and quotes" and "look how many ideas you developed!" It almost goes without saying that a teacher's written comments are extremely motivating to students; a well-phrased, encouraging comment not only reinforces students' thoughtful engagement during school, it can have good effects that last for years ahead.

Statement: Lyddie's outward appearance matches her inner qualities.

Written Response: I strongly disagree, because Lyddie only has one small dress, and she usually doesn't look very nice or respectful. People often stare at her and act very rudely toward her. She is really a girl with a lot of courage and determination. She treats people with respect, and helps people in time of need. For example, Lyddie helped out the men who could not push the carriage. She used her slip and the wheel became unstuck. Lyddie is basically living on her own at age 13, so she does not have a lot of time to take care of her looks. Looks shouldn't matter. "It's not on the outside, but on the inside that counts."

Experience with Stand and Deliver taught this student how to support her ideas in writing.

The Anticipation Guide

The Anticipation Guide (Readence, Bean, & Baldwin, 1989) is another effective tool to generate interest, invite individual perspectives, and add richness to thinking. Prior to the class reading and/or discussing the text, the teacher creates one or more strongly worded statements that introduce central themes or issues in the text.

Anticipation Guide statements encourage students to think deeply about what they really believe.

Building Literacy Through Classroom Discussion

Students either agree or disagree with the statement and explain themselves. Following the reading or discussion, or later at the end of the unit, students can return to the guide's statement and see if their thinking has changed.

The ideal Anticipation Guide statement will stimulate disagreement among your students, with one group vocally in agreement and another disagreeing with equal passion. For example, before reading *Romeo and Juliet*, a class might reflect in writing upon the statement "Agree or disagree: Love at first sight exists." In responding, students will draw upon their own knowledge of the world and other texts for evidence. The activity helps them in a number of ways. First, students hear different points of view on the issue before it comes up in the context of the reading, thereby opening their minds up to different possibilities as they read. Second, it clarifies the class's prior knowledge on the issue for the teacher, who can use that information in developing an EB guide and also in responding to students in the moment. After all, a reader who takes Romeo and Juliet's relationship at face value may miss the role of the family conflict in pushing the pair closer together and hastening the tragic outcome. Finally,

English Essay   w/c 𝓮𝓌

William Shakespeare called the title of this (peace) I selected "Two Songs by Amiens". In this grand classic, Shakespeare vividly paints the harshness of the winter season and how man thrives in it. The initial reactions that drew me to this masterpiece were the various crispy usage of imagery. It also gave me a chance to look at how old English was incorporated into writing. It has nice musical and cheerful tunes yet some serious stanzas.

This is the first kind of poem I have read in this style of writing. What I find mostly amazing is how the author connects jolly, happy tunes into serious stanzas with a flow. This is what tears apart this piece from any other poem I have read. This is the most unique feature of it plus the excellent usage of adjectives. An example of this would be the first verse of the second section: "Freeze, freeze thou bitter sky" Instead of using a word that is common in most poems to express the cold would be "chill" or "frost." In this occasion however, the author uses "bitter" therefore giving the sky a taste.

After reading this lovely piece, there were many pictures and scenes that formed in my mind. The most detailed image however was the winter wind slapping the roof of a small cottage and chilly air lurking everywhere. Inside a cottage was a man and his wife, Both comfortably resting and enjoying their lives. An another image that came to me was an image about a group of beggars stranded in the icy cold. All 6 were freezing but helpless, then suddenly all of them joined their hands and started to sing with glee.

Good organization of ideas. You've explained the poem with good support (A-)

Discussion, in tandem with writing, helps students learn how to organize their ideas, offer evidence, and try out academic language.

the activity helps students to see how their understandings change over time, as they return to the statements later and see if the reading or their classmates have altered their views.

Peer-Led Discussions

Once your students are fairly seasoned with participating in dialogic discussion—and they're familiar with using the four stances—try some student-led discussions. Partnership teachers found peer-led reading groups useful (Daniels, 2002; McMahon & Raphael, 1997). For example, while one class was reading a full-length novel, students periodically met in groups of three to five to discuss a chapter. One teacher, Annie, developed the following process to use envisionment building with small groups:

1. Hand-pick several discussion facilitators from the student leaders in the class.

2. While the others are getting into groups, take the facilitators aside and go over the Group Discussion Facilitator Guidelines with them (see right).

3. Everyone in the group gets envisionment-group questions, which include key questions drawn from your own guide.

Group Discussion Facilitator Guidelines

- You do not need to cover each question in each category; rather, see how the discussion is moving—address some questions and omit others.
- Begin your discussion with questions your group has about the story.
- If a question comes up that is not on the list, but is related to the novel, discuss it.
- Ask questions such as "Can you explain what you mean by that?" "Why?" "Does anyone agree or disagree? Why or why not?"

ENVISIONMENT-GROUP QUESTIONS

Stepping Into the Discussion
- What questions or opinions do you have about the novel so far?
- Is there any specific information that you would need to know more about in order to understand the novel?

Moving Through the Discussion
- Are the actions of the characters truly realistic? Why or why not?
- Is there a character you particularly dislike? Why?
- How is the main character changing? Do you have any concerns for him/her?

Stepping Out of the Discussion
- How does this novel remind you of any other literature you have read?
- How is this story similar to what happens in our lives today?

Taking a Critical Stance
- How would it make a difference if the book weren't written in the first-person perspective?
- How does the style of writing affect your understanding of the novel and the time period?

Building Literacy Through Classroom Discussion

4. The student facilitator uses the group questions to stimulate discussion.

5. When time is up, someone records, with the group's help, what was discussed. This is handed in to the teacher. Or when time is up, small groups move into one large group and debrief: What got talked about? What worked? What didn't? What did people disagree about? What questions remain for the class to discuss?

Students on the whole were able to hold their own in these small groups, and gained additional opportunities to speak with their peers in a more relaxed setting.

In classes where students use both small and large discussion groups, teachers have found it helpful to debrief afterward, reflecting on the advantages and disadvantages of small and large groups in terms of their understanding of the book. By combining both kinds of activities, teachers can provide multiple possibilities for understanding a text.

Cross-Genre Conversations

Part 3 of this book focuses on ways to pair texts to bring up different perspectives on issues discussed. These can be content-based—a text-book passage on Native Americans in the New World paired with a text on the same topic authored by a Native American, for instance. They can also be genre-based, showing students different modes of presenting similar ideas—a non-fiction article and a poem, for example. Juxtaposing texts helps students see them in dialogue with one another. Consequently, unexpected questions and insights may arise. When students are seeking multiple perspectives and speaking from a particular point of view, they also learn to distinguish between positions by evaluating the evidence against warrants of "truth."

A seventh grader looks up the meaning of a word that came up in a discussion about a book character.

To support one's envisionment with textual evidence is an important skill. We need to be able to reason with proof and to substantiate our thinking with appropriate information in every walk of life. This ability is often tested on high-stakes exams as well as in classroom unit exams. Classroom talk gives students a critical opportunity to practice supporting their ideas on a regular basis. While teachers regularly expect students to support their ideas with evidence in written work, they may be overlooking classroom discussion as a time when they can regularly reinforce this significant practice.

In discussion, the teacher elicits support for students' ideas in a number of ways: by upping the ante, by offering sample phrases as models, and by reinforcing the students' practice in providing textual evidence by incorporating it into regular written assignments.

Upping the Ante

The term *upping the ante* means raising the stakes. In a discussion setting, we can think of it as a technique that the teacher uses to push thinking to a higher level. Upping the ante is asking "students to address a more difficult task than they are currently addressing" (Roberts & Langer, 1991, p. 10). In the discussion of *Nothing but the Truth* above, Liz asks John to support his claim about a "rule." She says, "Find it. Show us textual evidence." Students skim through their text and locate the appropriate passage; they use the information to substantiate their comments and the conversation continues.

Often teachers up the ante simply by posing a question in reaction to a student's comments. Such a moment might be when a student expresses a conflict, a sense of confusion, or a strong conviction. There is usually something bigger and worthwhile to be discussed behind a comment like that. It's also a sure way to bring deeper understandings. You are truly intrigued by the student's idea, and ask: Why? What makes you say that . . . ? Is there something in the text, in the words, that makes you think that . . . ? Show us textual evidence. Your questions will echo in students' minds and help them to remember that they need to go back to the text to support their claims.

Model Phrases

The language that teachers offer to students is an important part of how they will interact in and learn from discussion. As Maloch (2002) noted in her study of literature discussion groups,

Model Phrases to Connect and Support

AT THE BEGINNING OF THE CLASS:

- Choose your best wonder question and bring it to the discussion.
- Your journal jots will be our springboards to discussion. Take a moment and finish your thought.

AS THE DISCUSSION BEGINS:

- Please acknowledge the thoughts and ideas that you are building upon and that you are embellishing. If someone comes up with something that triggers your mind and "snags" you, let them know. Let's try to be aware of where our thoughts are coming from because sometimes we borrow from others. They bring to us enlightenment. Say to them,
  - _____, I love that idea and I'd like to build on that.
  - _____, you made me think of something that I didn't think of before but it just popped into my head.
  - _____, I liked what you said but I respectfully disagree.

THROUGHOUT THE DISCUSSION:

- Anybody else want to share?
- Anybody else want to build on that? Anybody want to build from what _____ just said?
- Thank you for relating that to your personal experience.
- To stay on your point for a minute, _____, is there a word in this piece that made you think of that?
- So, if I'm understanding you correctly . . .
- Now this is a great point that _____ is bringing up; what about the other side of this?
- Does anybody want to share any other snags? Or confusions?
- Wonderful insight; can you expound on it, or build off it?
- Interesting. That's a good pickup from the book too. Thank you from quoting directly from the literature.
- If I can draw a connection over here from Student X to Student Y, you are really talking about.... So let's continue to watch that and maybe it will come up later in the conversation and we can pull some threads and draw them together.
- Let me compliment you for being aware of where your comments are coming from, and compliment people for saying "I agree" and "I disagree."
- Let's invite those of you who have not spoken yet.

The connector phrases (e.g., "I agree with" and "like X said") functioned as a sort of scaffold until students became more comfortable and strategic in their participation within the discussion. As they became more comfortable, these connectors were replaced by a range of connectors that emerged out of their own experiences and conversations. . . . By focusing students on "building" on one another's comments, [the teacher] began to push students past procedural or surface connections toward more substantive ones. (p. 107)

On the previous page are some phrases Partnership teachers used as models to show students how to connect and support their ideas. Although these work well as models for verbal dialogue, some teachers also printed up a list of phrases for students to have in front of them as they participated in the discussion.

In envisionment-building conversations, students' questions or initial written ideas generate the topics for discussion, which are then explored in depth with the help of the envisionment-building guide. With help from their teachers, students return to the text for justification of their comments, elevating the conversation.

Writing Assignments

A number of teachers successfully used envisionment-building strategies as a scaffold for writing by making direct connections between what students do

How to Write the Poetry Journal Jot
- First thoughts about the poem
- Meanings and messages
- Reactions and opinions
- Support for your thoughts, reactions, opinions using your understanding from the poetry guide questions

How to become involved when you read poetry
- **Step Into** the text by reading to know where it takes place, when it takes place, who is in the text and what information is important. What are some interesting details? What is the subject/topic? What images strike you? Why? What is the setting? Who is speaking?
- **Move Through** the text to understand what the text is saying. What messages do you find? Words? Whose voice do you hear? What meanings can you make from it?
- While reading the text and afterward **Step Out** and **Rethink** to make connections inside the text and outside the text. How does the text teach you?
- What themes are in the poem? Do you see any literary elements? Do you find the five senses? Are there similes? Why are certain words used? Do you find metaphors? Word pictures?
- Finally, **Step Out** and **Inspect** the text for deeper analysis and examination. Why is the poem structured like it is? Questions? Comments? What about the message relates to me, the reader? Why? Why did the poet select words to make specific images? How does the poem relate to your personal experience?

A teacher adapts the stances to help students write about poetry.

orally and what they need to do in writing. For example, Rosa, an eighth-grade teacher, decided to build on her students' research on the subject of immigration by discussing the poem "I am an American," by Elias Lieberman. To scaffold a thoughtful written response to poetry, she modified the envisionment-building stances to help students substantiate their comments with textual evidence. She gave her students a poetry guide handout with questions (see page 126).

You can see that Rosa has modified the way she uses the stances in the classroom. This tool helped her students to use details from the poem to substantiate and justify their comments. Here's a written response from John:

> The poem, "I Am an American," is a great poem about American pride. Elias Lieberman really shows his pride in America when he talks of his relatives dying in historical battles. Also, he talks of life in the horrid Russia, where his family members were viciously killed.
>
> Elias tells how his father thought of America, telling his son to die for the US flag. Elias Lieberman definitely is a very patriotic person.
>
> I also liked how he used metaphors like, "My father was an atom of dust, my mother a straw in the wind." He used this metaphor to explain what living in Russia was like. Nobody cared about just one person. Then, he said that his father became a man when he moved to America and his mother became a woman. This explains how many immigrants felt when they first came to America. My favorite part was when the author talked of how bad Russia was. It opens my eyes to other people's thoughts and feelings at the time of the Czarist Russia. This poem opened my eyes. I enjoyed its patriotism. Elias Lieberman is a very patriotic and talented poet.

In the past year I have made a vast improvement in reading. I feel more confident about it, especially when I am reading out loud. In past years I have always been scared of reading aloud, but this year I have gotten a chance to practice that skill. I have learned to analyze books more, especially using the sticky note method. The sticky notes allow me to record my feelings as I read, saving me the time of going back and re-reading. I have become so accustomed to thinking at a higher level that I even do it on books I read for fun. I appreciate what I read much more now than I ever did before. Reading has become more fluent and natural to me this year.

Writing in journals helps students to reflect on their learning.

Journals

Journals are a popular and effective method of getting students to write in middle school. When coupled with other strategies, journals can become more powerful tools. For example, journals with dual entries proved effective in one seventh-grade suburban classroom as they discussed and made sense of *The Giver*. It was customary, Carla says, that students in her classroom use sticky notes to write down any snags, surprises, questions, and comments as they were reading the novel.

I often use the sticky-note method with whatever we are doing to encourage students to jot their thoughts down, because if they don't the thoughts are fleeting. So they are thinking while they are reading, they are pondering, they are connecting, they are predicting, and they are addressing vocabulary they don't understand. All of these things they can bring to class conversation.

> Dear Journal,
> So far I think this is a intresting story. I was suprised a lot during chapter 3 although the biggest suprise was when Buck and Spitz fought. The fight they had was bloody and deadly. Buck won but he killed Spitz. Another suprise was how nice Francois and Perrault were to the dogs. They were not beat and they were feed at reasonable times. I noticed that Buck was more cautios and in a way became stronger not just fighting wise but he thought about things in a new way. To me that was suprising. It suprisied me that Buck didn't grow meaner as time went on, in my mind he almost grew nicer. Finally the last thing that suprised me was how all the dogs minded thier own buisness, they didn't mess with people, they left eachother alone.
> There were some connections throughout chapter 3. When Buck had to sleep out in the snow it reminded me of the story homeless. A few other connections were Zebra when Buck's feet were bleeding and Perrualt put little snow boots on him. When Buck came to Alaska it reminded me of the story Names+ Nombres. Connections aren't just in books they are in life. Like playing on a sports team, to gain thier respect you have to play really hard. Or if you go into a job interview you have to show them who you really are in order for them to hire you.
> I have a few questions about this story like why didn't Spitz like Buck? This question really makes me think, is Buck really a killer for killing Spitz? In my opinion I don't think so. I think it was all a matter of self defense. What are your feelings or thoughts on Perrualt? Are any of the other dogs scared of Buck? And would buck now be known as the leader?

In this journal entry, the text marks, envisionment-building guides, and discussion come together as a student interprets, connects, and asks questions.

Building Literacy Through Classroom Discussion

Students lifted ideas and questions from the sticky notes during their small-group discussions. They also built on and off these notes as they worked through their envisionments in the double-entry reading journal. Carla gave the handout to her students to instruct them in how to carry on a conversation inside their own heads and record it in their journals. Students used computers to write their entries, although these can also be easily done on paper as well.

As students kept the dual log, they were using writing to think through their understanding of the full-length novel, supported with observations from their sticky notes. They used the journal to bring ideas to the discussion, making it richer as a result. In this way, essential literacy skills—reading, writing, speaking and listening—are constantly growing in relation to and in response to one another.

Double-Entry Reading Journal

Format your notes in two columns. The right-hand column is for further reflection or commentary (discussion) about what you have already written in the left-hand column. This is a way of responding to your own writing, your questions, your observations, and your ideas. Use the following guidelines when writing a double entry.

Left side:

1. Notes on your first reactions to the reading.
2. Questions, problems, puzzles.
3. Observations of behavior of characters, setting details, descriptions, etc.
4. Quotations that are striking
5. Issues you see (ideas, insights, idea of friendship, courage, etc.)

Right side:

1. Reflections, comments on your notes after discussion.
2. Try to answer your own questions. Write all your ideas or possible solutions to the puzzles.
3. Write about any connections you see to the behaviors—why someone did something. Try to find some meaning or significance for the details you observed. How do they fit into the whole idea of the story?
4. Why was the quote striking to you? How does it apply to the story? Is it connected somehow?
5. Talk about why they matter, how the story made you think and theories you have about it. Is the story making a statement about something bigger?

A student mentioned that in her log she started to answer her own questions with a new question. That tells us that this student's mind is "on the quest"—moving and generating fresh ideas through these conversations with herself. Hence, ideas and understandings grew. Here is an excerpt from Ida's *Giver* journal:

1. Wow! There are a lot of rules.	Jonas has so many rules to follow. Yet he is in a very controlled area. Jonas goes to school, but what does he learn? More rules? It's stupid to have so many rules. I feel as if Jonas isn't even living; it's so perfect, that it's creepy. He lives a carefree life, and that's just not normal. Are they, the rule makers hiding something, and moreover who are they? Fun doesn't end when you turn twelve. Wow. That's what Jonas deeply feared the whole time—fun.

2. "Fun doesn't end when you become twelve." What does this mean to Jonas?

Would he miss it? Does Jonas have fun now? Is what we consider fun even allowed? What does he consider fun? Is it well mannered bike riding to the store so that he can trade one of his possessions for one that better fits his needs? With that idea of fun I'd ask to be released. Fun doesn't end when you turn 12; it starts.

> ## STRATEGY: Create constant opportunity for reflection and exploration to facilitate growth in understanding over time
> ## TOOLS: Pre and post T-charts, journal jots, note-taking, written reflection on discussion

During envisionment building, misreadings and wrong answers are seen as part of the process of coming to understand a text world. Provisional understandings, hunches and dead ends are part of reaching toward the horizons of possibilities (Langer, 1995). The more you read and discuss a text, the more fleshed out and solid your envisionment becomes.

Consequently, it's important for students to be able to reflect upon their growing awareness and to realize how it is that they have developed a more sophisticated understanding. If they pay attention to how their ideas are developing through talk, listening, writing, and reading, they can be more purposeful about their knowledge building in the future: paying more attention during class discussions, for example, or putting more details in their writing, or talking about the text at home before class.

Kevin, a seventh-grade teacher,

Give students ample opportunities to converse about their ideas.

wanted his students not only to read a short story and discuss it, but also to have ample opportunity to change and build their understandings. He planned to spend two days on the short story "The Five Dollar Dive," by Yvonne Nelson. It's a story of bullying with tragic consequences. After the class had discussed the short story, Kevin used a number of students' comments to create statements for a Stand and Deliver activity for

> **Reflection on Conversation:**
>
> **Think about our circle discussion of yesterday and our Five Corners activity today. What do you think of the issues now that you and your classmates have talked about them? Did someone's comments or ideas impact you? How? Do you look at the story and the characters in the story differently? Has it improved your understanding of the story? How? Explain? Any connections to you world that you can relate?**
>
> This made me realize what pushing people around can do. Even though Packy survived, he could have died. People say life is short so you have to try new things and take risks. I agree. But some risks can make life even shorter. This short story showed that you have to stand up to peer pressure. And never do anything that you dont want to do.

After one day of whole-class discussion and a second day of Stand and Deliver (called Five Corners by her teacher), a student reflects on how her understanding has changed.

the next day's lesson. During the activity, students offered and listened to different perspectives that challenged their own ideas or confirmed them with different evidence. Some students literally walked across the room as they were persuaded by stronger arguments about what the statements and the story could mean.

With the last five minutes of the class, Kevin asked his students to reflect on the conversations during the previous two days and to sum up their current understanding. Kevin asked his students to step back from their envisionments and write an expository piece summarizing the plot, discussing a metaphor, and explaining a theme in the story. One student wrote about metaphor this way:

> In this story the surface of the pool is a metaphor for life itself. The cliffs are like people at different levels of success and achievement. The higher the level you reach in your personal life, the more risk of danger or vulnerability you are open to. Choices you make can sometimes be unclear, like the view of the water from the highest cliffs. Harmful

or dangerous circumstances can sometimes sink you! This metaphor makes it clear to me that wise people must act with caution and look upon problems with a keen vision.

Kevin commented, "Excellent writing—deep thoughts from the pool of life –A".

Similarly, during the reading and discussion of *The Giver* in Carla's class (described above), she gave the following homework assignment: 1.What comment was powerful during the conversation? 2. Did anyone say anything particularly insightful? Jeremy wrote this:

CLASS DISCUSSION

Today in class we had a very in-depth conversation about chapter 8 in the book The Giver. There were many comments that caught my attention, but to me, the most interesting topic discussed was about the "Capacity to see beyond." Along with the reasons for the selection of Jonas as the next receiver and the eye colors of people in the community it took up most of the conversation time. The Capacity To See Beyond that Jonas need and supposedly has to be a Receiver was questioned in the discussion. We wondered if it was the ability to see color, read people's thoughts, or something else. Thelma also pointed out that on the cover there is a black and white picture with a tiny bit of color on the corner. Whether this has some significance or not in the book is still to be discovered. Another thing that caught my attention was the eye color. Jonas, the little baby Gabriel, and the old Receiver all have light eyes that aren't common in the community. We discussed this wondering if it was a coincidence or not. Lastly, our class discussed Jonas' job, especially the pain part. We had many questions about whether it was the kind of pain evoked by a physical object or if it was the pain of something emotionally. Maybe he would see something that he didn't want about the community that he lives in that he didn't think possible . . .

Although Jeremy's response is quite elaborate, you can quickly tap into students' thinking after a discussion by using simple three- by five-inch index cards. Ask students to jot down something they

Building Literacy Through Classroom Discussion

learned or an idea they have about the piece now. On the back, you can ask them to write a question still in their minds. This activity has come to be called a "ticket out"—because students hand their completed cards to you as tickets out of your room. (A variation is the "ticket in" that is done at home and handed in as students enter the room.) Below are some examples of ticket-out comments that show students' changing understandings after a class discussion of "The Lady and the Tiger," by Frank Stockton.

Another easy way to have students see growth in their understanding is to have them read the text twice, the first time with a pencil, and the second time with a pen. (A discussion may come in between the two readings, or afterwards). Ask them to note what they paid attention to the first time. How did reading the piece again help them to work out difficulties they had in their first reading, or to notice new things? This idea came from a teacher in a previous CELA study, Cathy Starr, who used it to great

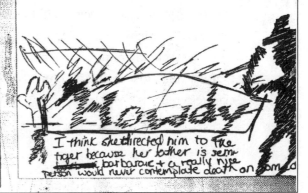

Using the Ticket Out strategy, four students express their opinions about the story "The Lady and the Tiger."

effect with her seventh-grade students (Rougle, 1999).

Reflection on Growth Over Time

Teachers who stress reflection on one's own thinking (metacognition) as a routine practice help their students to gain control of the thought process (Schoenbach et al., 1999). Over time, students can use this knowledge to become better able to regulate their own mental functioning. Metacognitive assignments may come at the end of a unit or marking period, asking students to reflect on areas of growth as

Students help one another figure out a challenging text.

well as areas to develop further. In discussion-based classes, it is natural to ask students to reflect on their participation in discussions as well as other class activities. Here is what a student had to say about her role during discussions:

> In class discussions, I think I said things that I thought were important. In group discussions, I think I said what I thought, and my group said what they thought, and we respected everyone's ideas. In class discussions, I think I tried to say stuff that was unique and that no one else had said. Overall I think I contributed in all class discussions.

Reading
- understand books better

- I get more out of my reading
- Readers marks helps w/
- I learned to wonder and reflect on the books

- Introduce to dif. ~~diff~~ genres

Writing
- I edit + revise more
- My writing is more clear & concise (MNA's)
- I learned to "work smart"
- How to organize a project (journals)
- ~~How to~~ mange time
- How to express feelings in poetry

Speaking
- build off ~~me~~ of other peoples comments and questions

- How to 'respectfully disagree' and state my opinion.

- Contribute to convo's more than last year

- Talk more :)

Listening
- follow conversations and move from 1 topic to another better

- take in what everyone else says and then talk.

- don't have to talk to be involved in convo.

- listen & understand other's point of view

As prewriting for an end-of-the-year reflection, a student jots down ideas of how she has grown. Influences of a discussion-based classroom are evident in all four modalities.

Conversation: Joyful As Singing

Building literacy through discussion begins with having a plan, preparing for, and orchestrating successful classroom discussions. It continues by focusing on goals that will move your students toward successful achievement in their reading and writing tasks: the ability to take multiple perspectives, to use textual evidence effectively in talk and in writing, and to develop new and changing understandings over time. In each of these cases middle school students are authoring comments, bringing their "valued voice," as Carla says, into literacy tasks. They are making their own meaning out of the texts and experiences—with support from their teacher and their peers. These critical literacy tasks are supplemented by an effective, motivational component: Students take pleasure in this kind of learning. Listening to students play with ideas, develop empathy and share laughter is a sure sign that you've found your footing with dialogic discussion. To quote Anton Chekhov, whose character in the short story "Ward No. 6" contemplates the enjoyment of conversation: "We have books, it is true, but that is not at all the same as living conversation in contact with others. If you will allow me to make a not quite apt comparison: books are the sheet music, while conversation is the singing."

Chapter Six
Sustaining Discussion

Reflection and troubleshooting

It was October of the fall semester, and we were having a teacher meeting at one of the schools participating in the CELA research to discuss how things were going. All of a sudden, one of the teachers, Ellen, blurted out, "What is this envisionment building, anyway?" Good question. What does it really mean, in terms of teaching and learning, in terms of class discussions? In the previous chapter we attempted to answer the question by focusing on the tools you can use to build visions of the text, but we know from our work as facilitators that it's wise to pause and make sure we can articulate our end goal.

The teachers at that particular meeting decided envisionment building meant *understanding*—understanding what happened in a text and how it relates to other texts, to your own life, to other facets of life and society. They said their role as teachers is to *enrich understanding*. We agree, and would even broaden this definition to include *developing understandings*. We make it plural to underscore that we want students to grapple with multiple viewpoints. We want them to read and consider fiction and nonfiction from the point of view of themselves, their peers, their teacher, the author, characters, their families, larger society, and so on.

The facilitator of a discussion has an enormous responsibility, then, to help students develop understandings in multiple ways. Students need to learn both how to articulate their understandings and how to allow them to be influenced by the ideas of their classmates. Fortunately, as you saw in Chapter 5, there are many tools and strategies to help you in this endeavor, including the envisionment-building guide. In this chapter, as in Chapter 3, we troubleshoot, addressing some of the questions that may arise in your mind during EB activities.

Q: I'm a visual learner. Can you show me how sustained discussions look, compared with question-and-answer sessions?

A: There are several metaphorical ways of thinking about the envisionment-building process. One way is to think about what would happen if you gave a student a large ball of string and asked him or her to hold one end and pass it to the next speaker, and so on. By the end of the discussion you would have a web of string in which all of the speakers are interconnected. This web contrasts with the traditional initiate, respond, evaluate (I-R-E) sequence (Mehan, 1979), which looks more like a wagon wheel in which the students are the spokes and the teacher is the center.

You can see from the visuals at right that the discussion model is more organic and free-flowing. Yet is has structure, its design created as the participants respond to one another.

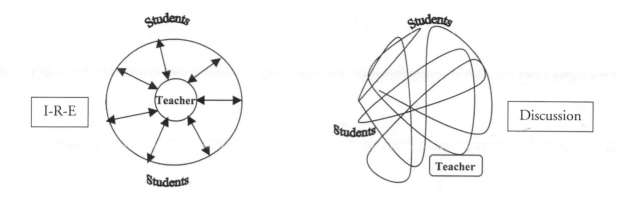

Q: How much should I try to adhere to my envisionment-building guide during an actual conversation?

A: The guide is just that, a guide. When we use them, we find they serve more as advance planning than anything else, helping us to think about the key points of the text and discern the relationships that are most important. During a conversation, we always start with questions related to the "stepping in" stance, such as these:

* What are you wondering about?
* What are your initial impressions of the story?
* What questions do you have?

When we start out this way, we find that most of the time, students bring up at least half of our questions *on their own* without prodding. We listen carefully to what's said in this initial volley, jotting down ideas as we hear them. We listen especially for those that we find promising for getting at some central/interesting issue in the piece. When there's a pause in the conversation, we jump in and say something like, "I'd like to go back to what Suzanna said about *x*. What did you think about that?" As the conversation moves on, we continue to listen carefully, probing students for evidence or further explanation, and raising the bar on students' comments when needed.

As the discussion continues, we glance at our prepared questions now and again. With part of our mind, we start to categorize the students' discussion in terms of what it tells us about their thinking. On the next page are some tips for hearing and providing scaffolding for student thinking, using the stances and the envisionment-building guide:

What you hear: A lot of questions or first impressions without much depth or substance to follow it up—a potpourri of tangential ideas.

What that tells you: Students are having trouble moving past the first stance.

Actions: Help students step in deeper by pausing the conversation, and returning to the text. Reread a section of it aloud that houses discussion points (ideas, themes, character dynamics), you want students to notice. Or you may ask your students to silently reread the text and find a quotation that they would like to share. If you think your students are stuck in the first stance because they are unsure of the narrative, take a little time to review/summarize the events of the story.

What you hear: Students spending most of their discussion time on plot points or mulling over what they think the characters are like.

What that tells you: Students are firmly anchored in the text, but they need to be encouraged to ponder the narrative's ideas, the author's intentions, and so on.

Actions: Raise the bar for students. Ask a stance-two question that is complex, or pose a related third- or fourth-stance question. An example of the former: During discussions of "Everyday Use," a short story by Alice Walker, students often focus on the older sister, Dee, *or* the younger sister, Maggie. When this happens, we stretch their thinking by asking, "Which character do you think deserves more sympathy, Dee or Maggie? Why?" This question meets the participants where they are—in the second stance—but asks them to rank their emotions for the two characters, and to look carefully at the text in order to support their decision. With younger students, the questions might be, "Which of these characters would you be friends with? Who would you not? Why?"

What you hear: An *absence* of voices making a connection between the text and the world. Students are not seeing what the text can teach us about real-life experiences. They are not lifting any ideas from the text and seeing how they mesh—or clash—with issues at home, or school, or in the media.

What that tells you: Students are still immersed within the world of the text. They need help stepping out to rethink some aspect of their lives in light of what they have just read.

Actions: Make the text-to-life connection occur by lobbing a second-stance question at them (catching them where they are), and then a third-stance question (anticipating where you'd like them to go). For example, imagine a discussion of *Nothing but the Truth* (Avi). One of your students has just commented that Philip isn't humming during the national anthem because he disrespects it—he just wants to get out of English class. Everyone, including you, agrees. You con-

nect with this conversation in the second stance by asking, "Is Philip being unpatriotic?" After students discuss this question for a while, they may by ready for a third-stance question that will compel them to make a text-to-life connection: "Could you see this happening in our society today? What does patriotism mean today? Is it similar to or different from the beliefs in this book?" Your students may stretch and leap to make these connections, yet they do hit the ball back, and the conversation continues with renewed energy, deepening analytical thinking.

What you hear: students remarking on the way the text is written. For example, "This chapter is more boring than the others"; "There are some weird vocabulary words in here"; "This part of the book is really violent."

What that tells you: Students are stopping short in their thinking, not yet using their experience as a reader to decide if their reactions to the book are because of the author's craft (or lack thereof)—or because of something else.

Actions: We don't often hear these kinds of comments in beginning discussions, because students, as relatively novice readers, are generally comfortable staying within the text world. If your students make comments like those above, push them to explore their assertions by posing questions such as, "Where do you see that happening?" and "Why do you think the author did that?"

Looking at matters of craft is a good conversational link to bring in when a topic on the floor seems to be stuck or done. You can always introduce it with open-ended questions such as, "What do you think about the way this book is put together? How would the story be different if it was told without any dialogue? Why do you think the author chose to write this chapter (this ending, etc.) the way she did?"

As we said earlier, third- and fourth-stance thinking deserve considerable time, and yet teachers often find themselves out of time. Not to worry. Develop a habit of glancing at your EB guide or notes a few minutes before you have to end the discussion. Are there big questions remaining? You can always pose one last question, if time permits. Then, it's time to take stock of the entire inventory of big questions with students. Point out to students what big questions were talked about— and mention a few issues that have yet to be discussed. You might write one of the unexplored questions on the chalkboard and ask students to write about it for homework. Or tell them to think about it, and that they'll be discussing it the next day as a warm-up. In the end you may have to let go of a few good questions; quality, not quantity counts.

Q: My students have begun talking. When should I interrupt?

A: Your students are beginning to develop their envisionments of the text. They're talking, perhaps asking questions, and perhaps sharing their opinions. Now your task becomes more complex, for all talk is not equal. Although each conversation is different, here is a list of guidelines on what to listen for, and how to respond effectively so that the energy of the conversation builds productively:

If you are hearing this:	You may need to do this:	Try saying or doing this:
A lot of similar responses	Up the ante—raise the bar on what students have been focusing on.	"It sounds like we're mostly in agreement about *x*. But what about *y*?" or "Can you find any evidence or connection to that idea in the story?"
A couple of students dominating the conversation	Support—invite more students into the conversation.	"Antonio and Maya—thanks. What about some others? Who would like to add to what has been said so far?"
Sweeping statements that are given without support	Up the ante—demand that students support their statements and/or think through their comments.	"Why do you think so?" or "Tell us more about that idea. Can you read us a passage that supports that idea?"
An argument	Encourage—provide ways for students to disagree appropriately, with evidence.	"I'm hearing some different opinions—great. Who has found some evidence for their argument?"
The conversation is dying down	Help—students probably need either a richer topic to sustain their focus, or more time in which to consider the issue.	Rephrase the topic in a more complex way (if needed), and/or say, "Let's take a five-minute time-out. Take five minutes to jot down some ideas about this question."

If you are hearing this:	You may need to do this:	Try saying or doing this:
A lot of comments about the students' individual lives, friends, family, or experiences	Orchestrate—connect their experiences back to the text or activity.	"Can you connect your experiences back to a character (a theme, an activity, etc.), What is similar? Different? What new questions do you have now?"
Students seem stuck on "what ifs"—speculating about a question that can't be answered	Orchestrate—refocus the question so that it is discussable.	"That's an interesting speculation. What kind of person might do what you're suggesting? Is our character that kind of person?"
A series of comments that are off track	Redirect—focus students on a question that is more directly related.	Invite student questions or ask a related question from your envisionment-building guide.
Information that isn't true	Clarify—ask for evidence, by inviting another student to provide the correct information, or by providing it yourself.	"Can you find a quote to support that?" or "Can anybody clarify this point for us?"
Stereotypes or racist/sexist comments	Tell—explain to students that these comments are not appropriate.	"When we talk about a group of people this way, it's a stereotype. Be specific in your comments—let's avoid generalizing about a whole group."

> **Q: Are misreadings possible? How do you know when a student is misreading the text, and how do you correct this wrong interpretation?**

A: In Chapter 3 we talked about clarifying incorrect answers—that is, answers where the reader is confusing some facts or terms or basic information about the text. In our example, Kent and his classmates were confusing the term "Elders" in *The Giver* with the term "elderly." The information

was evident in the text at a literal level; upon rereading, with guidance, the students should be readily able to find examples of the two terms being used differently.

What do you do, however, when someone has misread the text on an inferential level? Here's an example of such a situation. In some of our literature discussions with teachers, we used the Alice Walker story "Everyday Use," a text that always results in a powerful conversation. In a flashback within the story, a young girl is burned on her face during a fire and is rescued by her mother while her older sister stands inexplicably outside, watching the house burn. During one discussion of this story, a teacher speculated about the burning house: "Maybe the fire never happened; maybe it only happened in someone's mind." This idea sparked an animated discussion as people reconsidered the story in light of this possibility. Someone pointed out that the fire could be a metaphor for the older sister's feelings about her home and the poverty in which she lived. Upon reflection, we came to the decision that the evidence showed that the fire was a real event in the characters' lives, leading to the disfigurement of the little girl. Was the initial comment a misreading? Almost certainly. Yet this "misreading," posed to the group to wrestle with, provoked some thoughtful analysis of the story, leading to the discovery of the fire as a metaphor.

This example illustrates that the function of a good literary conversation is not for everyone to "get it right." The function of the discussion is to provide a safe place for the participants to work through their envisionments—their understanding of the text at that moment. Students' envisionments are likely to have holes or gaps in them—they may be only *partially* complete when they enter the discussion. A misreading at the inferential level can be an exciting opportunity for the class to do some critical analysis. Can they prove this idea right? Wrong? Is some variation possible? As long as students have enough time to follow it through, they will not leave having misinterpreted a key piece of the story. Rather, they will leave having investigated possible interpretations and having selected the one or ones that make the most sense, given the evidence at hand.

> ## Q: Do we need to come to consensus by the end of a discussion?

A: Judith Johnson, a poet and professor of English at the University at Albany, State University of New York, argues that consensus in academia and life in general is restrictive and narrowing. Rather, she argues for a "poetics of generosity" that "includes difference, accepts deviations, enjoys oppositions, as part of itself" (1999, p. 4). The reason such a poetics is possible is that good literature has the power to support differences in opinion, so readers can interact with it in different ways. Consequently, consensus at the end of a book discussion is neither necessary nor desired. Think

about rich discussions you've had with a friend; isn't it the continual push and pull of our views against others' insights that brings energy to conversation—and to life? Our students are no different; they talk and think about others' comments as they walk out of the classroom and into their dinner table conversations at home. Differences can and should coexist.

> **Q: What about the amount of time that discussions take? How will I address all of the content I need to cover to meet the state standards and prepare for the exams?**

A: The issue of time in relation to discussions is complex. Discussions do take up considerable class time, anywhere from 20 to 50 minutes, on average. Yet considering the content addressed in state standards, discussions turn out to be a very economical use of class time. This is because they engage students in multiple types of thinking in a short amount of time. This claim is easily tested. Without thinking of a particular standard to address, invite students to begin a conversation around a common text. Immediately afterward, take a look at the standards for English language arts for your grade level. It is likely that you will have addressed not only a number of the speaking and listening standards, but also several of the reading standards. Additionally, students will be better prepared to meet some of the requirements for writing. Developing skills with multiple standards simultaneously saves time in the long run (See pages 100–102 in Chapter 4 for more specific connections between literary discussions and the standards).

As for preparing students for state exams, that too is a complex issue. The stakes are high, with test preparation mandated more than ever. Yet research shows that such test preparation is not effective in the long run. In a study of 25 schools, including 14 that were succeeding academically despite challenges and 11 comparable schools that were not succeeding, Langer (2002) found that teachers and administrators at various sites prepared very differently for standardized tests. In the successful schools, those that were "beating the odds" (p. 4), teachers and administrators were working together to examine the tests and find ways to integrate the kinds of thinking required into the everyday curriculum. In these schools, "the focus is on the underlying knowledge and skills needed to do well in coursework and in life, as well as on the tests" (p. 17). By contrast, the less successful schools focused extensively on test practice, activities largely separated from the regular curriculum and from students' lives. Consequently, although class discussions do not at first glance appear to prepare students for standardized tests, they actually do an excellent job of enabling students to practice critical thinking and analysis.

> **Q: My students are having a hard time with the "stepping out" stance. How do I get them to connect the text to the larger society, when their knowledge of the world is still so limited?**

A: When so much of what students know about the world comes from television and the Internet, helping them to make connections between the text and their society can be challenging. But it's paramount, because if students fail to see the relationship between their in-school experiences and the workings of the world, then very little of what students learn in school gets applied to their lives. In short, they walk away with few true understandings.

Some teachers have had success in localizing their questions to students' immediate circle of friends and family and their community. For example, inner-city seventh graders who were reading *The Girl Who Owned a City,* by O. T. Nelson, had little knowledge of how city services would work without adults to run them; they had an excellent idea, however, of what their local neighborhood would be like without a police force.

In a different example, a teacher was surprised to discover that her students employed literate behavior with one another as they read, explained, traded, illustrated, and played with various anime figures such as Pokemon (Vasquez, 2003). Alvermann (2004) illustrates teenagers' extensive knowledge of video games, the Internet, and song lyrics. She suggests that teachers tap into this out-of-school knowledge by expanding the resources used in the classroom. For instance, teachers can encourage students to read from "a mix of trade books, textbooks, magazines, newspapers, student-generated texts, digital texts, hypermedia productions, visuals, artistic performances, and the like" (p. 34).

In addition, supplementary content knowledge, through nonfiction articles and/or interdisciplinary connections, can help. A seventh-grade teacher, whose students were reading *Holes* by Louis Sachar, brought in a newspaper account of excesses at summer youth camps ("Arizona Boot Camp Where Boy Died Reopens," Janofsky). Students read the article with interest both because it affected teens similar to them and because it shed new light on the situation in the novel. In another class, students read *The Devil's Arithmetic* by Jane Yolen after learning about the Holocaust/World War II in their social studies classes.

A different way to build content knowledge is to link your curriculum throughout the year, so that the text you read in September has themes or larger issues that are relevant to a text read in March. We'll look more at ways to build conversations over time in Part 3 of this book.

Q: I can't do an envisionment-building guide for each chapter of a novel. How do I pace myself and students through a whole novel and still take a dialogic approach?

A: Don't use an envisionment-building guide as a study guide.

Research has shown that students who work with study guides tend to focus their attentions on specific areas, learning about and remembering specific details, not an analysis of the bigger picture (Langer & Applebee, 1987). Moreover, study guides do not encourage further thinking on the topic, but close the conversation as soon as the question is answered. In other words, the student answers the question, knows that his or her answer is the "right" one, and mentally checks it off as "done."

One of the teachers we coached, Kendra, noticed that her students did not get invested in talking or thinking about the study guide questions she was using for *The Outsiders* by S. E. Hinton. During discussions, she would pose the study guide question to the students, and someone would answer it. Because the questions required one definite answer, there was little room for disagreement or elaboration. Kendra and her students soon grew to hate the study guide. She commented, "It was deadly, just deadly, for discussion." One day, she put the study guide aside and just asked students for their questions or comments about the chapter they had just read. A lovely conversation ensued, as students evidently had much to say about the book.

Kendra agreed to work with us on developing an envisionment-building guide for the book. Below you can see the questions we developed—in conjunction with writing activities—to help students step into the novel and make sense of the all-important first chapter. Adapt the basic ideas to any novel.

Writing to step into the book:
- What do you know about gangs? Are there any situations in which you would consider joining one? Why or why not?
- Reflection on a word: Outsider

Writing/Discussing to develop our understanding of Chapter 1
1. Draw a large question mark on your paper. Fill the space around the question mark with questions about the chapter. Only ask questions where you really want to know the answers.
2. What are your first impressions of Ponyboy? What interested, confused, or surprised you?
3. What do you think of the relationship between Ponyboy and his two brothers? Is it realistic?
4. Read these two statements by Ponyboy. What do you think he is saying? Do you agree or disagree, based on evidence from the chapter? Explain what you think.
   - "I'm not saying that either Socs or greasers are better; that's just the way things are." (page 6)

- "I lie to myself all the time. But I never believe me." (page 19)

5. Does this chapter change your opinions about gangs? Why or why not?

Writing to extend Chapter 1

- With a partner, draw a map that shows the relationships between the characters in this chapter. Label each character and write one or two adjectives to describe him/her. After you finish, look at the whole map you have made. What do you notice?

- If this chapter was happening in real life, and you had a choice of people to be, who would you want to be? Why? What did the writer do in the story to make you want to be that person?

After students have stepped into the book and are involved in and moving through the story, you can focus more on the important scenes and less on particular details, always opening with students' questions and comments. For example, below are some ideas for the last three chapters of *The Outsiders*:

Chapters 9-12

1. Immediately after you finish reading chapter 9, write a reaction to the chapter. What was on your mind at this point in the story?

2. In a small group, discuss: Who is ultimately most responsible for Johnny's death? See how many different possibilities you can consider on the way to making your decision. Which decision can you best support with evidence?

3. After reading the first paragraph of chapter 10, what do you think Ponyboy is thinking about? What is happening in his mind? How would a psychologist read this paragraph?

4. Compare Ponyboy's actions with the broken bottle on page 148 with his attitude toward the broken bottle earlier, on page 42. How has Ponyboy changed? What do you think is responsible for that change? Is it positive or negative, in your opinion? Support your answer with details from the story.

Note that envisionment-building guides for novels need to incorporate guiding questions that you want to remember as well as writing assignments to extend students' thinking.

Q: What are some ways to assess envisionment-building activities?

A: Earlier we shared a rubric that a teacher developed for her students to use in assessing group conversations. We suggested that evaluating each individual student's oral contributions to the discussion would be problematic both practically and conceptually, for not all participation is oral. Yet many teachers indicated it would be useful to be able to measure student contributions, especially when the discussion circle

is a recurring feature in the classroom. Perhaps the best way to assess participation, both from the speakers and the listeners, is to provide writing assignments that allow students to show you what they've learned from the discussion. Students at Pam's school had been discussing *Bud, Not Buddy*, by Christopher Paul Curtis, in class. Following the discussion, Pam developed some short essay questions that built on student discussions about the book. To increase the skills building she was providing through the assignment, she modeled its structure after the standardized test in her state. Here is a question from this assignment:

Although the novel Bud, Not Buddy depicts the hardships endured during the Depression, a careful reader will notice how strangers who are thrown together offer friendship, encouragement, kindness and support. Choose two of the following characters and explain fully how they help Bud Caldwell. In your answer be sure to:

- **Choose two characters (Bugs, Deza Malone, Lefty Lewis or Miss Thomas), and explain how each meets Bud.**
- **Fully explain how the two characters help Bud by showing friendship, support, encouragement or kindness.**
- **Use details from the novel to support your answer.**

Pam also used writing assignments to validate the stepping-out stance that she asked her students to adopt during envision-

> 3 <u>Lyddie</u> is considered historical fiction. What did you learn about life in New England in 1843? What were some of the advantages and disadvantages of the good old days? (Include questions that you still think about!)
>
> | Advantages | Disadvantages |
> |---|---|
> | Kids were allowed to be free and to work. + | Parents could leave their children alone to let them die. + |
> | The land was so spaced out that everyone had a ton of privacy + | Your neighbors were so spaced out your closest neighbor was at least 1 mile away sometimes. |
> | The air was very clean, (outside) not having electricity or a huge population + | No cars, they had to drive in carriages or buggys on horses, or walk. Their feet must hurt w/only leather shoes! |
>
> *Keep thinking true.* *Get deeper*
>
> In Lyddie's time, there were many advantages and disadvantages over today. An advantage is that kids were allowed to do anything but vote. They were even allowed to work. A disadvantage is that parents could leave their kids. Another advantage is that the air was so clean outside, without electricity or cars. A disadvantage was no cars. They either had to walk or ride a coach. Not many choices +

Written work extends discussion work; it invites students to support their answers with details, to think through their responses, and to articulate questions remaining in their minds. Thus, discussions help students to succeed on state exams.

ment-building discussions. Again structuring the prompts to look like the state exams, Pam asked students to apply their learning from the novel *Lyddie* (Paterson) to see what inferences they could make between the setting of the book and 1840s New England. Specifically, she asked them: Lyddie is considered historical fiction. What did you learn about life in New England in 1843? What were some advantages and disadvantages of the good old days? (Include questions that you still think about!)

On the previous page, you can see one student's response to this question.

Q: Is discussion appropriate for struggling readers?

A: Although there's always the temptation to provide simpler work and basic tasks for struggling learners, we need to remember that these students also need the benefits of the kind of complex thinking that is provided through literature discussions. Literature discussions—those that are authentic, incorporate uptake, and use student comments and ideas as a substantial part of the content—lead toward student achievement, though they rarely happen with struggling learners (Nystrand, 1997). Discussions have the potential to increase engagement with the material—and this, in turn, aids learning. In a study of eighth-grade students, Nystrand found that the level of engagement among students is important in helping them to learn: "Not surprisingly, we found that disengaged students failed to learn much. Students who were off-task in class, and who did not turn in their work, were seriously impeded" (p. 273). Given that struggling readers already have reason to be disengaged from school, it follows that teachers who use discussion to foster engagement have a powerful tool to increase their motivation and, in turn, their learning.

In addition to motivation and engagement, struggling readers need something else: explicit instruction and practice in literary thinking. Lee (2004) suggests that with struggling readers, many of whom are African American and Latino students from low-income families, what is important is (a) valuing the cultural knowledge students bring into the classroom and (b) explicitly showing students how to connect and use that cultural knowledge to "play the game of literary criticism" (p. 20). Lee recommends beginning literary discussions around texts, such as song lyrics, of which students have extensive knowledge. Within this familiar context, students begin to discuss literary elements such as symbolism and irony. By engaging students in discussions around these texts, and through the explicit sequencing of instruction in how to participate, Lee found that: "students with histories of low achievement in reading become intensely engaged in literary analysis. They produce interpretations that are quite often profound. They learn to play the game of literary criticism in

ways that capture the most rigorous norms of the discipline." (p. 20)

What kinds of explicit instruction are helpful for struggling readers? Greenleaf et al. (2001) describe a number of instructional strategies that are effective with struggling readers (and are effective strategies for more successful students, too). Many of these strategies will assist students to access texts and thereby improve their ability to participate in class discussions alongside their peers:

- reciprocal teaching strategies (questioning, summarizing, clarifying, predicting)
- direct instruction in examining text genres (modeling, Think Alouds)
- development of technique (note taking, paraphrasing, identifying root words, prefixes, suffixes, breaking down the complexity of words and sentences)
- developing fluency/self-knowledge as readers (keeping a metacognitive log about challenges that occurred during reading and writing reflective letters to teachers about progress) (pp. 95–96).

Other techniques (described in Chapter 2) that we have found effective for struggling readers include the use of sticky notes and the use of reader's marks.

Q: I'd like to extend envisionment-building techniques into my writing assignments. Can you give me ways to do that?

A: One simple way to develop literary understanding is to use journal prompts that tie in to the four stances. These allow students to use their writing time to devel-

---

Journal Starters for Responding to Literature

1. So far I think this book is . . . Explain your opinion by giving specific examples to tell more about the story or the writing style.

2. One character that I see myself in is . . . Tell why by giving examples of the way that character is like you.

3. If _____ (a parent, older brother or sister, friend) were reading this book, he/she would think it was . . . because . . .

4. A question that's on my mind after reading this part is . . . Tell why you want to know this! What are some possible answers?

5. If I were telling this story, I would . . . Explain what you would do differently or keep the same.

6. Reading this book reminds me of . . . Tell more about what it reminds you of—another book, an experience, a place, a person—and why!

7. The part I just read makes me think a little differently about . . . because . . .

8. My feelings toward (character's name) have changed since the beginning of the book . . . Explain how your feelings have changed.

9. A part of this book that I really don't understand is . . . because . . .

10. If I read another book by this author, I would know it was the same author because . . .

11. Tell what you have noticed about what kinds of things this writer does in a story that might be different from other writers you have read.

op questions and ideas of their own or to answer some thought-provoking questions that you have provided. On the previous page is a list of journal prompts that we developed for use with literature; some will work for nonfiction, as well.

Partner Letters. Partner letters are another effective writing assignment to try. Several teachers in the project used these successfully. A seventh-grade teacher, Katrina, successfully developed this idea around free choice books: students chose someone who was either reading the same novel, a different book by the same author—or a completely different book. They completed the letters outside of class, exchanging them with their partner in class. In the letters the students were asked to "engage your partner in a dialogue that is thoughtful and meaningful."

Two other teachers, Annie and Connie, used partner letters during a Revolutionary War unit. Students had read historical fiction in small groups, each group reading a different novel. During the reading of their novels, each student was paired up with someone who was reading a different book. Writing from the point of view of a character, students wrote three formal letters, sharing information about their circumstances. Partners asked questions in their replies, and compared and contrasted their lives. During the "mail delivery" days in class, students enthusiastically waited to receive their letters, quickly unfolding them to read what their partner had written.

Partner letters developed because teachers tried out some ways to extend the talk in writing, finding that the idea of a dialogue between and among students can be continued beyond the oral conversation. In Part 3 of this book we look at other written assignments and find ways to connect them to a larger conversation that extends beyond any individual discussion.

Q: With this kind of discussion, I'm afraid that students won't notice what I want them to. How do I make sure to "fit in" the parts that I feel are essential?

A: The easiest way to make sure that these larger issues are covered is to draft them into envision-ment-building questions to have in hand during the conversation. Students won't hit all of the important points in this one discussion, but you can focus them on the central points and make sure they haven't missed a key element of the text.

Having students write and ask questions themselves will increase the chances that they'll touch on some of the main issues themselves. Then you can extend students' thinking by upping the ante to get at some of the larger, more complex issues that students are not likely to notice. For example,

teachers who want students to notice the symbolism in Harper Lee's *To Kill a Mockingbird*, might be tempted to ask, "What symbols are there in *To Kill a Mockingbird*?" This is likely to be interpreted as a test or display question, and students will stop talking or at best will revert to guessing or waiting to hear the "right" answer. On the other hand, a prompt such as, "What questions do you have so far?" may elicit a question about the tree where Jem and Scout keep finding their little treasures. The teacher can then up the ante by asking, "What's important about that tree? Why didn't Harper Lee have them find these treasures somewhere else, like in a box or on the sidewalk?" or some similar question. Students will explore the idea of the tree as an important image, and the teacher can provide them with the terminology for "symbol" so that they can use it to explain their thinking. The bottom line is that envisionment building does not mean abandoning all teacher knowledge in favor of student talk. Students will be able to do more with teacher comments or questions, though, if they are hooked onto the students' points or questions, using uptake to connect the ideas and then returning them to the students for further exploration.

Coming Full Circle:
The Beauty of Defined Roles

In the space within the discussion circle, diverse experiences, student understandings, and teacher knowledge meet. Envisionment building offers an approach that is both teacher friendly and student friendly. It's teacher friendly because it provides a role for the facilitator's knowledge and experience. It's student friendly because it provides a role for students, inviting them to share *their* knowledge and experience with one another and with you. Students learn from their teacher and from one another, and they become participants in literary conversations.

In the last part of this book, we look beyond the individual discussion toward a discussion-based curriculum. What might a curriculum look like if it regularly incorporated discussion? How might the curriculum itself become a yearlong conversation, in which texts speak to one another and ideas build over time? How might writing assignments, oral discussions, language study, and diverse texts be integrated together to produce a more coherent program? We begin, in Chapter 7, with a conceptual overview of what it means to think about curriculum in terms of a conversation.

Part Three

Extending Discussion

Chapter Seven

Connecting Middle Schoolers to the World

How to guide these discussions over time to become a larger significant conversation

For many, curriculum evokes an image of a teacher plan book, designed with a grid that neatly catalogs the activities, readings, and assignments students will do in a course. However, what if the curriculum were less like a plan book and more like an interactive website—flexible, informative, and interlinked to related ideas? Participants—the students and teacher—could be actively involved in shaping the information and in learning about the ideas under study. With their thinking stimulated and their learning represented, participants could enact a curriculum that has significance for them. Achieving such a feat is not easy, however, as Mary Adler discovered in her first years of teaching:

In my first year of teaching eighth-grade English, I did what many other new teachers do when it comes to planning curriculum: I went to the book room. Looking around at the tattered and unevenly numbered piles of books available for teachers to use, I gathered together one of each book that looked interesting (or that I remembered from my Adolescent Literature class) as well as copies of the textbooks, and took them home for the weekend. I also borrowed copies of the books I was required to teach in eighth-grade honors—*The Crucible* by Arthur Miller and *To Kill a Mockingbird* by Harper Lee, books that I feared were going to be very challenging for my students. Finally, I asked what students would be doing in their history class and looked at the state and district standards to see what skills I was required to cover in the eighth grade. This confluence of information made curriculum development both very simple and complex. Simple because I picked books that "fit"—fit the chronological history curriculum, fit the requirements, fit into the marking periods. Complex because it seemed like I would have to learn to juggle while teaching—to get the students interested, teach the skills they needed to know, maintain discipline, prepare students for high school literature classes, and help them become readers (!) in the process.

It took three years before I began to see some connections between the texts in my curriculum. In honors class, for instance, I typically began with *The Crucible*, since it addressed the Puritan period, which was being studied in history class. We had many discussions about evidence used during the witchcraft trials, and how people manipulated information for their own gain. I gave the students a map showing the relationship between land ownership and accused witches; working with this graphic, the students were able to see that the accused were often isolated, were women, and/or were owners of land that others wanted. "Was this a fair system?" my students wondered. "When the system is unfair, is it okay to lie to protect yourself? Should the protagonist, John Proctor, have lied to save his life, at the expense of his name?" The questions and observations that came from students helped

Building Literacy Through Classroom Discussion

me to see my curriculum as more than what was in my plan book—it was "alive," enacted through the people in my room. They also helped me to see that students could read and enjoy challenging texts, especially ones that possessed conflict and ambiguity.

Over time, I noticed that our talk kept returning to the same themes—justice, dignity, fairness, and a related issue, manipulating others. In the spring, when my students and I read *To Kill a Mockingbird*, another novel with a jury trial, we picked up the same chain of conversation we'd been having throughout the year. By the third year of teaching, I was able to refer students back to *The Crucible*, asking them what had changed in jury trials (as depicted in the literature), in the last 300 years—and what remained the same. With these discussions as a foundation, students went on to write research papers and problem-solution essays about our justice system today.

What I came to understand was that the required texts could be used as part of a larger conversation. I had learned to think of my classroom materials not as too hard or too easy, but rather as "appropriate or inappropriate according to the questions that are asked and the conversations that are generated around them" (Applebee, 1996, p. 28).

Big and Little Discussions

In the first months of our work together on the Partnership for Literacy project, we talked a lot about the three key concepts we wanted to bring to the participating teachers: dialogic discussion, envisionment building, and curricular conversations. We realized we needed a way to distinguish which kind of discussion we were talking about: Was this a single class discussion—a dialogic interaction—or was this number of discussions that together created a "bigger" conversation? We found ourselves referring to them as "little c" and "big C" conversations. The "little c" related to developing understandings over a relatively short period of time—one or two class periods. These conversations are essential to the day-to-day learning in the classroom and, over time, they develop a classroom culture in which student voices are part of a larger community. "Little c" conversations are described in the first two parts of this book.

In these last three chapters, we want to turn to the "big C"—the conversation that connects the individual day-to-day understandings into a larger idea or issue that is bigger than any one discussion. The metaphor comes from Arthur Applebee's (1996, 1997) conception of a curriculum that is enacted through conversation. He argues that it is through classroom discourse that students learn about the ways of knowing, ways of thinking, and ways of doing that are central to the discipline. Over time, students engage in "little c" conversations that teach them overtly about content (topics,

issues), and more tacitly about process (ways of thinking, talking, and doing). Taken together, we can think of this progression as a curriculum—a curriculum that is constructed.

Achieving curricular cohesion takes time; it often takes a couple of years of practice before a teacher feels in the groove of it. In part, this is because curricular conversations (the "big C's") depend on the individual conversations (the "little c's") to give them life and shape. Until the dialogic discussions are running smoothly (dancing in and out of the four stances), there is little foundation on which a curriculum can be built. That's why we've structured the book to put this concept of curricular cohesion last. In chapters 8 and 9, we'll also provide support in terms of strategies and tools that help extend and sustain the curriculum over time. But first, let's look at the concept.

Curriculum as Conversation

The early meaning of the word *curriculum* was "a course one runs around" (the Latin word meaning "to run" is *currere*). From the physical act of racing around a circular path, the word *curriculum* evolved to stand for a mental pursuit: a course of study in ancient European universities and a prescription of content and syllabi in American secondary classrooms. In English, the word may evoke a tradition that looks more to the past by teaching texts (reciting and memorizing), from the literary canon (works by mostly dead white men), than by helping students participate in what Arthur Applebee (1996) calls significant conversations in the field—discussions in which students are invited to examine modern life and also to imagine the future.

Linking Past and Present to Inform Our Future

A number of researchers (Applebee 1996; Dewey, 1938; Dyson, 1993, 1994; Eisner, 1994; Hynds, 1997; Stock, 1995; Wells, 1999) offer a vision for thinking about teaching as a process by which students actively participate together with the teacher in a curriculum that is part of a "living tradition." This humanistic approach encourages students and teachers alike to redefine ideas, reformulate knowledge, and reinterpret texts. Participation—the "doing"—is what makes it a living tradition that has the power to transform: the power to transform knowledge, our own understandings as teachers, and our students' lives.

What's Up, Romeo?

Consider how we commonly teach Shakespeare's *Romeo and Juliet*. Students are often invited to read

Building Literacy Through Classroom Discussion

it aloud, and then engage in discussions of the play's characters, setting, and themes. They may be asked to compare the play with a film version, or maybe even with *West Side Story*. True enough, students take away something of value, but two important results aren't achieved—or achieved with enough impact. Students' knowledge is not enacted, and students may not connect Shakespeare's themes to their own lives in enduring, applicable ways. And thus, the playwright remains somewhat of an irrelevant relic in students' minds; his value resides in school, not in their world.

But suppose you have students read aloud a Shakespeare play, staging at least part of it. During this staging, students try out different intonations and body movements to see how these improvisations influence our understandings of a scene's import or the characters' motives. Your students gather in small groups, and each group stages one act in a modern setting that strongly reflects the conflict. Maybe it's the dynamic between the son of a military family and the daughter of a family who marched in rallies against war, or particular groups at odds in your town. Who knows, maybe it's even a clash between the son of an environmentalist and the daughter of a logging family. Suppose students do not, however, have liberty to change Shakespeare's language itself. These acts are staged together and the class talks about how effective this new staging is and what they learned about the play by doing the project. How did the language adapt? Then, perhaps, they see *William Shakespeare's Romeo & Juliet*, directed by Baz Luhrmann, and discuss whether the contemporary setting works with the original dialogue.

All these drama activities compel students to consider such questions as, Do conflicts between families and/or cultures exist as markedly today as they did in Shakespeare's day? What are some examples students can think of? Were students startled when they found that characters in the movie *Romeo and Juliet* used guns, when the original language refers to swords?

These "little c" discussions can lead to a "big C" conversation that explores a question such as this: Is Shakespeare from "back in the day"—part of the old tradition—or is there something in Shakespeare that speaks to our lives

A student is ready—with mind, voice, pen, paper, and life experience—to tackle Shakespeare and make it her own.

today? This conversation might in turn embrace related "big C" ideas: Why do the younger and the older generations not see eye to eye? Is love blind, or does it see most deeply? How is violence related to love? Who makes the decisions we live by? Can we change our fate?

With this kind of teaching, Shakespeare is not part of a dead tradition—or, as Applebee (1996) put it, a "deadly" one (p. 33). Rather, Shakespeare speaks quite readily to contemporary problems and issues. In such a case students are learning to "do" or perhaps to "make" English rather than to "study" or "remember" it. (Thanks to Dr. Jacquelyn Kilpatrick, English Professor at California State Channel Islands, for modeling teaching possibilities with Shakespeare).

Effective Curricula: Integrated, Diverse, and Highly Interesting

There are many ways to structure a curriculum. These approaches are enacted and received differently by students and thus lead to varied kinds of learning (Applebee, 1996, pp. 69–79). Here are some common ways educators organize curricula:

- **Catalog:** a list of texts, skills, and/or activities with no relation between them
- **Collection:** a set of texts that explores a particular topic
- **Sequence:** a chronological or hierarchical order of study
- **Episodic:** a sequence of units that are self-contained but that relate to a larger idea or topic
- **Integrated:** units or topics are discussed in relation to a larger topic as well as what has come before, so that understanding of the larger topic grows and changes over time

As we have seen in our work with the Partnership teachers, student learning is stronger and more durable with integrated curricula. Why? Because in integrated—and to some extent episodic curricula—students are explicitly and frequently asked to connect and use the ideas they are learning about. Not only does this help to reinforce skills and content, but it also naturally promotes higher-order thinking, for students are engaged in comparing, analyzing, and even synthesizing information across texts to come up with an understanding that is larger than that of any one text. It's also an efficient and exciting way to teach, because you do not have to constantly begin again, engaging students in new topics.

However, as we suggest in Chapter 8, teachers do not need to start with an entire integrated curriculum to produce connected learning over time. Why not start with a few paired texts and test the idea by exploring a topic over a week or two? Then, try extending it to a unit of several weeks in which students explore a larger issue through a series of conversations, writing tasks, and activities. Then, look across units and see if you find connections there. When planning such a unit, you may want to consider the

features that make such curricula work. Effective curricula do the following (Applebee, 1996, 1997):

- extend beyond the classroom into the community, history, other past and/or present texts, and/or current events or situations
- reflect a diversity of voices or genres
- provide a sense of continuity over time
- sustain high student interest and involvement in the ongoing conversations
- focus and develop domains (topics, issues, concepts) that are significant

Addressing a diversity of voices is an important feature to consider for both urban and suburban schools. Our students live in a society in which race and culture mix and sometimes clash; they desperately need the opportunity to hear and respect other voices and experiences. They also need to see that schools value and accept different voices and cultures, including their own. As Melissa, a seventh-grade teacher in an urban school in New York, put it, "I attribute a large portion of my success to highly engaging literature, written at an appropriate reading level, starring protagonists with whom students could relate" (Anderson, 2002, p. 5).

Melissa achieved startling results by teaching the novel *Money Hungry* (Flake), a story about a 13-year-old African-American girl who speaks in African-American Vernacular English. Although Melissa had only one copy and had not intended to read the whole text aloud, students were so involved with the story, and with a heroine who experienced issues and situations familiar to them, that they insisted that she read the entire book. (Later, students lined up to check the book out, reading it over and over again). Here's an excerpt from an article about Melissa's class, which appeared in *English Update*, a newsletter put out by CELA.

> The protagonist, Raspberry Hill, was discussed in relation to characters in other books. Moreover, each reviewed skill, such as using figurative language, was linked back to Flake's book, and new readings helped students think about their interpretations of *Money Hungry*. As students read other engaging texts, they began making connections across genres and selections. For instance, they noticed that the suspense techniques used in *The Girl Who Owned a City* by O.T. Nelson (studied in April), were not that far removed from those in *Money Hungry*. (Anderson, Adler & Morrill, 2002, p. 4).

Making the most of her students' enthusiasm, Melissa used the text as the basis of a larger conversation that was ultimately about how writers use literary techniques in different ways.

Curriculum Planning: Five Areas to Ponder

We've discussed varied ways of structuring curricula, advocating for more integrated, connected learning. We've discussed some of the features of effective curricula, especially the importance of including diverse voices and genres. These are conceptual pieces that are important to think about for the larger picture but that may not help you as much in the curriculum-planning phase. There are five areas to ponder when rethinking curriculum. These five areas apply to both the "little c" and "big C" conversations, so they can be used at any point in the process (adapted from Applebee, 1996, pp. 51–65):

1. **Quality:** Is the material you want to use clear and accurate, and on point for the conversations you want to have? (Have you chosen works that are most central to the conversation?)

2. **Quantity:** How much material are you thinking of using? Is there enough to sustain a discussion? A series of discussions/activities? Or is there an overwhelming amount of material?

3. **Relatedness:** Are the different components you're thinking of using substantially related in some way? You'll want to avoid tangential or superficial relationships because these will not yield deep connections or new ideas about the topic or issue under discussion.

4. **Manner:** How are you thinking of teaching the material? Are you asking authentic questions that have more than one "right" answer? Are you providing enough scaffolding so that students can engage with the texts and get the skills they need to participate in more cogni-tively sophisticated ways? Are students' voices or experiences an important part of the discoveries you expect them to make?

5. **Significance:** Does it feel as if students are pursuing important questions of some depth? Are they using literacy skills to do so? Are they bringing their personal experience and knowledge to bear on the problem or idea you are collectively exploring? Are students reading critically with a developed awareness of other texts?

Within a curricular conversation, students can look across texts, discuss their choices, and pose questions to one another.

The Role of Writing in the Larger Conversation

To develop curricular conversations that deepen over time, teachers need to provide enough structure so that students can progress in their learning (see no. 4 above). To provide this structure, it's helpful to have a sense of the end goals for the conversation. (Though the goals are likely to be amended, it is helpful to have them in mind when you begin.) With these goals in mind, the next step is to think about the kinds of skills and knowledge students need to get there. For example, if students will produce an analytical essay at the end of a unit, then they will need practice with analytical thinking and use of textual support. This practice can be provided through journal jots, learning logs, and discussion throughout the unit. Then students can use their journal and other written work to help them construct a more formal essay.

In previous chapters we explored ways to scaffold student learning with an array of facilitating techniques. Now, we want to emphasize the role of writing. Assigning informal writing frequently is an extremely effective way to scaffold for your students. With each assignment, whether a two-minute fast write or an essay, students gain practice with tasks that later may be assessed more formally. Writing is thinking, and so it is an excellent tool for getting students to make connections within and across texts. Logically, then, different kinds of writing push different kinds of thinking. In a study that looked at the relationship between writing and learning, Langer and Applebee (1987) found that "different kinds of writing activities lead students to focus on different kinds of information, to think about that information in different ways, and in turn to take quantitatively and qualitatively different kinds of knowledge away from their writing experiences" (p. 135). Specifically, they found the following:

- Short-answer questions are good for recall in the short term but do not promote analysis or reconsideration of the text.
- Writing summaries or taking notes helps students to pay attention to the whole text, but only on a surface level.
- Essays requiring analysis promote more retention of less information; in wrestling with a few complex ideas, students do more rethinking of the information and hence retain it longer (pp. 135–136).

Langer and Applebee's findings make perfect sense: The more you work with something and manipulate it, the better you understand it and remember how it works. This is probably why we are not issued our driver's licenses on the basis of watching videos and taking a multiple-choice exam. Rather, we are asked to get in the car and maneuver it in complex ways. It is not expected that we will know how to drive immediately, but rather that we will be taken out a number of times and allowed to practice in different neighborhoods and driving conditions. Like driving practice, writing assignments give students the opportunity to navigate their thinking process along various routes and give them the confidence to eventually sustain their thinking over a longer piece of writing.

Many writing assignments may be informal—students can complete them in their journals—for the express purpose of giving students time and space to explore their thoughts before or after discussing a text or topic. This writing need not be graded for content; feedback can be given in the form of peer response, or the teacher might respond periodically with a sentence or two, so that he or she doesn't get bogged down in marking up papers or writing extensive comments.

This kind of preparatory writing helps students develop or reformulate ideas and thereby stimulates complexity in student reasoning (Langer & Applebee, 1987). Writing can also be used to review ideas on a particular topic within the larger conversation. Finally, writing assignments can encourage the reformulating of ideas.

In the box at right, we share some ideas for writing aimed at these various purposes.

Writing Ideas

For exploratory purposes
- Freewrite: response to literature
- Converse in writing with someone who takes a different view
- Journal jot
- Question mapping (begin writing questions you have about the idea or topic; continue to expand your questions in certain areas; choose one or two to explore in writing; share with the class)
- Brainstorm relationships or possible metaphors for thinking about connections

For reviewing information
- Retelling of relevant story
- Notes in preparation for class discussion
- Dialogue (double-entry) journal (statement on left, evidence on right, or other configuration)
- Learning logs ("Take five minutes at the end of class to jot down what you learned in today's session.")
- Summary
- "Reflection on what I learned during the class discussion"
- T-charts (see Chapter 8 for some ideas)
- Newspaper article describing the text, situation, or experience

For rethinking, connecting, or analyzing across texts
- Personal narrative
- Autobiographical incident and reflection
- Analysis of an interview
- A persuasive speech
- Editorial
- Compare-and-contrast essay
- Analytical essay about a larger theme and how it develops across the texts
- Letter to or from a character
- Rewrite the story or text from the point of view of a different character or person
- Research paper

Conflict on the Mississippi

In the autobiography "Cub Pilot on the Mississippi", Samuel Clemens (Mark Twain) experiences both internal and external conflict. Internal conflict happens with one character that is trying to decide what is the right thing to do in a situation. External conflict is conflict that happens between two or more people or things trying to settle an argument, trying to survive in nature, trying to survive in society, etc.

During the course of the story, Samuel experiences internal conflict. One example of internal conflict that Samuel experiences is whether or not he should express his feelings towards pilot Brown. He really dislikes Brown because Brown gets on his back about everything he does. Samuel is afraid that if he expresses his feelings towards Brown that Brown will get on his back even more and give him an even harder time if he does something wrong. Another example of internal conflict that Samuel experiences is that he is dreaming of killing Brown. Samuel really wants to kill Brown but it is illegal to harm a pilot while they are on duty. He is also afraid that if he gets thrown off this boat that he may not be accepted onto another boat and he would have to find another career.

During the course of the story, Samuel also experiences external conflict. An example of external conflict is Samuel vs. Brown in the pilothouse. Henry tells Brown that he told him to dock. Brown insists that Henry did not tell him and goes after him with a ten pound piece of coal. Samuel could not just sit there and watch his brother get attacked so he did the first thing he could think of. He attacked Brown with the stool he was sitting on. He hit Brown with it making him fall to the ground. He then got onto Brown and started to pound him.

During the end of this story, the conflicts are resolved. Samuel finally expresses his feelings about Brown by taking out his anger on Brown in the pilothouse. He also gets to hurt pilot Brown like he wanted to. The surprise at the end of the story was that even though Samuel was the one who broke all the rules, Brown was still the one to leave the ship.

A class discussion of Twain's "Cub Pilot on the Mississippi" got students to consider characters at odds with one another. The discussion served as a kind of prewriting exercise for a final paper on internal and external conflict.

Final Draft

"…Serve as the watchdog of society…to satirize its silliness, to attack its injustices and to stigmatize its faults" is a perfect description for John Steinbeck and his books. The Pearl by Steinbeck proves this statement to be true because violence and predudice are all in the novel, which also occur in society. The doctor symbolizes prejudice because he is prejudice against Kino and all the poor civilians. The trackers and Kino symbolizes violence because they have violent ~~because~~ tendencies. His books demonstrate what major conflicts have gone on in societies throughout history.

Steinbeck must think that the main problems in society are prejudice and violence because he accentuates them throughout the story. Prejudice is demonstrated by the doctor because he turns down Kino when he has no money. When Kino showed the doctor what he had to pay for treatment, the servant said "the doctor has gone out" (page 12). This is just a really mean thing to say to someone who is poor and will probably have no money. But when Kino finds the pearl the doctor suddenly wants to help him. Just because someone is poor that does not give people the right to judge them based on that fact.

After students had successfully related a quotation to a text in discussion, Liz, their eighth-grade teacher, removed the scaffolding. She assigned students to write an essay relating a Steinbeck quotation to *The Pearl*. This student paid special attention to the social issues of prejudice, violence, and poverty— not a surprising focus, given a larger conversation on human nature.

Developing a Big Conversation: One Teacher's Story

Now, let's look at how one teacher wove writing, reading, and discussion together to create a larger conversation in her eighth-grade classroom. Liz, a popular seventh-grade teacher, agreed to her principal's request midway through the Partnership to switch to the eighth grade the following year. It was a big shift for her, but the school needed another eighth-grade teacher, and it meant that she would be able to keep her seventh graders for another year. It also provided a wonderful opportunity to plan curriculum in a territory as yet unknown.

Selecting books that have enough legs. Mary met with Liz over the summer to help plan the curriculum. Liz's main concern at the time was finding quality, meaty texts that students could really sink their teeth into. As a seventh-grade teacher, she had grown fond of *Tuck Everlasting* (Babbitt), *The Giver* (Lowry), and *The Call of the Wild* (London). Would the eighth-grade books appeal as much? What would she do with *The Pearl* (Steinbeck) and *The Devil's Arithmetic* (Yolen), two required texts that year? *The Pearl* tells the story of a fisherman who unexpectedly discovers a valuable pearl and then must cope with the resulting tensions in his village, family, and community. Liz knew from other teachers that students sometimes had a difficult time connecting with the book, especially in light of its challenging vocabulary. *The Devil's Arithmetic*, by contrast, focused on the Holocaust, which was a compelling topic to most students—but which seemed a vastly different topic from the other texts in the book room. Also, Liz needed to choose other texts to use during the year—she was considering Avi's *Nothing But the Truth* because she felt students would connect with the main character, a student who makes up a story to get out of his English class and then watches the situation spiral out of control.

Linking the books by theme. Liz had many options to use in planning her curriculum. However, as part of the Partnership work, she had also agreed to work on developing a curricular conversation to see what kinds of coherence could be made between the major texts in the course. This was daunting because at first glance, *Nothing But the Truth* had little to do with *The Pearl* or *The Devil's Arithmetic*. Because *The Pearl* seemed to be of greatest concern to Liz, Mary and Liz began by discussing that novel. What were the themes that seemed worth exploring? Following is a partial list from that first brainstorm:

- Greed can destroy/ruin
- Influence of pride or "hubris"
- A strong sense of family and community—the "song"
- Testing strength of character
- Exploring the human condition

With these initial themes in mind, they considered the other texts being offered. Which threads seemed to apply to more than one text? As they discussed *Nothing but the Truth*, they discovered other themes. Here are a few:

- How do our individual backgrounds and experiences affect our notions of the truth?
- What is it that causes us to behave the way we do?
- Is there one truth?
- What does it mean to tell the truth?
- Is it in our human nature to twist things to our advantage?
- How much of the "truth" is affected by our perceptions?
- How do we "flavor" the truth?

Note that the themes above are not yet "kid friendly"—they're ones Liz and Mary thought about as readers themselves. This is important! When you are planning your curriculum, always start out as a reader. As a professional in the field of English, chances are good that your thinking will reflect your years of experience in the discipline. Chances are also good, therefore, that the questions you ultimately explore with your students will represent significant issues in the field as opposed to questions that represent what we think students "ought to know about" or "should know" in adolescence, such as more didactic themes like "Taking Responsibility" or "Consequences".

Finding the theme at the heart of it all. After looking at the thematic questions from *The Pearl* and *Nothing but the Truth*, Liz and Mary realized that the term *human nature* kept coming up. They played with some related questions, including, "Can human nature be changed?" and "Is evil inevitable? If not, what can we do about it?" and "What motivates us as humans?" Eventually, Liz decided to ask a simpler question: "What is human nature?" Students would explore this question over time with a variety of texts across genres.

Turning the theme into the "big C" question. Now that Liz had her larger question, she wondered how best to begin the conversation. Human nature, after all, was a complex and abstract idea, seemingly far removed from the life of the average eighth grader. Mary remembered a college philosophy class in which she had read about a great debate on the subject of human nature between philosophers Thomas Hobbes and Jean-Jacques Rousseau. Hobbes felt that human nature was essentially evil and self-serving, held in check only by society's laws and expectations. Rousseau, in his early writings, felt that people were essentially good, and that evil or corruption was the result of a corrupt society. Liz liked the contrast in these positions. She wondered if her students could handle 17th- and 18th-century philosophy, though. Liz realized that she would have to do some serious scaffolding to help students develop the facility to work with the material and to develop interest in the topic.

Making it real, making it appeal. Liz set aside the first two weeks of the semester to focus intensely on developing an understanding of the theme of human nature. She posted large photographs of Hobbes and Rousseau on her bulletin board along with short quotations illustrating their contrary positions. When students entered class in the first day, they were given Journal entry #1: "What is human nature?" Surprisingly, students had quite a bit to say about their understanding of this abstract topic. Here are some of the students' ideas, raised in discussion after writing:

Human nature is...
• "Natural habits"
• "Instincts—what children do"
• "Basic flaws in humans"
• "An excuse that people say—'It's just human nature'"
• "Something you just do"
• "Something physical—it's your body growing"
• "Your reaction to situations"

Asking students to take a stand. That first week, students did a number of other activities designed to help them explore the topic. They participated in a "Stand and Deliver" exercise (see pages 117–118 in Chapter 5 for details) in which they agreed or disagreed with the statement, "All people are born good." In the ensuing conversation, students brought up many issues important in their own lives, some of which would come up later in the texts they would read, including issues of corruption, the role of parents in shaping their children's beliefs and attitudes, the influence of society's expectations on a person's behavior, and the role of genetics in shaping a person—the nature/nurture argument.

Inviting writing. Students also worked together with a partner (and a dictionary) to rewrite a paragraph on Hobbes' and Rousseau's philosophies in their own words. For homework, they had to decide whether they agreed with Hobbes or Rousseau—are people good or evil at heart? They were then asked to look through the newspaper to find an article that illustrated their opinion, providing evidence that people had an essentially good or bad nature.

Sadly, the events of September 11, 2001, unfolded during this first week of instruction, creating a real-life context in which the discussion of human nature that was happening in Liz's classroom took on a new and painful dimension. The concept perhaps helped students to articulate some of the questions and concerns that arose as they watched the horror replay day after day on television. As with the articles they searched for in the newspaper, students were seeing a connection between class assignments and what was happening in the world outside of school.

Using the theme as a way to view literature characters. As the curriculum took shape over the next few months, Liz found that the theme of human nature worked well to shape a debate over the motivations and actions of various characters in *The Pearl* and *Nothing but the Truth*, and over the Holocaust events portrayed in *The Devil's Arithmetic*. Having not taught this curriculum before, she relied on her students to give her feedback on what they were discovering. This feedback helped her to adjust her plans to fit the learning that was happening in the moment. Generally speaking, her students signaled to her that they were keeping the "big C" question alive in the natural course of their conversation. Said Liz:

> It is very rewarding for me to hear students refer back to the theme of human nature or Hobbes and Rousseau in our discussions. In fact, they expect it. One student asked me, "Ms. B, are we talking about that human nature thing again?" To which I heartily responded, "Yup!" That "human nature thing" allows them to make connections necessary for higher-level thinking and conversation. Granted, not all students share their views and participate in the class, but at least they are aware of what makes a good literary discussion.
>
> I also learned never to underestimate middle school students; they are extremely thoughtful and if you let them, they will teach you a lesson or two about human nature.
>
> —Elizabeth Benedetto, ELA 8, Green Fields Middle School

Benefits of Curricular Conversations

One of the challenges of trying something new, as Liz did with the curricular conversation, is that it becomes more difficult to measure success. In her reflection, Liz comments that her curriculum allowed students "to make connections necessary for higher-level thinking and conversation." We think she's right. Seeing curriculum as a discussion that extends across days, weeks, and even semesters brings coherence and sharpness to both the teacher's and students' thinking and learning about their subject matter. This raises a larger question: *How is the thinking produced through curricular conversations different from the thinking developed through a more conventional curriculum?*

As a way of answering this question, let's compare two curricula—a typical genre-based middle school curriculum and a curricular conversation (using Liz's human-nature curriculum as an example)—and explore what kinds of learning are likely to result. Specifically, we're wondering what students really learn about when "doing" English. What have they learned to know, do, and say in English class? In Applebee's (1996) words, this is important because "what we learn is a function of how we learn it" (p. 62). When evaluating the benefits of curriculum, it's important to look at not only the content (or what is covered), but also the process (or the ways students are asked to think about and use the content).

Team Effort

The role of collaboration has been proven to be essential in solving the problems and developing high-quality thematic units. In a study of middle school teachers, Athanases (2003) commented, "Middle school teachers shouldn't be alone in this work; they need teams and support" (p. 117). We hope that you will find a colleague to work with during your summer planning. A useful piece to help think about the power of teacher reflection is Carol Rodgers's (2002) article "Defining Reflection: Another Look at John Dewey and Reflective Thinking."

Dialogue is as critical for teachers as it is for students. Above, Eija collaborates with a teacher in her classroom. Below, Mary and Mark Jury (left, from the Reading Department at the University at Albany) talk with teachers during a Summer Institute.

Knowledge From a Typical Genre-Based Curriculum

Let's imagine Classroom X, in which students follow a standard genre-based curriculum, studying "the novel" followed by "the short story" and then, perhaps, "poetry." In such a class students are likely to participate in a question-and-answer format in which the teacher is looking for pre-specified answers—in Chapter 1 of this book we call this pattern of speaking *monologic*. Students are expected to recite information and facts about the texts and to remember this information on comprehensive end-of-unit exams and study guides that include multiple choice, fill in the blank, and short-answer questions. In this classroom, the unit is self-contained—when the unit on the novel is finished, students no longer are expected to return to the information they learned.

In this classroom, then, what are students learning about? What have students likely learned is important in "doing" English? It is important to

* identify the background of the author.
* identify traits of a character.
* identify key elements of the genre (theme, setting, iambic pentameter, etc.).
* define vocabulary words.
* define literary terms and locate examples.
* remember facts and details about the story.
* answer questions.
* use writing to prove knowledge of the story.

Let's compare the knowledge and learning in this genre-based curriculum with a curricular conversation, using our example above from Liz's curriculum on human nature. Here we see a classroom in which students engage in thematically related envisionment-building discussions that continue over time. In this type of curriculum, students are expected to take a stand on an issue, defend their opinion in front of their peers, and listen to their classmates' ideas. In this classroom, what have students likely learned is important in "doing" English? It is important to

* recognize conflicting approaches to an issue.
* define vocabulary to understand challenging texts.
* express thoughts clearly in speech and in writing.
* support ideas and opinion with evidence.
* apply themes from a work (or works) to a larger issue and back again; make connections to previous texts, personal experience, or real life.
* evaluate characters based on their motivation and actions.
* pay attention to authors' craft, including use of literary devices, by comparing texts and tech-

niques and considering their effect on the reader.

* anchor new information in previous discussions or examples.

* ask questions; learn from and with others.

Although students studying the human-nature curriculum may not have studied the literary elements such as theme and character in the same way as in the first example, they did learn to identify such elements because they needed to use them in an argument or question about the larger issue. It is possible, in a well-structured, scaffolded curricular conversation, for students to learn all of the basic information we would expect English students to know. They then learn to take this information and use, question, and explore it in comprehensive ways. For example, Liz's students learned skills in reading nonfiction (a newspaper article), through the lens of human nature. The challenge of finding and reading an article that promoted a particular point of view about human behavior helped them to use this basic literacy skill in making connections to the real world outside of the classroom.

We suspect that learning is more comprehensive within curricular conversations because students have a sort of "schema"—or organizing principle—developed already. In other words, students in Liz's class had already explored the idea of human nature and now read new information with that concept already firmly in place. The new information was added to the old, strengthening their overall understanding and making it more complex. In a sense, students were, as Applebee (1996) puts it, developing "knowledge-in-action"—learning to speak about topics or issues that are significant to their lives but also in ways that are appropriate to the discipline. By contrast, in the first example students were being taught in a different tradition, in which they were primarily asked to study and remember information for the purpose of completing study guides, textbook questions, or unit exams. Applebee describes the drawbacks of this sort of curriculum this way:

> [It is] a curriculum that construes knowledge as fixed and transmittable—as something 'out there' to be memorized by students. It is appropriate to a curriculum of the names and dates in literary history or of the rules of grammar and rhetoric, of phonics and vocabulary practice. Such a curriculum of knowledge-out-of-context may enable students to do well on multiple-choice items. It does not enable them to enter on their own into our vital academic traditions of knowing and doing. (p. 33)

The kinds of thinking described above are essential for students to develop in secondary schools if they are to do well in college. A recent survey of faculty of the California Community Colleges, the California State University, and the University of California identified the higher literacy skills expected of

successful college students. Specifically, faculty identified a number of "dispositions and habits of mind that enable students to enter the ongoing conversations appropriate to college thinking, reading, writing, and speaking" (Intersegmental Committee of the Academic Senates, 2002, p. 13). These include the following "broad intellectual practices"—practices highly consistent with discussion-based classrooms:

- Exhibit curiosity
- Experiment with new ideas
- See other points of view
- Challenge their own beliefs
- Engage in intellectual discussions
- Ask provocative questions
- Generate hypotheses
- Exhibit respect for other viewpoints
- Read with awareness of self and others (p. 13).

One exciting part of being English teachers is our ability to help our students understand and participate in our favorite discipline. When we do so actively and cohesively, we also help students to develop lifelong literacy skills—"habits of mind"—that will help them to succeed regardless of the field which they will eventually enter.

Curricular Conversations That Invite Multiple Voices

Liz's curriculum was effective for her students, who came from primarily suburban, white lower-middle-class and middle-class families. Many of the students' family members were serving or had served in the military, and so discussion of human nature in times of conflict was especially relevant to them. Had Liz's students been from low-income or immigrant families, including African-American and Latino students, they would have contributed different experiences and "funds of knowledge" to the conversation (Moll, Amanti, Neff & Gonzales, 1992). Carol Lee (2004) provides an example of such a curricular conversation in high school classrooms.

Lee (2004) describes how exploring the idea of symbolism across works helped students to learn more about how authors use metaphor to reveal new meaning and relationships beneath the surface. Lee developed this curriculum using *cultural modeling*, a simple and powerful technique. First, the teacher identifies important issues within the discipline that students need to know to become highly literate in the field. Lee identified symbolism as a key element that students need to be able to recognize, explore, and use if they are to succeed in English. Second, the teacher taps into the cul-

ture of the students in the classroom to enable them to discuss this issue in texts and contexts that are most familiar, extending over time into other, less familiar works.

Lee recognized the prevalence of symbolic talk, called *signifying*, within the tradition of African-American discourse. Signifying is "a form of ritual insult, a language game played across generations within the African-American community" (p. 19). However, Lee also realized the African-American students in her study were largely unaware of their facility with symbolic language to convey meaning in a complex way. Studying symbolism over time, therefore, had a triple effect: (1) It enabled them to actively participate in a significant conversation in the field; (2) it made it possible for them to use their own out of school knowledge, language, and experience as a scaffold to explore this academic concept in effective ways; and (3) it provided a way for the students to make use of their academic knowledge to understand their own cultural practices in a new light.

Lee (2004) began the conversation with a range of texts that students knew and liked: rap videos and lyrics and short film clips, all incorporating symbolism. For example, she engaged students in a discussion of metaphorical meanings in the lyrics to "The Mask" by the Fugees. Following this, students studied literature from authors closest to the African-American tradition, beginning with Toni Morrison's *Beloved*. Once students were comfortable analyzing these texts for their symbolic and metaphorical qualities, they looked at such elements in more canonical works, including those by Shakespeare, Dante, and Ellison.

Middle school teachers can also adopt a cultural modeling approach by engaging in a dialogue with their students and finding out what experience and knowledge they bring to the classroom. Students can then be invited to actively participate in a curricular conversation in which they have something to offer and something to learn. As Ladson-Billings (1994) puts it: "A hallmark of the culturally relevant notion of knowledge is that it is something that each student brings to the classroom. Students are not seen as empty vessels to be filled by all-knowing teachers. What they know is acknowledged, valued, and incorporated into the classroom." (p. 87)

Patricia Lambert Stock (1995) has also written about the idea of a curriculum that develops out of students' experiences. Stock worked with high school teachers to enact a dialogic curriculum, using Bakhtin's notions of dialogue as a springboard for a course that began with students' family stories and extended outward to other texts. Stock, like Applebee (1996), Lee (2004), and Ladson-Billings (1994, 1995), points out how critical it is to enact a curriculum that provides a central place for students to share and explore their knowledge. By engaging your students in regular discussions in your classroom, you are already giving them an important voice in your day-to-day curriculum. In Chapter 8 we offer some ideas for ways to take this pivotal foundation and extend it further over time.

Chapter Eight

Across the School Year

*Strategies for linking individual lessons and units
to create a coherent curriculum*

It's not like you get better just by practicing. You can get better by knowing the world better, figuring things out. And then having something to say.
— Yo-Yo Ma (Hirshey, 2005)

How does the idea of curricular conversations (Applebee, 2004) help you figure out what to teach and how to teach it so that it has coherence over time? In the previous chapter we described how to choose an overarching theme to help you bring together texts, compelling ideas, and discussion under one canopy. In this chapter, we'll look at how the curricular conversations that ensue "light up" the canopy. Comment by comment, text by text, ideas within this thematic sphere get illuminated, and the effect is like hundreds of little lights winking on. Students become energized and invested in the conversation because *their* curiosities, experiences, and ideas move it forward.

First, we'll look at ways to find texts that have the sufficient wattage to illuminate your curriculum. We'll also guide you to see how using a variety of texts, from a variety of genres, can engage [students] in ethical and philosophical reflection on the values and beliefs of their own cultures, of other cultures, and of other times and places. (National Council of Teachers of English, 1996, p. 30)

The Case for Embracing Many Genres

Why use a variety of genres to create a coherent curriculum? In a nutshell, every genre and subgenre stimulates different kinds of thinking and responses in a reader's quest to make meaning. Adding a work from a different genre brings another opportunity for reflection, as the texts under study respond to one another in different ways. For example, nonfiction requires students to read for detail in order to interpret factual events. To read nonfiction effectively, students also need to evaluate the basis for the facts—trustworthiness—and whether the author imparts a fair perspective on the subject matter. (This type of thinking pertains to the third and fourth stances.) Nonfiction invites students to make comparisons across texts. For example, one might compare a narrative nonfiction treatment of a Civil War battle with an encyclopedia account of it. Expository texts also lend themselves to discussions of rhetorical argument and bias. Works of poetry and fiction stir our emotions and invite readers to think about how language affects our feelings about a subject. Discussions often pursue matters of craft and questions about the author's intent. Art, photography, and video stimulate students to think about the power of visual images to convey ideas and emotion. More specifically, these forms of communication invite students to critique the media's use of the visual to communicate. As well, English language arts standards support

the use of texts of various genres. Take a look at a few eighth- and ninth-grade standards from California, among the most rigorous in the nation (Stotsky & Finn, 2005). Students are expected to:

A student deeply engrossed in writing.

- find similarities and differences between texts in the treatment, scope, or organization of ideas;
- synthesize the content from several sources or works by a single author dealing with a single issue;
- paraphrase the ideas and connect them to other sources and related topics to demonstrate comprehension;
- compare and contrast the presentation of a similar theme or topic across genres to explain how the selection of genre shapes the theme or topic.

STRATEGY: Develop two-day assignments that enable students to see connections between texts
TOOLS: Pair texts within or across genres; prompts; draw upon student writing for initial ideas and connections

Although the use of multiple texts can be very powerful, it can also be challenging at first for students and for the teacher to think in terms of two or three works rather than one. We suggest that you start small—think of one lesson that invites connections to be made and extend it over two consecutive days of discussion. Plan activities that build natural bridges across the two days. Write out your plans in the form of an EB guide, so you'll have a discussion map at your fingertips. Here is how you might organize these two days:

Day one: Have students read the first text in school using a reading strategy such as text marking, a T-chart, or sticky notes to record their comments as they read. They may discuss the text in pairs or in small groups if time permits, or they may have a quiet written conversation with a partner. Then, for homework, have students revisit their notes and write their initial impressions of the text in their journals.

Day two: The next day, have students read the second text and jot down their initial impressions, as well as any wonder questions, or language that "snags" them (see pages 128–130 in Chapter 5 for a review of all the active reading strategies mentioned here). Next, have them gather for a whole-class discussion, where they explore their questions for each text. If students are more comfortable discussing just one text before moving on to discussing the other, that's okay. You can sense when they are ready for you to interject a comment that prompts them to compare the texts.

The cross-text discussion often takes off at this point. If not, you can use the cross-text questions that you prepared in advance as part of the envisionment-building guide. In the ensuing discussion, both texts are used as a reference point. Details from the stories are used as evidence to build coherence and an understanding of a bigger idea.

Super Sleuthing: Finding Related Texts

Finding two texts to pair is a matter of building up a good bank of pieces—and luck. For example, a quick glance at the day's newspaper may yield a perfect piece. Textbooks that you have at your fingertips often contain shorter pieces well organized by theme; just be sure the piece offers enough depth and ambiguity to engage students and generate good discussion. Here are some additional suggestions for finding shorter texts that work together:

- **Pair two works by one author** (a poet, journalist, short story writer, essayist, children's book author, lyricist, or even an artist). Students may look across works to explore that author's style, purpose, underlying beliefs, thematic concerns, and so on.
- **Pair an article that evaluates or defines a genre with a short example of the genre.** (For example, team up an article by Mary Higgins Clark on suspense writing with a short mystery story). Students can apply the evaluative article to the example, learning more about the genre and also deciding whether the criteria are justifiable. This could extend into a larger unit in

---

QUICK CHECK
for Orchestrating
Discussions of Two
or More Texts

❑ Have you asked questions that prompt students to compare the two texts?

❑ Have you used the four stances to help you frame your questions?

- Have you asked for initial impressions? (first stance)

- Have you enticed students to share their developing understandings? (second stance)

- Have you invited students to step outside the text? (third stance)

- Have you challenged your students to take a critical stance? (fourth stance)

which they read a full-length mystery and analyze how it is written—followed, perhaps, by their own mystery stories. Sleuth out rich sources of writers-on-writing pieces—*Writer's Magazine* and *Poets and Writers* are two of many. And many contemporary writers have written compelling books on genre and craft, including Eudora Welty, Stephen King, Anne Lamott, and Georgia Heard.

A student reads a question from his journal to jump start the conversation.

* **Pair two texts that take different perspectives on a compelling topic.** (For example, students might wrestle with two takes on gender roles, education, child rearing, aging, or other contemporary issues. The divergent views might arise from different cultures, time periods, generations, and so forth.) A little later in this chapter we'll look at how gender roles are portrayed in "The Indian Child" (Niethammer), a short anthropological piece about a Native American tribe, and the poem "From Unveiled" (Saroyan) which describes a Middle Eastern family's traditions.

* **Pair two works that have the same theme.** A classic pairing that has worked well with middle school students is the lyrics of "Cat's Cradle" by Harry Chapin and the poem "Do Not Go Gentle Into That Good Night" by Dylan Thomas. Although the poem is more challenging than the song, the common theme of aging and how it affects the parent-child relationship provides a scaffold that can help students to make sense of and appreciate both pieces. As a variation, pair a short text with a piece of music or a painting that addresses the same theme.

* **Pair texts that give voice to often marginalized voices.** One of the most common ways to focus a study like this is by having students read fairy tales from around the world. This opens students up to perspectives outside of the western canon. Ladson-Billings (1994) offers a poignant example of a teacher who read *Mufaro's Beautiful Daughters*, an African Cinderella story by John Steptoe, as a way of convincing her class of African-American students that princesses

did not all have long blond hair (p. 92). (Another picture book useful in this regard is *African Princess: The Amazing Lives of Africa's Royal Women* by Joyce Hansen).

We've also seen readers respond powerfully to Jamaica Kincaid's (1991) essay, "On Seeing England for the First Time," in which Kincaid describes how her entire educational experience in Antigua was designed to pay homage to England, a place she came to hate. Such an essay could be paired with a text having to do with education, patriotism, self-image, immigration, or coming of age.

* **Pair texts on an important topic from different disciplinary perspectives.** Juxtaposing texts from different disciplines opens up new understandings about the topic and the discipline. For example, consider the topic of Christopher Columbus. Chapter 16 of a common middle school history textbook, *A History of Us* by Joy Hakim, presents Columbus in a particular way that foregrounds his accomplishments and relegates his harsh treatment of the Taino natives to one paragraph buried at the bottom of page 4. Another history text, Howard Zinn's *People's History of the United States*, begins with a positive description of the native people and an excerpt from Columbus's journal, in which he writes, "They would make fine servants." (p. 1) Finally, a children's picture book by Jane Yolen, *Encounter*, takes a wholly sympathetic view of the native people, as personified by the child who is the narrator. The opportunity to explore these diverse perspectives on Columbus helps students to think not only about the topic, but also about rhetorical strategies and uses of information.

Multiple Voices: Seeing History Through Short Stories, Memory, and the Evening News

Here is an example of how a teacher culled texts from different disciplines. About two months into the fall semester, Kevin decided to have his seventh graders participate in a whole-class discussion of Julia Alvarez's short story "Snow." He had read it and facilitated a conversation about it with his colleagues, so he was excited about using the text in his class. In this 1960s-era story, an immigrant girl learns in school what nuclear fallout looks like. When it starts snowing outside, the new girl is frightened. Having never before seen snow, she thinks a nuclear disaster has occurred.

Kevin decided to foreground the reading and discussion by involving artifacts from the cold war era in which the story is set. He displayed large posters of President Kennedy on the wall. Kevin then asked his students to interview their parents—and, if possible, grandparents, about what they remembered of the Cuban missile crisis. Before reading the story aloud, Kevin showed the class an excerpt of

a 1962 newsreel, which included the president talking about the crisis. He then led a brief discussion about the television footage, encouraging students to also share their relatives' memories of the event. He even drew a giant mushroom cloud on the chalkboard.

As students read the story, all this knowledge danced in their heads. History had been given to them through the authentic voices of their relatives, news reporters, Kennedy, and the voice of their teacher. It had been made personal, immediate, and relevant, and so when students discussed the story, it was perhaps easier for them to relate it to their own fears about war and other precarious situations or misunderstandings in their lives. For example, a student from Puerto Rico who had joined the class a short time earlier shared how he had never seen snow coming to this northeastern town. It was the first time he had spoken in a discussion.

Zoom Lens on a Poet: Discovering Craft, Discovering Voice

Janet introduced her seventh graders to a study of several poems by the same author, William Carlos Williams: "The Red Wheelbarrow," "The Locust Tree," "This is Just to Say," and "Between the Walls." The four poems were all short and filled just two pages. Janet instructed her students to read the poems with a pen in hand. As is customary in her room, Janet had prepared a T-chart to help students with the reading, thinking, and commenting on the poems. On the left-hand side students were asked to write a reaction across the texts: "What are your initial impressions? What questions do you have?" Her students, experienced with this kind of discussion and with writing on T-charts, were able to come up with a variety of initial reactions and questions:

> MIKE: Short but sweet. Doesn't seem like they're connected. They should flow but they do not. Why?
>
> KURT: I am wondering why his poems are so short in length. What are these stories supposed to mean? He used a color in three out of four poems. It seems that these poems have random things. What does the word cinder mean?
>
> JESSICA: Is William Carlos Williams making lists?

Janet used the students' questions to jump-start a discussion about the poems individually and then collectively. Afterward, students wrote on the right side of the T-chart, detailing what they had learned. This enabled Janet to find out how their understanding was enriched as a result of the conversation. Below are the comments of a student, Dave, before and after the discussion:

After the initial reading: I am thinking that this poet is using metaphors or past life experiences. The poem that really threw me off was the Locust Tree in flower. I can't tell what he's doing. Although I'm starting to think he is using a metaphor.

After the first discussion: I have come to the conclusion that his poems are based on past life experiences. Also I think he's using metaphors to prove something about those experiences. Why did he choose these topics to write about?

After the second discussion: I take back everything I said before. I now believe that he is using metaphors to give us advice. This idea is only a start. I believe his writing is very brilliant. I also believe his writing is left without an ending for a reason.

Dave's comments suggest that over time and through repeated discussions, he and his classmates were coming to understand Williams's craft, what kind of poet he is, what his style is like, and what kinds of subjects he writes about, among other things.

The Poet and the Anthropologist: Under the Canopy of Childhood

At another point in the year, Janet introduced her students to a text pairing that crossed genres and focused on a theme that adolescents have personal knowledge of: childhood. First, students read Carolyn Niethammer's "The Indian Child," a short anthropologist's account of childhood among a Native American tribe. Then, students read and discussed Gladys Alam Saroyan's "from Unveiled" (2002), a poem from the point of view of a Middle Eastern girl describing her family's traditions. The class took down information from the poem, connecting it to what they knew before and asking questions. When students discussed the first text, they were struck by the differences between their lives and the lives of children raised in the Native American community.

The next day they moved to discuss the poem in light of their previous discussion of the article. The seventh graders had noticed that in the poem, the mother treated the brother and the sister differently. As the sister explained, "The trick was to pick the kibbe with the hidden coin. I never won. / My brother won every time." (p. 3) Students discovered that this differed from the treatment of females in the nonfiction piece, in which Native American children referred to all of their female relatives as mother. In that community, children had many who cared about them. This fact made the students think hard about and even disagree on the desirability of a custom like this. A lively discussion ensued as students pondered the consequences and used examples from their own lives as a way to argue the pros and cons of the situation.

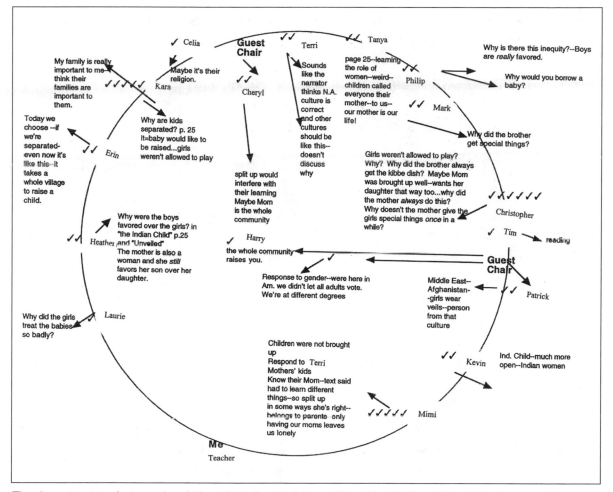

This discussion map shows students' ideas about the parallel texts "from Unveiled" and "The Indian Child."

If students had read only the poem, their thinking would have stayed confined, closer to the ground. But by juxtaposing the poem with the nonfiction, Janet invited her seventh graders to filter information through three distinct lenses: the two genres, and their own experiences.

Interestingly, the strong voice of the girl in the poem added another dimension—gender. Both boys and girls remarked on the mistreatment of the female child in the poem during the discussion. Rich conversation does this; surprise layers get added. After the two-day discussion, some students expressed strong opinions on how they would bring up their own children in the future. A boy wrote in his journal that if he had a son and a daughter, he would absolutely treat his children equally.

Students were participating actively, shaping the conversation with ideas evoked by the texts and in response to their peers' comments.

> **STRATEGY: Scaffold skills to build on the kinds of knowledge you have previously taught**
> **TOOLS: Goal setting and curriculum planning**

During an after school meeting with a seventh grade teacher, Lani, we noticed that something was bothering her. She was restless, shuffling papers. She took out some notepaper and picked up her pencil. Gathering the courage to ask what was clearly a difficult question, she finally said, "I need you to tell me what scaffolding is . . . I keep hearing the word, but I'm not clear on what it is or how I'm supposed to do it." At that moment we realized how difficult these terms are, and how too often teacher-educators take it for granted that everyone knows what they mean.

What did we say? Together with Lani, we worked out what exactly we meant by scaffolding: extra support, a way of structuring your curriculum day by day and week by week so that students get extra help early on to help them accomplish what they are not ready for on their own. Students can be scaffolding for each other. (That is why discussion in large and small groups is so helpful, as are strategies such as paired or buddy reading or reciprocal teaching.) The teacher can provide scaffolding by adding in extra steps such as whole class modeling for writing assignments, think alouds to develop reading comprehension, or writing process techniques to help improve writing between drafts. The most important distinction we could make for Lani was that scaffolding helps students learn the skills they need to know on the way to learning about the important stuff—so that they get the payoff—the right and ability to participate in discussions about meaningful topics that matter.

The concept of a curricular canopy, or umbrella, will be helpful to you in thinking ahead about what your students might need. By thinking through various texts and planning a larger discussion that helps to connect them, you anticipate where students will need assistance. Then you insert the supports—scaffolding—to assist them with the process.

The recently retired CELA Outreach director, a former middle school teacher, had these thoughts about the challenges of using scaffolding: "It isn't enough to support students; that support must be carefully structured and gradually removed as the students begin to internalize the structure. Building scaffolding for my classes meant I needed to think about the problems the students might have . . . to develop strategies that would help them overcome these difficulties, and to design activities that would make these strategies clear as the year unfolded. " —Elizabeth Close, personal communication

QUICK CHECK
for Scaffolding Students

❏ Have you provided extra guidance with new or difficult tasks or texts?

❏ Have you built on knowledge/skills students have learned previously in this class?

❏ Have you asked students to support their statements with evidence when writing and speaking?

❏ Have you helped students to reflect on their learning process?

Below is a partial list of scaffolding activities for reference.

Scaffolding Activity	Purpose
Student questions	Clarify and expand envisionments.
Journal writing	Focus thinking; think about changes over time.
Readers' marks	Pay attention to text features; identify what students know and do not know and what "snags" their interest.
Stand and Deliver	Hear different perspectives on an issue and present evidence for your own position.
Debate	Rehearse arguments on two or more sides of a question.
Sticky notes	Pay attention to style/structure/language.
	Identify problems, gaps, and areas of understanding.
Think Aloud strategies	Model/internalize the mental processes of good readers.
Open Mind	Develop understanding of character motivation and development.
Buddy reading	Build fluency.
Reciprocal teaching	Develop comprehension skills (prediction, summary, etc.).
T-Charts	Collect and focus student thinking.

Close adds an important consideration when using scaffolding—it is not the end result, anymore than construction scaffolding is left up once a building is finished. It's a helpful reminder to pull the supports away over time so that students can experience more independent success.

> **STRATEGY: Plan curriculum that is flexible yet complex enough to sustain conversation over time**
> **TOOLS: Regular reading, discussion, and writing of students' ideas; select texts/units based on a larger idea; consider an introductory unit to begin the conversation**

Whether you're planning the next day's lesson or setting curriculum goals for an entire semester, always keep the "big C" in mind. Ask yourself such questions as, What is the larger conversation about? What have we been discussing so far? What is logical to do next? At this point, it might make sense to do the following planning:

1. Make a list of the major texts you're already using which have worked to engage your students. Be sure that the texts you want to use are accurate and rich enough in language, plot, character, and/or information to support extended discussion.
2. Identify options for full-length texts as well as shorter readings.
3. With a colleague, start discussing the texts you've used. What are these texts about? Make a list.
4. Try out some big ideas that snag you and that work with the texts you already use. Jot the ideas down; try casting them as an authentic question—a real topic of inquiry. Test out the idea as you apply it to different books. (It may be that the idea doesn't have legs.) Keep refining the idea. How does it change and grow and become more complex in order to apply to more works? Will this idea resonate with students' cultural backgrounds and experiences? Will they be able to conceive of this issue as significant in some way?

After reading Text 1:	*After reading Text 2:*	*After reading Text 3:*
What important facts or ideas were in the text? What have I learned?	What facts or ideas are challenged? What new information do I have?	What new information and perspective do I have now? What questions do I have?

A T-chart scaffolds for students as they consider larger ideas across texts.

Building Literacy Through Classroom Discussion

5. Perhaps introduce the "big idea" you want to work with in an introductory unit lasting a week or two. This gives you time to explore the concept on its own and really invest some energy into it before you dive into the texts. For example, a ninth-grade English teacher (Applebee, Adler, & Flihan, 2005) developed a yearlong curricular conversation around the larger theme of tolerance. Because tolerance is an abstract concept, she spent several weeks in September helping students to think it through, using popular films, student experience, simulations, and various texts to help create a shared understanding. This worked so well that students were still talking about tolerance in June.

6. One way to introduce the unit is to use the Reflection on a Word activity (Himley & Carini, 2000; see Chapter 2 for specifics) to help students "till the soil" around the topic.

Rescuing Reluctant Readers: One Teacher's Story

As we have tried to indicate, building a larger curricular conversation takes time. With only a year or two actively working in the project, Partnership teachers did not often have the occasion to completely rework their curricula. Rather, they began in small ways (similar to strategy no.1), and slowly built connections over time. In this section we offer an example of a teacher working in an urban school who achieved remarkable results with his students by daring to give them authentic texts on a

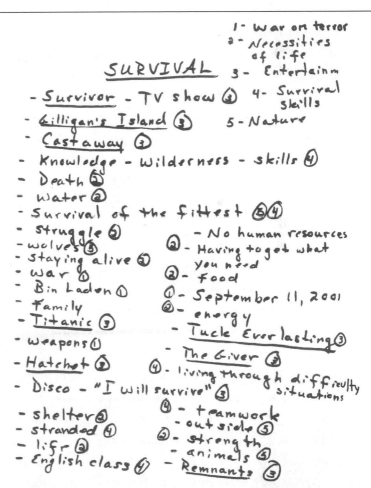

Eighth graders generated this Reflection on a Word at the beginning of a unit on "Survival."

topic that challenged them to rethink their own self-concept.

Bill, a young enthusiastic teacher, was assigned to teach students, some of whom had repeated eighth-grade English more than once. The school tried to solve the problem of low achievement by grouping students who had failed before into one team. Bill was determined to support his students, to invite their voices and help them to learn. However, this was a challenge when students did not believe in their own capacity to learn. They talked about themselves as "dummies" and had internalized the stigma that followed the designation to this team.

Many of these students were aliterate adolescents (Alvermann, 2004), those who might know how to read but who chose not to. However, from the beginning of September, Bill treated his students as readers. He told them they were readers and asked them to keep track of everything they read outside of school. He asked students to make a list of anything and everything they read at home during one week. Students brought sports magazines to school as well as books. They wrote about their favorite reading materials, and Bill posted these reading logs on the bulletin board outside the classroom for everybody to see.

In the classroom, students continued talking about reading. They had a discussion about what makes reading difficult and what makes it easy. Then they went on to read an article in the *New York Times* (Gall, 2002) about Afghan women who were illiterate but had newly acquired the right to learn to read. The article had compelling pictures that interested the students. After a little hesitation, they read with great curiosity (and their teacher's help), about adult women across the world who wanted to learn to read. Throughout the ongoing discussion, students' own experiences as readers outside the school were acknowledged and their voices legitimized. They

QUICK CHECK
for Planning Curriculum

✓ What materials might help develop and sustain this conversation in a meaningful way? Are the materials

- ❏ clear and accurate (nonfiction) or rich (fiction)?

- ❏ related and connected to the broad theme?

- ❏ Related texts of different genres?

- ❏ Texts that offer contrasting perspectives?

- ❏ Pieces told by authors of different cultures?

- ❏ Nonfiction articles or documentaries?

- ❏ Multimedia (Internet, film, music)?

✓ What issues and subtopics are appropriate for conversations to explore within this theme? Are these issues and topics

- ❏ culturally significant?

- ❏ open to active interactions among teachers and students, among students, among teachers and texts?

expressed enjoyment at learning about and connecting to other peoples' struggles to read. These teenage girls and boys, some of whom were parents themselves, aspired to more in their lives just as the Afghan women did. The power of reading was uncovered by the overarching conversation. A student mentioned, for instance, that he has the power to move beyond his neighborhood, that he does not have to live there forever. For Bill's comments on his students' reactions to the article, see below.

In His Own Words

Bill wrote an article about his reading unit in CELA's Fall 2002 issue of *New(s) From the Field*. In Bill's words:

"As with many teachers, I found myself facing another group of students this year who found little appeal in reading. Realizing that this challenge would be an obstacle for my curriculum, I decided to share this challenge with my students in the hope that we could explore their issues about reading. What I had intended to be a short unit has branched into a major theme of the year. As we read about Fredrick Douglass and Harriet Tubman in literature circles, we began to discuss the importance of reading as well as education then and now. While our conversations were rich in thinking as students began finding their connections to the text and enhanced their understanding of the texts, they were left feeling the insignificance of the topic in today's world.

"Eija Rougle, my Cela facilitator, who had been observing our discussions, offered me an article that discussed women in Afghanistan learning to read after being freed from the Taliban's restrictions. I was apprehensive at first, considering the reading level of my students and the reading level of the *New York Times* article, but all reservations were put to rest when I experienced the enthusiasm of the students over the topic. They helped each other through the reading and seemed interested in figuring out parts of the reading on their own. Initial discussions focused on misconceptions and negative feelings students had towards the people of Afghanistan. Further discussions led students to talk about issues in reading and education and they applied these to their own communities. They talked about literacy volunteers, their own parents/family members not being able to read, charter schools, libraries . . . students had no trouble when writing (paired writing on paper, journals, essays . . .) entered into the assignments. Many seemed appreciative for the opportunity to work through their ideas on paper. Students connecting themes/topics that were first introduced in September clearly showed me students' ability to absorb, understand, and think beyond the text. And the response I received when I recently assigned students their first book report showed me much more."

— Bill Hoffman, ELA 8, Milltown Middle School

More themes with staying power. As you might imagine, there are many "umbrellas" such as literacy as a route to personal liberty that can help students connect with significant disciplinary and/or global issues. Other themes that have potential to develop over time include the following:

- the rights of women/voices not heard
- civil rights/racism/discrimination
- encountering and/or being the other (adapted from the College Board's Pacesetter Project)
- how we shape and are shaped by our environment
- crossing borders/coming to a new land
- personal change and growth over time
- justice and liberation
- resistance to oppression (including references to the Holocaust/genocide)
- results and effects of conflict/war on individuals and communities
- what makes different genres work? Comparing, analyzing, and trying our hand at them. (Mystery or suspense, humor, science fiction/fantasy, etc.)

> **STRATEGY: Use assessment to stimulate knowledge-in-action rather than knowledge-out-of context.**

TOOLS: Writing assignments that build on student experience and understanding and also invite critical connections across texts

As teachers worked to change the way students talked about texts over time, many found that assessments that used to work seem oddly out of place in this new configuration. Perhaps this is because the typical school assessments ask for students to provide information in discrete chunks—that is, to provide answers that are isolated within a single text, unrelated to students' lives outside the classroom or even to other texts read in class. As Applebee (1996) notes, "Much of the testing in American schools and colleges emphasizes knowledge-out-of context instead of rewarding students' performances within culturally significant domains of knowing and doing" (p. 116).

In building a larger conversation, then, think of assessment as an opportunity for students to show you what they have learned over time in your classroom. How have they put the pieces together? What connections have they made within and across texts? A central way to enable students to express this knowledge is through extended writing activities. As we mentioned in Chapter 7, writing is helpful throughout the conversation—before, during, and after key texts, depending upon

your purposes and the kinds of thinking that you would like students to gain or demonstrate. Varied genres of writing help students develop different rhetorical skills and think about alternate aspects of the text/larger conversation. Some of these genres are represented below. What is important, regardless of the specific assignment, is that students "get going composing" long enough to enable them to develop fluency with both language and ideas.

Writing Genre	Purpose
Written conversation	Create a first exploration of ideas.
Written response to text/art/film	Make personal and informational connections.
Comparison/contrast essay	Look for features across texts.
Expository essay	Analyze and prove a larger point with evidence.
Book review	Take a critical look at how a text is written.
Persuasive essay, letter, or speech	Select and present convincing evidence/arguments.
Poetry	Pay attention to language and imagery.
Personal narrative	Reflect on personal experience in larger ways.
Fiction	Learn about story content, structure, and language.
Biographical sketch	Use vivid, specific language to describe.
Descriptive writing	Pay attention to detail and sensory language.
Summary	Understand and retell the main points in logical order.

As we worked with teachers on building a larger conversation about ideas and text relationships, we began to see a secondary conversation developing over time, relating to the skills students needed to effectively participate in these discussions. Their teachers were working to provide students with the necessary scaffolding to succeed on various tasks, including longer writing assignments. When planning, these teachers frequently asked themselves, What will students need extra help with during this task? and What have they already learned that they should be applying to this task on their own? These issues represent one of the more complex tasks a teacher must attend to, for it requires a constant state of awareness of where students have been and where they are headed. Fortunately, the students themselves often engage in dialogue to express where they are having frustration and/or success. The teacher can tap this with a "ticket out" activity, having students write one sentence about what they have learned in class that day. On the reverse side, students write a question about what they learned or about the topic. They hand them in to you on their way out the door.

A standard form of scaffolding involves providing students with assistance in generating and shaping their ideas for writing. As they develop facility with this, however, it's important to remove the scaffolding and let them try their own ways of generating a draft, perhaps followed by a brief discussion in which students can articulate a description of techniques that they have found useful. It's also likely that students will benefit from one another's feedback—and yours—in making revisions to the writing they have begun. Mini-lessons about grammatical or formatting elements can be integrated into instruction as they come up in students' work, with reminders to students of the skills they have already learned so that they can keep using these techniques to improve their written product. There are many excellent references for teachers to use in helping students through the writing process, including Kirby, Kirby, and Liner's (2004) excellent book *Inside Out*, now in its third edition, as well as works by Ralph Fletcher, Donald Graves, Nancie Atwell, and others.

QUICK CHECK
for Assigning Writing

What extended writing experiences will help my students to find out about and engage with this theme? Do these assignments

- ❏ enable and support student participation?

- ❏ allow room for students to develop their own understandings?

- ❏ provide students with extended practice in exploring a larger idea or concept through writing?

- ❏ logically follow from and build upon classroom reading, discussing, listening, and informal writing experiences?

- ❏ include scaffolding necessary to help students succeed?

Writing With Built-In Scaffolding: One Teacher's Story

Courtney, a seventh-grade teacher, wanted her students to be able to use the knowledge they had developed throughout the whole year. Courtney and the other seventh-grade teachers at her school had decided that the end-of-year assessment would be an extended essay on the topic of character change and growth over time. Students could compare several different characters they had read about with one another as well as with their observations of their own growth and change over the year. However, Courtney was worried that students would forget central characteristics of the characters that they read about throughout the year. She developed some scaffolding to help: a chart in which students recorded information about the key character(s) at the end of each major text. The chart looked something like this:

Title	Name and description of key character	How did this character grow or change over time? (Give a couple of examples.)	What connections (similarities and differences) do you see to other characters you've read about this year?	What connections can you make to your own life experience?

Students kept the chart in their portfolios and took them out to fill in regularly over the course of the year. This had the additional benefit of generating periodic conversations in which they revisited previous works to look at character development.

Prompts for end-of-unit or end-of-year reflection. Finally, we'd like share some prompts that you can adapt for almost any extended writing assignment that invites students to revisit what they've learned.

- What have you learned this year about _____ , across our texts?
- How have you changed or revised your original beliefs?
- What insights does this give you about our society/human nature?
- Across the texts we've read, whose voices have you heard most strongly? What did they say?
- Whose voices did you hear less of? What would they say if they were included?

When in Doubt, Look at the Core Four

Though there are many places to start in developing a more cohesive curriculum, we've suggested four:

1. Begin with discussions of short, related texts.
2. Provide scaffolding to build on previous skills and prepare students for an upcoming task.
3. Structure curriculum to provoke a larger conversation.
4. Use assessment, particularly extended writing assignments, as a way to help students actively rethink course material.

As more coherence develops, so will the benefits—perhaps the first time a student spontaneously refers back to a previous concept or text. The teacher's planning will be living on in the current conversation. But we know that despite these successes, there will be bumps in the road. In the next chapter, we reflect on the challenges that are likely to come up.

Chapter Nine

Extending Discussion

Reflection and troubleshooting

In this chapter, as in chapters 3 and 6, we are using a question-and-answer format to respond to real questions that middle school teachers raised as they grappled with the concept of curricular conversations in their own classroom.

> **Q: I have a great thematic curricular conversation happening, but I was disappointed on our unit test that students didn't make the connections. I think it's pretty obvious. Why are they missing it?**

A: What you are doing is probably pretty unusual for your students—that is, in most of the classes they've had up to this point, connections are not terribly important. What has been important is remembering the information in time for the unit test, getting it down properly, and then gearing up to remember the new information for the next unit or marking period. So unless you regularly make the connections obvious, they may remain in your head rather than in students' heads.

How can you make connections overt to students? Their first exposure to the curriculum comes when they enter your classroom. If you have your own room with bulletin board space, use it to spell out the topic of the larger conversation. If your larger theme, for instance, is "Coming to a New Land" (stories and nonfiction about immigration and conquest), put the title up on the bulletin board. See what else you can put around it to help students think about what "a new land" might be—a map of the United States with key arrows, for instance, accompanied by pictures of some of the authors of the immigrant stories that you're going to read. Students' work can be posted on the same boards.

Don't underestimate the power of the bulletin board and a pack or two of sticky notes! A number of Partnership teachers used the sticky-note strategy quite successfully to sustain students' awareness of the larger conversation. One teacher had students generate ideas about the topic, using sticky notes and colored markers and then invited students to stick their thoughts up as part of the ongoing discussion. Let's imagine that during the second semester, you decide to keep the same conversation described above, but

Sticky notes of students' ideas can sustain students' awareness of the larger conversation.

extend it some—now "a new land" is more of a metaphor . . . for crossing borders of race, class, age, and/or gender. You give students large sticky notes or index cards and ask them to brainstorm all of the ways in which people cross borders or enter uncharted territory. They begin by putting ideas from the first semester, like "travel to America" or "explorers find a new country" but then may move on (perhaps with some help), to topics like "first woman in medical school," "the bus boycott," and "getting your first apartment on your own." You've used the common classroom space to begin charting your conversation; the words and ideas can remain up as a reminder—or can grow and change over time.

Other ways to introduce students overtly to the larger conversation:

- ☀ **Tell students about the unit you've been planning.** Explain to them what they'll be reading and doing this semester and why you've put the texts in this particular order. It's rare that students know what they'll be doing or reading next.

- ☀ **Regularly incorporate questions about the big conversation into the small ones.** It's hard to remember to bring up the "big C" when the detailed, individual conversations are so focused and interested. Envisionment-building questions have the advantage of tapping the fourth stance (see Chapter 4), which ask students to think critically across texts.

- ☀ **During class discussions, when students have not addressed the larger idea, you can ask about it with a straightforward question.** For example, Margaret, a seventh grade teacher, opened her class one day by asking students to respond to this statement in their journals: "People never change." After students had written for five to seven minutes, she asked them to pull their chairs into a circle for a discussion of the short story "Shells" by Cynthia Rylant. Surprisingly, although students had just written on the topic of change, they did not once connect that topic to the story. They seemed to view it as a disconnected assignment and left it behind once they had moved into the story world.

    Toward the end of the conversation, Margaret casually asked students, "So, what did you think about that sentence on the board?" They had a lot to say about the sentence, mostly generalities about people they knew and how some are spurred to change by sudden events (such as September 11), or how some do not change regardless of what happens to them. Margaret responded, "One thing I need to say before we go. One thing we'll keep seeing is how kids change as they grow up—you'll change, too, by June. We'll be learning about growing up and how people change as they grow older. So keep an eye out for this in everything we read." Although students were not yet making the connections she hoped for, she was providing support by making the larger theme clearer (in talk and in writing). Over time, this helped them to

pull themes out of the texts as they were reading them, to make the connections on their own.

 ☀ **Clarify the connections through writing assignments.** These can be as informal as a journal jot or homework assignment with the prompt: "Write about the connections you see between this article and the last story we read." They can also be more formal: "Think about some of the borders you will have to cross in the next few years. In what ways do you think your experiences will be similar to or different from the characters we have read about in this unit? What can you learn from the characters' experiences that will help you to deal with the challenges you will face?" When regular writing assignments ask students to make connections, they begin to snowball in discussions, too—students begin to see the relationships where previously they only saw a class assignment. They may even find that it's fun to use information they already have in new ways.

> **Q: How can I keep the information we've studied and the conversations we've had fresh and alive in my students' minds so they won't forget them and will be able to make connections as we move on?**

A: Here are several ways to help your students keep their ongoing conversations in mind over time:

 ☀ Include overt questions about connections to previous texts or experiences in your envision-ment-building guide (especially in the critical-stance portion). Begin lessons by asking students to recall and connect information (orally or in a quick write).

 ☀ During the lesson, you can jot down notes about important points that you want to refer to again. At the end of the lesson, you can review these notes with students, taking stock of the ideas thus far and foregrounding their connections to the larger theme.

 ☀ Use the classroom environment to publish student ideas and work that support the larger theme (like road signs on the highway). One teacher we know printed students' insights that emerged from class discussion on large pieces of paper and hung them on a clothesline above the classroom. These were "snags," or specific, striking thoughts, that gave people a fresh way to think about the topic.

 ☀ Students can return to earlier journal entries and reread them, marking their thoughts in a dif-ferent-colored pen or using sticky notes to identify connections they had previously made and to update their thinking. This would work well in conjunction with a portfolio or other reflective activity in which students are asked to write about what they have learned over time.

> **Q: What do I do if my students lack background knowledge for a particular work? Should I avoid using texts that describe events about which they have no knowledge?**

A: You know your students. Although they may not know explicitly about a particular time period in history or a literary reference, you can trust your relationship with them and know that you will be able to help them connect to practically any topic. Moreover, a text about unfamiliar events can be an opportunity to build important connections and understandings. Though it may be frustrating at first not to lecture on this new information, it is important as always to invite students' questions and wonderings first. Even misunderstandings, or hunches about the work can be fruitful stepping stones.

Arthur Applebee (1996) writes:

> The quick reaction is that we must turn explicit attention to this missing background if we want the texts to be read and appreciated. The immediate danger with such an approach, however, is that this "background knowledge" can easily become a new knowledge-out-of-context, or more or less disembodied set of information to be taught and learned. We gain knowledge-in-action in any arena, through gradual immersion in new conversations rather than standing alongside and being told about them. (p. 123)

Here's an example. In an adolescent literature course at the university, Mary's students were assigned to read *The Watsons Go to Birmingham—1963*, by Christopher Paul Curtis. It turned out that most of the students were unaware of an important historical element of the novel, the bombing of the Birmingham church that killed four young girls. With this novel, it can be problematic if readers do not realize that Curtis is referencing a real event. Students were helped enormously by the curricular conversation, which was supported by additional texts (a period newspaper article, Web sites promoting the film *Four Little Girls* by Spike Lee, photographs from the time period, and Norman Rockwell paintings). These texts broadened the dialogue and provided students with important perspectives on the event. For instance, the attitudes, underlying tone, and word choice of the newspaper account were striking to many students, who commented that it seemed itself to reflect the racial tensions of the day. Older students who had lived through this time period, those who had lived in the South, and those whose parents remembered the incident were able to dialogue with those who lacked understanding of the event, offering critical personal and emotional details.

Q: I teach five classes, and I find that discussions of the same book or theme go differently with each group. So how can I plan my next teaching moves for a discussion?

A: It *is* a lot to keep track of. Preparation is so helpful here—by thinking about the text(s), developing authentic discussion questions, and deciding on larger questions or issues that resonate for you. Then step back, use wait time, and let students bid for the floor. Your ears will tune to students who pose provocative, interesting comments. With your help, other students will build off or on these comments and you will start hearing topical threads that you can amplify with your questions. Here are some additional tools that may be helpful:

- Try "mapping" the conversation in each class period. Mark on the sheet (with shorthand) the gist of what was said and by whom. You might draw a circle and write students' names on the seating chart quickly while the students are writing their initial impressions/questions. See Chapter 8 for an example. Some teachers prefer simply to take notes in a spiral binder, jotting the speaker's name on the left and bulleting key points on the right. If you do this, try using a different binder for each class period. When the bell rings, you can easily pick up the corresponding binder and begin class by reviewing the last set of notes with students, reminding them of the points that were made in the previous discussion.

- You may make a chart or ask a student to be a scribe during the last five or ten minutes of the period, as you take stock of the conversational threads/big ideas discussed. These ideas are then posted on a bulletin board for other classes to view. You'll most likely get five somewhat different idea charts of conversations. These charts are also wonderful displays of the multiplicity of ideas and perspectives discussed in different classes. They will add richness to the growing conversation. Some similarities will run across classes, though, and these may turn out to be potential seeds for common writing assignments in the future.

- Ask students to map the conversation. They can quickly write their peers' names and put a check mark on a discussant. More important, they will keep track of ideas in the comments and then can go back to build on or off these ideas. Toward the end of the period, save some time for the student reporters to talk about what they heard during the discussion. This is a good tool to develop critical listening and note-taking skills in an authentic context.

Q: How do I connect class discussion to writing, especially since I can't plan in advance what students will say?

A: This is a dilemma that several Partnership teachers grappled with. What they found was that with practice, they could predict some basic points that students were likely to make about a piece, and they could pull questions as needed from the envisionment-building guide to help students get at some of the essential issues in the text. Actually, they found that developing the discussion questions was a helpful tool in thinking through the writing assignment to follow.

As a last resort, let's imagine that you have prepared prompts for an essay or other writing topic, and you discover about halfway through the conversation that students are not talking at all about a central topic that you've assigned for the writing. It's perfectly fine to be up front with them about this; they're counting on your expertise to help them focus their discussion in just this way. All you need to do is say, "Okay. Let's take stock of where we are. I hear Steve saying x and Molly saying y. What about z (the central topic)?" Students can wrestle with z for a while, an activity that will prepare them well for the writing assignment to come.

Q: How can I have a whole-class conversation when students have read different books in their book groups? Isn't that confusing? Why not just keep the discussion in small groups?

A: First, it is important to select book groups on a common topic so that there is a strong connection among texts. Some common topics may be historically based and serve as interdisciplinary texts, such as the Revolutionary War or colonial period, the Native American experience in early America, or the Civil War. Other topics might focus on common issues such as survival, civil rights, the women's movement or women's rights, or the immigrant experience. Second, make it clear to students that you are assigning them different books on a similar subject, and that one of your reasons for doing so is to have them investigate different experiences during this time period or varied ideas about this topic.

While groups are reading their books, you can have them hold small-group envisionment-building discussions (see Chapter 3 for ideas on this), or you can use another technique such as literature circles (Daniels, 2002). Your purpose would be to have students engage in student-to-student discussion about the book, beginning with their questions.

However, student ideas can also be shared across groups in a whole-class setting. Here's one way to do it: Ask the groups to each write a summary of their common book for others to read. (Scaffold summary writing here if students need it.) Then, provide students with copies of the text summaries so that everyone has a general sense of the story lines. Alternatively, have someone from each group do a short book talk. (We have found that this step is not really integral to the overall success of the cross-text discussions, but it seems to relieve some students' anxiety at having to talk about texts without any prior knowledge of their plot lines.) At this point students have a shared knowledge base and should be able to take off in a more in-depth discussion.

As a next step, try a jigsaw. Have the expert groups discuss their common text and come up with a larger theme or two that they feel runs throughout their book. Then have the experts move into mixed groups where they share their larger themes with one another across texts and see what their ideas have in common. The mixed groups then share these themes with the whole class while the teacher takes notes. This provides important scaffolding as you move into the whole-class conversation. Once students have finished reporting across texts, you'll have a big list of thematic connections on the board. This list can begin the whole-class discussion: Which themes do students feel hold up for the book they read? Can they narrow the list to a few larger themes that they feel are important? And then, the really hard questions: What do these themes tell you about this time period/topic/issue? What are these various authors telling us? How does this message connect with our lives today in some way? Or with other texts, with popular media, with the news?

This process, of course, requires more work and time than a straightforward single-text discussion or activity. Why go to all the trouble? Because of the potential benefits—and they are many: increased peer motivation for reading, accessible texts that unobtrusively differentiate instruction, increased time for individual practice in discussion, and a less stressful small-group environment that may encourage shy or reticent students to speak up. The issue of accessible texts is probably the largest benefit. This strategy allows struggling readers to read at their own level but also to participate and see connections on an equal footing with their peers. For example, when the jigsaw is underway and students are in mixed groups discussing their books, the struggling reader has the chance to be an expert too, teaching the others about themes in his or her book. His or her voice is needed to see connections across the texts. In the process of reading an accessible text and understanding it, the struggling reader gains fluency and develops literacy skills, including envisionments of the story world.

Q: What happens when topical connections become superficial or trivialized?

A: Many students are, unfortunately, accustomed to making superficial responses in school. This happens when there is a focus on a recitation of facts (Nystrand, 1997). When students first generate their own questions, some will bring this tradition with them. For instance, the first questions a group of students asked about an article on Eleanor Roosevelt were "What was her father's name?" and "What was her mother's name?" These were easily answered and dispensed with. Then somebody asked, "Where did she get her strength?" With that question, conversation took off. When the focus is on meaning making, or building envisionments of the story world, the social environment in which discussion takes place creates a synergy that pushes students to reveal deeper questions. With time, students learn to look for big ideas and depth in conversation. Here are some things you can do in the meantime to hasten the process:

- Your role as a facilitator of discussion is critical; you are, as a Partnership teacher put it, in the driver's seat. If students ask superficial questions, make a point of clarifying and reminding them of what kinds of questions are big thoughtful questions and what kinds of questions can be answered quickly. Sometimes the quick questions need to be asked as clarification—if so, they can be answered and then left behind in favor of richer inquiries.

- Model thoughtful questions; if possible use a question from a student and point out how that question provokes good thinking.

- Encourage students to go deeper. For example, in a discussion of Langston Hughes's short story "Thank You Ma'am," about a boy who is caught trying to steal a woman's purse in order to buy a new pair of shoes, a student asked, "What kind of shoes did he buy?" You can honor the question by asking the students to predict a response, and then move on. You might also ask the student to explain why that question is important to her or him. How does the answer add to our understanding of the story? It may be that the question is part of a larger idea that the student needs help in articulating. In this way, you are supporting and scaffolding student thinking rather than putting him or her on a spot.

Q: Does everything have to be related to the larger question? (Poetry, interdisciplinary units, research paper, test preparation, etc.)

A: It is true that in the ideal world, the exploration of the curricular conversation would move smoothly forward, neatly building scaffolding and moving seamlessly from one text to the next.

However, schools are not ideal—and even in the best-run, most organized school environment, other things will come up: testing schedules, a required research paper, your beloved poetry unit, an interdisciplinary unit with a team teacher, or even the DARE program. All are conspiring to derail the larger conversation!

We can compare this to a stimulating telephone discussion with a friend. When interrupted, we don't try to work it into the discussion, too. Rather, we say, "I'm sorry, my toddler was asking for a piece of cheese," and then ask, "Where were we?" Your friend reminds you, and off you go again, back into your conversation. Similarly, in the classroom, students understand that sometimes things interrupt—and then continue again.

Here's an example. Annie, a seventh-grade teacher, found a way to use a topical interruption to her curriculum to maintain her students' skill with discussion and reflective thinking. Although students were working on an interdisciplinary research paper that did not easily fit into her regular curriculum, Annie brought continuity to the classroom by hosting a discussion in which students reflected on the process of writing the paper. Students had a lot to say about writing research papers. Of interest to Annie was their universal agreement that they had learned a great deal from the project. They also had some good ideas about how the teachers could structure the workload better. By using the discussion-based format for the activity, Annie was able to remind students about standard process in her class and pave the way for a return to her regular curriculum.

Q: Should I stay away from charged or controversial questions, texts, and topics? How should I approach a controversial issue if I want to include it in a conversation?

A: Your willingness to use controversial materials and topics probably depends on the community in which you teach, your own comfort level, and the text-adoption practices at your school and/or in your district. What do you do if you have an issue or topic that you feel is worthy of discussion, but you are concerned that your choice of texts/topics will become part of a parent/community debate? Do you self-censor and drop the text and the topic or do you have other options? Here are some thoughts:

    Find out what process your school or district uses to adopt texts and other materials. See if the resources you plan to use are already adopted or can legally be put through the process. Talk with colleagues who know the community and school about your idea and gauge their reaction. A negative reaction from a colleague does not have to be your deciding factor, but it may help to have any relevant information about similar efforts at your school.

- Communicate with those who are involved. If you are concerned that you may encounter some parent objections, present your idea first to your department chair and your principal or other administrator who works with language arts. Point out the strong points of what you are trying to do, including any titles of quality literature or nonfiction, any standards your unit will address, and strengths in terms of student interest, real-world connections, active learning, and student growth in empathy and compassion. If you have the support of the administration, then communicate with parents. Send home a list of titles that you may use. Explain your good reasons for using them and the benefits to students. Have students bring back a permission letter that tells you their parents are aware of what you are doing and are in support.

- See the NCTE's (n.d.) position/guideline paper, "The Students' Right to Read" for guidelines on dealing with censorship issues (http://www.ncte.org/about/over/positions/category/cens/107616.htm).

- Keep in mind that what is controversial varies by community, approach, and beliefs. Different communities hold different values on the purposes of education and the meaning of literacy. Know your community and what its values are and consider these in your planning—think about ways to bring these beliefs or understandings into your curriculum and provide students with safe opportunities to examine them. As Applebee (1996) points out:

> When traditions of knowing are in conflict, educators are forced to recognize that the curricular choices they make reinforce one set of values at the expense of another. American schools are founded on the premises of tolerance, diversity, nonsectarianism, and inclusiveness; they have characteristically stressed qualities of thoughtfulness, reflection and independent thinking. Such characteristics, however, are themselves values that are not universally accepted within American society. (p. 120)

Afterword

Like you, Partnership teachers have followed a path toward discussion-based teaching. Though each stop on the journey was customized to teachers' own interests, teaching background, and students, each was supported by the principles that shape this book—dialogic discussion, envisionment building, and curricular coherence. Below, we hear Rosa reflecting on her experience with discussion-based teaching in an urban middle school:

> There are number of things I learned personally and professionally through this CELA experience. One personal realization is that an old dog can learn new tricks. I have changed the way I read personally thanks to specific journal jot questions; I now take time to think through the four stances as I read; when I write about what I read, the stances help me question, respond, analyze. All of this personal change is reflected in my professional behavior now. When my classes read text with me, we all dig in with our own questions about the text and our surprises, thoughts and reactions. My students now text mark, too! Now, in years to come, this will be my first technique—teaching reading strategies that do lead to writing strategies. Vocab markers, conversations based on student questions, journal jots, graphic organizers . . . all new ways of learning that will become part of my teaching style next year and will help me develop further.

We find Rosa's comments remarkable because they show optimism, growth, newfound strength and skills at a time when teachers are under fire. Her comments and those of the other teachers we worked with suggest to us that you can always count on true, meaningful conversations to produce good thinking and learning, especially when you're talking about topics that matter—to you and to your students.

With conversation, good things happen. Students read, write and speak more thoughtfully, for real purposes, and in the interest of advancing their knowledge and self-identity. As authors collaborating on this book, we have relied on the power of our own ongoing discussions to both refine our current knowledge and stimulate the formation of new and unforeseen ideas. Although we had an outline when we began writing, we were constantly surprised and delighted by the crystallization of new thinking that emerged when our two voices came together.

We hope that you will use this book together with your colleagues to similarly experience the benefits of a good conversation.

Literature Cited

Alvarez, J. (1991). Snow. In *How the Garcia girls lost their accents* (p. 167). New York: Plume/Penguin.

Avi. 1991. *Nothing But the truth: A documentary novel.* New York: Orchard Books.

Babbitt, N. (1985/1975). *Tuck everlasting.* (1st Paperback Ed.). New York: Farrar, Straus, Giroux.

Bambara, T. C. (1996). The war of the wall. In *Deep sightings and rescue missions.* New York: Pantheon Books.

Bauer, M.D. (1986). *On my honor.* New York: Clarion Books.

Chapin, H. (1988). Cat's cradle. On *The gold medal collection* [CD]. New York: Elektra/Asylum Records.

Christopher, J. (1967). *The white mountains.* New York: Macmillan.

Cisneros, S. (1991). Eleven. In *Woman hollering creek, and other stories.* New York: Random House.

Cisneros, S. (1985). My name. In *The house on Mango Street.* Houston: Arte Publico Press.

Clark, M. H. (2000). Suspense. In *Literature and thought: Mysterious circumstances* (pp. 43–45). Literature and Thought Series. Logan, IA: Perfection Learning.

Collier, J. L. & C. C. (1974). *My brother Sam is dead.* New York: Scholastic.

Curtis, C. P. (1999). *Bud, not Buddy.* New York: Delacorte Press.

Curtis, C. P. (1995). *The Watsons go to Birmingham—1963.* New York : Delacorte Press.

Flake, S. (2001). *Money hungry.* New York: Jump at the Sun/Hyperion Books for Children.

Fugees. (1996). The Mask. On *The score* [LP]. New York: Columbia.

Gall, C. (2002, September 22). Long in Dark, Afghan Women Say to Read Is Finally to See. The *New York Times,* p. 1.1.

Gardner, M. (1941, January 31). The dinner party. The *Saturday Review of Literature,* 25 (5).

Hakim, J. (1995/2002). A new land is discovered. In *A history of US.* (3rd Ed.). Oxford: Oxford University Press.

Hansen, J. (2004). *African princess: The amazing lives of Africa's royal women.* (L. McGaw, Illus.). New York: Hyperion Books for Children.

Hinton, S.E. (1967/1997). *The outsiders.* New York: Puffin Books.

Hughes, L. (1994). Mother to son. In A. Rampersad (Ed.), *The collected poems of Langston Hughes* (p. 30). New York: Alfred A. Knopf.

Hughes, L. (1996). Thank you ma'am. In A. S. Harper (Ed)., *Short stories by Langston Hughes.* New York: Hill and Wang.

Janofsky, M. (2001, September 7). Arizona boot camp where boy died reopens. The *New York Times,* p. A10.

Kincaid, J. (1991). On seeing England for the first time. *Harper's Magazine,* 283 (1695), 13.

Kipling, R. (1894/1995). Rikki-Tikki-Tavi. In *The jungle book: The Mowgli stories.* (J. Pinkney, Ill.). New York: William Morrow.

Lee, H. (1960/1988). *To kill a mockingbird.* New York: Warner Books.

Lee, S. (Producer, Director) & Blanchard, T. (Writer). (2000). *4 little girls* [Motion Picture]. New York: HBO.

Lieberman, E. (n.d.) I am an American. In *I am an American, and other collected poems* [LP]. New York: The Spoken Word.

London, J. (1963). *The call of the wild.* New York: Macmillan.

Lowry, L. (1993). *The giver*. Boston: Houghton Mifflin.

Luhrmann, B. (Director) & Shakespeare, W. (Writer). (1996). *William Shakespeare's Romeo & Juliet* [Motion Picture]. Beverly Hills: Twentieth Century Fox.

McKissack, P. C. and F. L. (2003) *Days of jubilee: The end of slavery in the United States*. New York: Scholastic Press.

Miller, A. (1953/1976-77). *The crucible: A play in four acts*. New York: Penguin Books.

Myers, W. D. (2003). *blues journey*. Ill. by Christopher Myers. New York: Holiday House.

Niethammer, C. (1977). *Daughters of the earth. The lives and legends of American Indian women*. (pp. 23–36 excerpted). New York: Simon and Schuster.

Nelson, O. T. (1975). *The girl who owned a city*. New York: Dell.

Paterson, K. (1991). *Lyddie*. New York: Lodestar Books.

Perry, Y. N. (1994). The five dollar dive. In *The other side of the island: A collection of short stories*. Santa Barbara : John Daniel & Co., 1994.

Rockwell, N. (1964, January 14). The problem we all live with. *Look* (cover illustration).

Rylant, C. (1985). Shells. In *Every living thing: Stories*. New York: Bradbury Press.

Sachar, L. (1998). *Holes*. New York: Farrar, Straus and Giroux.

Salinas, M. (1986). The scholarship jacket. In M. C. Boza, B. Silva, & C. Valle (Eds.)., *Nosotras: Latina literature today*. Tempe, AZ: Bilingual Press/Editorial Bilingue.

Saroyan, G. A.. from Unveiled. In (N. S. Nye, Ed.), *The flag of childhood: Poems from the Middle East* (p. 3). New York: Aladdin Paperbacks.

Shakespeare, W. (1954). *The tragedy of Romeo and Juliet* (Ed. R. Hosley). (Rev. Ed.). New Haven: Yale University Press.

Six dead after church bombing. (1963, September 16). The *Washington Post* [Electronic version]. Retrieved March 8, 2005 from http://www.washingtonpost.com/wp-srv/national/longterm/churches/archives1.htm.

Soto, G. (1990). Seventh grade. In *Baseball in April and other stories*. San Diego: Harcourt Brace Jovanovich.

Steinbeck, J. (1947/1992). *The pearl*. New York: Penguin Books.

Soto, G. (1995). Oranges. In *New and selected poems* (pp. 72–73). San Francisco: Chronicle Books.

Steptoe, J. (1987). *Mufaro's beautiful daughters*. New York: Lothrop, Lee & Shepard Books.

Stockton, F. R. (1968). The lady or the tiger? In *The storyteller's pack, a Frank R. Stockton reader*. New York: Scribner.

Thomas, D. (1971). Do not go gentle into that good night. In *Collected Poems of Dylan Thomas: 1934–1952* (p. 128). New York: New Directions.

Twain, M. (1885/1996). *Adventures of Huckleberry Finn*. New York: Random House.

Walker, A. (1988). Everyday use. In Prescott, P. (Ed.). *The Norton book of American short stories* (pp. 714–721). New York: Norton.

Uchida, Y. (2002). Prisoner of my country. In *Glencoe literature: The Reader's choice* (Course 3, Grade 8). New York: Glencoe McGraw Hill.

Williams, W. C. (1986–88). *The collected poems of William Carlos Williams*. (A. W. Litz & C. J. MacGowan, Eds.). New York: New Directions.

Yolen, J. (1988). *The devil's arithmetic*. New York: Viking Kestrel.

Yolen, J. (1992). *Encounter* (illus. by D. Shannon). San Diego : Harcourt Brace Jovanovich.

Zinn, H. (1980/2001). *A people's history of the United States*. (v. 1). New York: Harper Perennial.

References

Adler, M., Rougle, E., Kaiser, E., & Caughlan, S. (2003/2004). Closing the gap between concept and practice: Toward more dialogic discussion in the language arts classroom. *Journal of Adolescent & Adult Literacy*, 47, 312–322.

Allington, R. L. & Johnston, P. H. (2001). What do we know about effective fourth-grade teachers and their classrooms? In C. Roller (Ed.), *Learning to teach reading: Setting the research agenda* (pp. 150–65). Newark, DE: International Reading Association.

Alvermann, D. E. (2000, July). *Grappling with the big issues in middle grades literacy education*. Keynote address presented at the meeting of the National Educational Research Policy and Priorities Board's Conference on Curriculum, Instruction, and Assessment in the Middle Grades: Linking Research and Practice, Washington, D.C. Retrieved February 28, 2005 from http://www.middleweb.com/alvermann.html

Alvermann, D. E. (2004). Adolescent aliteracy: Are schools causing it? *Voices in Urban Education*, 1(3), 26–35.

Anderson, M., Adler, M., & Morrill, L., (Fall, 2002). Keeping expectations high while helping lower-achieving students meet them. *English Update*. New York: Center on English Learning & Achievement, 1–5, 8.

Applebee, A. N. (1986). Musings . . . principled practice. *Research in the Teaching of English*, 20, 5–7.

Applebee, A. N. (1996). *Curriculum as conversation: Transforming traditions of teaching and learning*. Chicago: University of Chicago Press.

Applebee, A. N. (1997). Rethinking curriculum in the English language arts. *English Journal*, 86(5), 25–31.

Applebee, A. N. (2002). Engaging students in the disciplines of English: What are effective schools doing? *English Journal*, 91(6), 30–36.

Applebee, A. N., Adler, M., & Flihan, S. (2005). Interdisciplinary curricula in middle and high school classrooms: Case studies of approaches to curriculum and instruction. Manuscript submitted for publication.

Applebee, A. N., Langer, J.A., Nystrand, M., & Gamoran, A. (2003). Discussion-based approaches to developing understanding: Classroom instruction and student performance in middle and high school English. *American Education Research Journal*, 40(3), 685–730.

Athanases, S. Z. (1993). Adapting and tailoring lessons: Fostering teacher reflection to meet varied student needs. *Teacher Education Quarterly*, 20(1), 71–81.

Au, K. H. (1993). *Literacy instruction in multicultural settings*. New York: Harcourt Brace.

Bakhtin, M. M. (1981). Discourse in the novel. In M. Holquist (Ed.), *The Dialogic imagination: Four essays* (C. Emerson & M. Holquist, Trans.). (pp. 259–422). Austin: University of Texas Press.

Bakhtin, M. M. (1973). *Problems of Dostoyevsky's poetics*. (R. W. Rotsel, Trans.). Ann Arbor, MI: Ardis. (Original work published 1929)

Bereiter, C. & Scardamalia, M. (1987). An attainable version of high literacy: Approaches to teaching higher order skills in reading and writing. *Curriculum Inquiry*, 17(1), 10–30.

Bloom, B., Mesia, B. B., & Krathwohl, D. (1964). *Taxonomy of educational objectives.* New York. David McKay.

Brown, A. L. & Palincsar, A. S. (1986). *Guided, cooperative learning and individual knowledge acquisition* (Technical Report No. 372). Cambridge, MA: Center for the Study of Reading.

Bruer, J. (1994). Classroom problems, school culture, and cognitive research. In K. McGilly (Ed.), *Classroom lessons: Integrating cognitive theory and classroom research* (pp. 273–290). Cambridge, MA: MIT Press.

California State Board of Education (1997). *English-language arts content standards for California public schools, kindergarten through grade 12.* Sacramento, CA: California Department of Education.

Cazden, C. B. (2001). *Classroom discourse: The language of teaching and learning* (2nd ed.). Portsmouth, NH: Heinemann.

Chekhov, A. (1964). "Ward No. 6." (Additional Trans. E. Rougle). Retrieved 2/25/05 from http://endeavor.med.nyu.edu/lit.med-db/ webdescrips/chekhov813-des-.htlm

Collins, J. (1982). Discourse style, classroom interaction and differential treatment. *Journal of Reading Behavior,* 14, 429–437.

Daniels, H. (2002). *Literature circles: Voice and choice in book clubs and reading groups.* Portland, ME: Stenhouse.

Dewey, J. (1938). *Democracy and education: An introduction to the philosophy of education.* New York: The MacMillan Company.

Dyson, A. H. (1993). Social worlds of children learning to write in an urban primary school. New York: *Teachers College Press.*

Dyson, A. H. (1994). The Ninjas, the X-men, and the ladies: Playing with power and identity in an urban primary school. *Teachers College Record,* 96(2), 219–239.

Edelsky, C. (1999). *Making justice our project.* Urbana, IL: NCTE

Edelsky, C. (2004). Democracy in the balance. *Language Arts,* 82 (1), 8–15.

Eisner, Elliot W. (1994) *Cognition and curriculum reconsidered* (2nd ed.). New York: Teachers College Press.

Finders, M. (1997). *Just girls: Hidden literacies and life in junior high.* New York: Teachers College Press.

Fine, M. & Macpherson, P. (1993). Over dinner: Feminism and adolescent female bodies. In S. Biklen & D. Pollard (Eds.), *Gender and education: Ninety-second yearbook of the National Society for the Study of Education.* (pp. 126–154). Chicago: University of Chicago Press.

Freire, P. (2000). *Pedagogy of the oppressed.* (M. B. Ramos, Trans.). New York: Continuum Publishing Co. (Original work published 1970)

Gall, C. (2002, September 22). Long in dark, Afghan women say to read is finally to see. The *New York Times,* p. 1.1.

Gardner, H. (1993). *Multiple intelligences: The theory in practice.* New York: Basic Books.

Gentile, C. A., Martin-Rehrmann, J., & Kennedy, J. H. (1995). *Windows into the classroom: NAEP's 1992 writing portfolio study* (NAEP Publication No. 23-FR-06). Washington, DC: National Center for Education Statistics.

Giroux, H. A. (1993). *Border crossings.* New York: Routledge.

Greenleaf, C., Schoenbach, R., Cziko, C., & Mueller, F. (2001). Apprenticing adolescent readers in academic literacy. *Harvard Educational Review* 71(1), 79–129.

Hamburg, D. (1992). *Today's children*. New York: Random House.

Hillocks, G. (1995). *Teaching writing as reflective practice*. New York: Teachers College Press.

Himley, M. & Carini, P. F. (2000). *From another angle: Children's strengths and school standards: The Prospect Center's descriptive review of the child*. New York: Teachers College Press.

Hirshey, G. (2005, January 30). You get better by knowing the world: An interview with Yo-Yo Ma. *Parade Magazine*, p. 5.

Hynds, S. (1997). *On the brink: Negotiating literature and life with adolescents*. New York: Teachers College Press.

Intersegmental Committee of the Academic Senates (ICAS). (2002). *Academic literacy*. Sacramento, CA: Author.

Johnson, J. (1999). *The poetics of generosity*. Retrieved October 1, 2004, from http://www.albany.edu/~jej84/chimeras.htm

Kincaid, J. (1991). On seeing England for the first time. *Harper's Magazine*, 283(1695), 13.

Kinney, D. A. (1993). From Nerds to normals: The recovery of identity among adolescents from middle school to high school. *Sociology of Education*, 66(1), 21–40.

Kirby, D., Kirby, D., & Liner, T. (2004). *Inside out: Strategies for teaching writing*. (3rd ed.). Portsmouth, NH: Heinemann.

Kirby, D. & Liner, T. (1988). *Inside out: Developmental strategies for teaching writing*. (2nd ed.). Portsmouth, NY: Boynton Cook.

Ladson-Billings, G. (1994). *The dreamkeepers*. San Francisco: Jossey-Bass.

Ladson-Billings, G. (1995). Toward a theory of culturally relevant pedagogy. *American Educational Research Journal*, 32(3), 465–491.

Lampert, M. (1990). When the problem is not the question and the solution is not the answer: Mathematical knowing and teaching. *American Educational Research Journal*, 27(1), 29–64.

Langer, J. A. (1990). The Process of understanding: Reading for literary and informative purposes. *Research in the Teaching of English*, 24(3), 229–60.

Langer, J. A. (1995). *Envisioning literature: Literary understanding and literature instruction*. New York: Teachers College Press.

Langer, J. A. (1999). *Beating the odds: Teaching middle and high school students to read and write well*. Report No. 12014. (2nd rev. ed.). Albany, NY: Center on English Learning and Achievement. Retrieved June 8, 2005, from http://cela.albany.edu/reports/eie2/index.html

Langer, J. A. (2002). *Effective literacy instruction*. Urbana, IL: National Council of Teachers of English.

Langer, J. A (2004, May 4). *Developing the literate mind*. Speech presented at the Conference of the International Reading Association. Retrieved October 20, 2004 from http://cela.albany.edu/researcher/langer/IRA_Develop.pdf

Langer, J. A. & Applebee, A. N. (1987). *How writing shapes thinking: A study of teaching and learning*. (NCTE Research Report no. 22). Urbana, IL: National Council of Teachers of English.

Lee, C. D. (1992). Literacy, cultural diversity, and instruction. *Education and Urban Society*. 24(2), 279–91.

Lee, C. D. (2004). Literacy in the academic disciplines and the needs of adolescent struggling readers. *Voices in Urban Education*, 1(3), 26–35.

Maloch, B. (2002). Scaffolding student talk: One teacher's role in literature discussion groups. *Reading Research Quarterly*, 37(1), 94–112.

Markova, A. K. (1979). *The teaching and mastery of language*. White Plains, NY: M. E. Sharpe.

Marshall, J., Smagorinsky, P., Smith, M. (1995). *The language of interpretation: Patterns of discourse in discussions of literature*. (NCTE Research Report No. 27). Urbana, IL: National Council of Teachers of English.

McMahon, S. I. & Raphael, T. E. (1997). *The Book club connection: Literacy learning and classroom talk*. NY: Teachers College Press.

Mehan, H. (1979). *Learning lessons*. Cambridge, MA: Harvard University Press.

Moll, L. C., Amanti, C., Neff, D., & González, N. (1992). Funds of knowledge for teaching: Using a qualitative approach to connect homes and classrooms. *Theory into Practice*, 31(2), 132–141.

National Council of Teachers of English. (n.d.). The students' right to read. Urbana, IL: Author. Retrieved March 8, 2005, from http://www.ncte.org/about/over/positions/category/cens/107616.htm

National Council of Teachers of English & International Reading Association. (1996). *Standards for the English language arts*. Urbana, IL: IRA and NCTE.

National Reading Panel. (2000). *Teaching children to read: An evidence-based assessment of the scientific research literature on reading and its implications for reading instruction*. (Report No. NIH-00-4769). Bethesda, MD: National Institute of Child Health and Human Development.

Nystrand, M. (1997). *Opening dialogue: Understanding the dynamics of language and learning in the English classroom*. New York: Teachers College Press.

Noddings, N. (1995). Teaching themes of care. *Phi Delta Kappan* 76(9), 675–79.

Plisko, V. W. (2003, November 13). *The release of the National Assessment of Educational Progress (NAEP) the nation's report card: Reading and mathematics*. Retrieved February 22, 2005, from http://nces.ed.gov/commissioner/remarks 2003/11_13_2003.asp

Polanyi, M. (1959). *The study of man*. Chicago: University of Chicago.

Ramirez, J. D., Yuen, S. D. & Ramey, D. R. (1991). *Final report: Longitudinal study of structured English immersion strategy, early-exit and late-exit transitional bilingual education programs for language-minority children. Executive Summary*. San Mateo, CA: Aguirre International. Retrieved February 25, 2005, from http://www.ncela.gwu.edu/pubs/ramirez/longitudinal.htm

Readence, J., Bean, T., & Baldwin, R. (1989). *Content area reading: An integrated approach*. Dubuque, IA: Kendall/Hunt.

Roberts, D., & Langer, J. A. (1991). *Supporting the process of literary understanding: Analysis of a classroom discussion* (Report Series No. 2.15). Albany, NY: National Research Center on Literature Teaching and Learning.

Rodgers, C. (2002). Defining reflection: Another look at John Dewey and reflective thinking. *Teachers College Record*, 104(4), 842–866.

Rosenblatt, L. M. (1994). *The reader, the text, the poem: The transactional theory of the literary work*. Carbondale, IL: Southern University Press.

Rougle, E. (1999). *A lifelong middle school teacher never stops learning; The case of Cathy Starr*. (Research Report No. 12005.). Albany, NY: National Research Center on English Learning and Achievement.

Saroyan, G. A. (2002). From unveiled. In N. S. Nye, (Ed.), *The flag of childhood: Poems from the Middle East*. (p. 3). New York: Aladdin.

Schoenbach, R., Greenleaf, C., Cziko, C., & Hurwitz, L. (1999). *Reading for understanding: A guide to improving reading in middle and high school*. San Francisco: Jossey-Bass.

Smagorinsky, P. (2002). *Teaching English through principled practice*. Upper Saddle River, NJ: Merrill Prentice Hall.

Stevens, J. (2003, November 13). *Statement on NAEP 2003 mathematics and reading results. National Association of Educational Progress*. Retrieved February 22, 2005, from http://www.nagb.org/release/statement_11_03.html

Stock, P. (1995). *The dialogic curriculum: Teaching and learning in a multicultural society*. Portsmouth, NH: Boynton/Cook.

Stotsky, S. & Finn, C. (2005). The state of state English standards. Washington, D.C.: Thomas B. Fordham Foundation. Retrieved 2/26/05 from http://www.edexcellence.net/institute/publication/publication.cfm?id=337

Tompkins, G. E. (1998). *50 literacy strategies: Step by step*. Upper Saddle River, NJ: Merrill.

Vasquez, V. (2003). What Pokemon can teach us about learning and literacy. *Language Arts, 81*(2), 28–35.

Vygotsky, L. S. (1978). *Mind in society: The development of higher psychological processes*. Cambridge, MA: Harvard University Press.

Wells, G. (1999). *Dialogic inquiry: Toward a sociocultural practice and theory of education*. Cambridge, UK: Cambridge University Press.

Wertsch, J.V. (1991). *Voices of the Mind: A sociocultural approach to mediated action*. Cambridge, MA: Harvard University Press.

Wilhelm, J. (1997). *You gotta BE the book: Teaching engaged and reflective reading with adolescents*. New York: Teachers College Press.

Williams, J. (2004). *Soundings, a world premier: A note from the composer*. Retrieved January 5, 2005, from http://jwfan.net/modules.php?op=modload&name=News&file=article&sid=398

Wood, D., Bruner, J. S., & Ross, G. (1976). The role of tutoring in problem-solving. *Journal of Child Psychology and Child Psychiatry*, 17, 89–100.

Index